As It Is

in the

Days of

Noah

Printed in the United States of America

ISBN 1-57558-25-X

Cover design by Christi Killian
Cover photograph © 1998 by Dwayne N. Moore Photography

As It Is

in the

Days of

Noah

Dr. N. W. Hutchings

Dr. N. W. Hutchings, 1998

Foreword

This is a story as told by the author about himself.

Although I have probably written over one hundred books, there is no self assurance that any of them contain anything of great importance. In fact, I am not sure the readers will find anything in this book that might be considered of importance. However, one day before the Lord calls me home I might write something of importance. Therefore, I would pray the reader will read this book with considerable attention to each page and chapter, because if I should write something of importance in this book I would regret it being missed.

I have been urged from time to time to write my autobiography. The reason I have delayed this boresome task is that in sharing the mundane affairs of my seventy-five–year existence on this planet, I would have to tell the whole truth, at least to the satisfaction of my conscience. It is very easy, and quite pleasing, to share the mountain top accomplishments of life, but then who wants to hear about the swamps, snakes, and alligators. Therefore, in order to placate my solemn sense of moral duty to tell the whole truth, and at the same time not drag the reader into the depths of manic depression, I will linger on the mountain tops, and hastily run through the mire and muck of the hinterlands.

Should anyone be offended by any particular subjects or references in this book, personal or otherwise, no apology is offered. Any seventy-five-year-old should be entitled to offend a few people.

The final straw that broke my will against writing about myself was something my son-in-law, Bill Uselton, said: "Dad, if you will not write an autobiography for yourself, or for those to whom you have ministered, you should at least leave something in writing about yourself for your grandchildren."

That was really hitting below the belt. Nevertheless, this self-serving essay is dedicated to my three daughters; Carol, Cheryl, and Cathy (whom I often, when disturbed, called Ham, Shem, and Japheth); my stepchildren: Pola, Poline, Sothea, Sothy, and Phaly; and, of course, my grandchildren: Jennifer and Kelly, and step-grandchildren, Kevin, Stephen, Elizabeth, and Matthew, and any other grandchildren that may be born hereafter—for better or worse.

It is the hope of the author to take the reader, or readers if more than one, through seventy-five years of the most exciting time in the history of mankind since Adam looked at Eve and asked, "What's for dinner?"

What has happened in my lifetime? Radio, television, laser, x-ray, organ transplants, split atoms and nuclear weapons, space travel, satellites, computers, genetic engineering, and cloning, to name just a few. I learned to drive in a Model-T Ford, speeding down the country roads at thirty miles an hour, but Adam could mount a horse in the Garden of Eden and go thirty miles an hour.

The prophet Daniel said that knowledge would increase, many would run to and fro, and the end would come like a flood. You and I, and everyone who has lived through this fantastic era, have been privileged and blessed of God. No man or woman who lived prior to the twentieth century could have seen what we have seen or experienced. Jesus said: "When you see these things coming to pass." For the first time in history we can see on television, right from our living rooms, practically everything and anything of importance within minutes after it happens, from anyplace in the world.

Before we get into preaching, perhaps we should get on with the story and begin at the beginning. To coin a phrase,

"Noah W. Hutchings, this is your life. . . ."

On the Banks of the Kiamichi River

Me and Geneva, 1923

According to my State of Oklahoma birth certificate, I was born December 11, 1922. The place of birth was a farming community which still exists today, Messer. Messer is approximately eight miles northeast of Hugo in a section of southeast Oklahoma called by area natives, Little Dixie.

My year of birth was only thirty-three years this side of the great 1889 Oklahoma Land Run. The Oklahoma Territory had originally been given to the five civilized tribes: Cherokee, Choctaw, Chickasha, Creek, and Seminole. These American Indian tribes had been moved forcibly by the U.S. government in the 1830s from the southeastern states to Oklahoma Territory. Because of the great sufferings and loss of life in the move, the Cherokee Indians called the journey the Trail of Tears. The Indians had been promised that Oklahoma would be their nation and home forever. The territory was divided into three areas: the Cherokee Nation, the Choctaw and Chickasaw Nation, and the Creek and Seminole Nation. Little by little the land was taken away by the federal government for homesteading. The Oklahoma Land Run of 1889 pretty much ended the Indian's hope of ever living in peace in their own country. At the turn of the century most Indians were on reservations because they had sold their land for a few dollars, which was then invested in whisky and unsound investments. A few retained title to their land and attempted to take up the white man's ways.

My father's name was Thomas Clyde Hutchings, and my mother's maiden name was Mattie Askew. The Hutchings branch to which my father belonged came from Georgia.

Thomas Hutchings   *Mattie Askew Hutchings*

Grandpa Jack Whitecotton

Greatgrandma Betty Whitecotton Hutchings

In England during colonial times those who could not pay their debts were put into debtors' prisons. At some point before the Revolutionary War, England took the poor souls in the debtors' prisons and by ship emptied them out on the Georgia shores to fend for themselves. Evidently some of them must

Grandpa Askew

Grandma Askew

have lived, because many of them, including a few Hutchings, ended up in north Texas and southern Oklahoma. The Askews were of Scottish descent and settled in Alabama. Why the Askews were in Alabama is something I have never tried to find out, either for lack of time, or interest, or both.

When I was born, the fourth child, my Grandma Askew had previously been foiled in her determination to name her grandchildren after biblical characters. She was determined with me that this was not going to happen again; she had the name already picked out—Boaz! At that time neither my father nor mother were Christians, and they probably did not know the name of Boaz from Bohunk. In any event, Boaz, to my mother, sounded neither human nor animal, so she balked. Grandma had a second choice picked out just in case—Noah! My mother did not connect Noah with the Bible. The only Noah she knew about was Noah Webster, the man whose name is associated with the compilation of the dictionary. Thus, I was named Noah Webster Hutchings. I am sure that Boaz of Bethlehem was a fine, outstanding, charitable gentleman, but I have been grateful that my name was given as Noah instead of Boaz; although I am not sure I would have picked Noah either, had I been given an option.

The community of Messer was on the banks of the Kiamichi River, a very beautiful stream that originates in the Kiamichi Mountains in east central Oklahoma. The land in the Messer community was sandy and replete with flinty gravel, which in due course was later turned into a maze of gravel pits. It is too bad that this did not happen before my father wasted several years trying to grow cotton on a rock pile.

Hugo, which had a population of five thousand in 1922 (and by the grace of welfare and dependent children's aid has not gained or lost in population since), is the capital of Choctaw County, which is in one of the five Indian nations that once comprised the state of Oklahoma. The Choctaw Indians were shorter in height than the members of other tribes. They also had a reputation of being lazy and ad-dicted to fire water, although I am sure these social laxities did not apply to all.

My first memories of early childhood must date to when I was three and four years old. The house we lived in, in 1926 or 1927, was unpainted. It had two bedrooms on one side of a breezeway, and on the other side was a living room, kitchen, dining room, and another bedroom. The house also had a fireplace, and I remember on Christmas morning the family sitting around the fire, eating fruits and nuts, while I played with a toy monkey that would climb up and down a string when the string was pulled.

The house was near the main road that ran in front of an eighty-acre farm. The property belonged to an Indian woman whom we called "Old Sofie." Old Sofie owned a house at the back of the farm, although she did not do any farming herself.

Old Sofie was really not that old, probably in her

middle forties. She was slim and tall with a regal bearing. Sofie did not appear to be a member of the Choctaw tribe, and I would guess that she was either a Cherokee or Creek. She wore red dresses down to her ankles, and her long black hair was worn in two braided strands that reached down to her waist with red ribbons at the end. Sofie kept pretty much to herself, with Indian visitors occasionally dropping by her house. Every so often we would see a different Indian male move in with her, and I would hear my parents discuss Sofie's new man. She doubtless either received Indian grant money from the government, or a pension. My father was not charged rent, as she only wanted someone to take care of her farm.

In the middle twenties very few farm families owned cars, probably not more that one in ten. The horse and buggy, or wagon, were still the main mode of transportation. I remember no one in the Messer community having a radio. At the time, we were considered in the upper middle class because we owned a Victrola record player. My older brother and sister, Reghal and Juanita, were then in their teens, and would buy Jimmy Rogers records, and neighbors would drop by to hear the latest recording of this famous country ballad singer.

There was a silent film movie theatre in Hugo, but as far as I remember, no member of my family ever went. There were a few stage presentations at the Messer schoolhouse, and one that I recall was an Indian war-dance staged by real live Indians. Oklahoma was granted statehood in 1907, and we were still held spellbound by stories of Indians on the warpath scalping the palefaces. So when the Indians, skimpily dressed in brief leather skirts, began dancing, chanting, and waving their tomahawks, I ran and stood by the door, ready to make a rapid escape in the event they started scalping people for real.

One example of the difficulties of some phases of life on the farm in the twenties was the potty-training of children. There was no inside plumbing, so potty-training began with what we called the "slop jar." The "slop jar" was a two-gallon pot with a rounded flange. After a child finally graduated from diapers and learned how to balance his or her body

on this contraption without turning it over, then there was a graduation to a second stage of potty-training, the outside privy. Poor families had one-holers; the middle-class had two-holers, and

A two-hole outhouse

the very upper-class had three-holers. As I think back, our outside toilet was a two-holer at Old Sofie's place.

One of the common cliches was, when the whereabouts of someone was asked, the response would come, "He's gone to - - - - (toilet), and the hogs ate him."

I am usually extremely busy in the office. Getting out publications, books, mailings, and producing a program every day requires twice as much time as I have to give. When anyone calls for me, the secretaries or wats line operators are specifically instructed to find out their names and their business. So one day, a man who had been calling and pestering me about a relatively minor matter, called for the third time. When my secretary buzzed me and announced the name of the caller, I replied in a rather unfriendly voice, "Tell this bore I have gone to - - - - (toilet), and the hogs ate me." Behold, this person was already on the line. Subsequently, I had a most difficult and embarrassing few minutes attempting to explain why I might get eaten by the hogs in going to an outside toilet.

The second stage of my own potty training was most difficult. Living near the river, there was an abundance of poisonous snakes—copperheads, rattlesnakes, and water moccasins. We kids were continually warned to watch out for the snakes. For a three- or four-year-old to pull up on the boarded seat, and then keep from falling down through the hole was one problem. Another problem for me was that there was no light, and I could just imagine a snake in the hole waiting to bite me. So one day when I felt the urge to relieve myself, instead of going to the outhouse, I simply sneaked under the front porch steps. These steps had no backing, and anyone using them could see right through. So while I had my pants down, about a dozen women came up the steps to go into the house. My mother was holding a sewing bee that day, and I could hear chattering and laughing, along with the rising voice of my mother in great displeasure. While my mother knew little of Bible verses, she knew intuitively and experientially that sparing the rod spoils the child. My mother was determined not to raise spoiled kids, but before Mama could find the razor strap, my Grandma Askew hurriedly rushed her namesake behind the smokehouse and pointed out to me where I could take care of my required duties without having to use the toilet.

I remember another occasion where I narrowly missed the strap. One morning Mama discovered she had run out of coffee. She asked me if I could go about three blocks down the road to Mrs. Rhodes house and borrow a cup of coffee. I assured her I was big enough to do the job. After receiving the coffee from our neighbor, I started back. Then I got a brilliant idea. There were some deep wagon tracks in the dirt, and so I sprinkled the coffee in the tracks and then covered it with dirt. When I entered our house with an empty cup, my mother wanted to know where the coffee was—"Didn't Mrs. Rhodes have any coffee?" I informed her I had indeed gotten the coffee, but I had put it into the wagon tracks. When she asked why in the heavens I would do such a thing, I responded, "So that we could raise our own coffee, and I would not have to walk to our neighbors in the cold for coffee anymore." I escaped a spanking, but I did receive a lesson in agriculture from my dad.

Another pleasant memory from our few years on Old Sofie's place was related to a dear black lady whom everyone called Aunt Rose. Aunt Rose was a kind, heavy Mary Poppins. When Aunt Rose was walking down a road with all her possessions in a large sack on her back, it was to be known that she was going to a home where there was sickness, or a mother was about to give birth to a new baby. Aunt Rose never asked for money. She never asked permission. She just came and stayed as long as she was needed. Then, without telling anyone she was leaving, she would simply pack her bag and go without saying a word.

When my younger sister Sue was born, Aunt Rose came unannounced. She washed the clothes, ironed, cleaned the house, baked gingerbread, and made delicious rhubarb pies. Us kids secretly hoped that Mama would quickly get pregnant again so that Aunt Rose would visit us once more. I do not remember much more about Aunt Rose. I do know that she had a son, and I have often wondered whatever happened to her.

My Grandpa Hutchings lived on the Kiamichi River at Hutchings' Landing. I do not remember much about how he looked except that he was fairly slim, and I believe he wore a partial beard. One day my mother was sewing, and I looked out the front window to watch the snow coming down from the sky. I saw my grandpa walking down the road, but before he turned to come up the lane to the house, he parted the wires on the fence, took a few steps, and lay down on the south side of a large log. I told my mother that Grandpa had lain down behind the log. She looked, did not see anything, and thought I was just wishing that Grandpa would come see us. About an hour later, he did knock at the door. The only explanation for Grandpa's behavior, that I could later reason, was that his heart was bothering him, and he just could not go any farther. It was not long after this incident that Grandpa Hutchings died of a heart attack.

Family life at the Hutchings' home in those earliest years of my life, now that I look back, do not seem unpleasant. However, there were times when there was considerable quarreling between my father and mother. It is not known to me what prompted this infrequent anger and turmoil, except that my father was weak when it came to alcohol.

I remember riding to town with Daddy on a wagon loaded with cotton. After waiting in line to get to the cotton gin, my dad would take me downtown for a bowl of homemade stew or a hamburger. This was an exciting treat for me. However, when he went by himself so-called friends would get him drunk and then swindle him out of his money in crooked card games or dominoes. On such occasions,

Daddy would be late coming home, and my mother would be waiting under a tree in the front yard. As the light from the sun began fading in the west, we could hear my dad's voice yelling at the horses and cracking the reins on their backs. A few minutes later we could hear the sound of the wagon bumping along the road as the horses were pushed to run as fast as they could.

After stopping at the barn, the harness would be taken off the horses and my father would stagger to the house. We knew that an intense and severe argument would follow, as my mother tried to find out if he had paid the note at the bank, or used all the money for booze and gambling. My father's drinking and poor management resulted in suffering for the entire family, and this was most likely the reason we had to move almost every year.

The year I reached the age of five, my dad moved the family to another farm one-half mile up the road. It was the Turner place, and I do not know the reason for the move. Perhaps my father and Sofie had a problem between them, or perhaps Dad just liked the looks of the rocks better on the east side of the road. That winter I had my sixth birthday, and in the fall I enrolled in the first grade at the Messer grade school. The Messer grade school was an excellent one at that time. It had three large classrooms, while many schools only had two rooms, or even one room. The first year in school I definitely learned two things: there was no Santa Claus, and if I went a week without making a one hundred on a spelling test, I would get a whipping—which I did receive on one or two occasions.

The year was 1928. Dad said the market for farm products was good. Cotton was twelve cents a pound, and corn was one dollar a bushel. The time to make a fortune was at hand. Dr. Harris, who was also a large land owner, had arranged a loan at the bank for more livestock and farming equipment, but we had to pack up and move again to a place called Boggy Bottom ten miles southwest of Hugo. Little did my father and mother realize at the time the disappointments and hardships that would lie ahead during the next two years.

Boggy Bottom

In the fall of 1928 my father and mother readied to move to a community ten miles southwest of Hugo called Boggy Bottom. Boggy Bottom got its name from the Boggy River. The Boggy River headwaters began between Atoka and Seminole in the foothills of the Kiamichi Mountains, and its entire course covered only about eighty miles before it met the Red River. The Red River is the southern border between Oklahoma and Texas.

My parents were anxious to move and left behind most of the skimpy cotton that had not been picked. With a new bankroll to purchase needed livestock and farming tools, there was now an excellent chance to really improve the economic status of the family. Much of the land my father was to farm was virgin, rich bottomland adjacent to the river. The house and barn were average for farm rental property at that time. The house had three small bedrooms, a kitchen, and a combination dining and living room. The family at that time was composed of my father; mother; older brother, Reghal; two older sisters, Juanita and Geneva; my younger sister, Sue;

and Harold, who was less than a year old.

The prices for farm products had actually risen in 1928, so my dad and older brother went to work clearing the land. This entailed cutting the trees with a crosscut saw, then cutting the roots of the stump, either pulling them out of the ground with tackle using mules to provide the power; or, if the stump was large and stubborn, dynamite was used. Small trees and brush were eliminated by using axes, and then after a couple of months the entire pile had to be burned. Also, plowing new ground where there had been trees and brush, with only mules and plows, was an extremely difficult and frustrating job. The entire family had to pitch in and work. I was too young to contribute much to the actual farm work; however, I was expected to feed the chickens, watch after the cattle, and slop the hogs.

My older brother had attended high school in Hugo when the family lived at Messer. After we moved to Boggy Bottom, my oldest sister went to live with a family at Soper so that she could attend high school. So after we got settled in at the new place, my sister Geneva and I had to enroll at school and try to make up for the time lost. The school we went to was simply called the Oklahoma School. It was a one-room schoolhouse and one teacher taught all eight grades. Because of the distance, my sister and I rode horses. One was a large black male, Nick, and the other was a small mare we called Cricket. The schoolyard was fenced, so we would take off the saddles during school hours and the horses could graze or rest until we were ready to go back home. I can remember the cold winter days with the wind howling from the north. We would get to school so cold and numb that we literally had to fall off the horses, our hands, arms, and legs being frozen stiff.

There were times when the horses were not available for us to ride, so the only other option was to walk. There were no school buses in 1928, at least in Boggy Bottom. The road to school was dirt and wound mostly through heavy forest. At Messer the locals were mostly white with a respectable representation of Indians. In Boggy Bottom there were no Indians, but the whites were outnumbered by the blacks, who lived mostly in small cottages in the woods. We were quickly oriented by Boggy Bottom whites that we were to be deeply afraid of the blacks. So in walking to and from school, often in the waning daylight, Geneva and I would get on the opposite side of the road as close to the ditch as we possibly could, when passing a black's house or meeting one in the road. Even when we were at home and blacks were seen coming up the road, we would run into the house. When mother would ask why we had run into the house, we would respond that a black cloud was coming down the road. I do not remember a black ever assaulting a white, doing any harm to whites, or bothering whites—but, that is just the way it was. That is the way we were taught. So the blacks kept to themselves and the whites kept to themselves. In looking back, it does seem strange that we would have forgotten so soon that our beloved Aunt Rose was also a black person.

When the first cold norther of the winter came in late November of 1928, my dad killed and butchered a couple of hogs. The hams, shoulders, and sides were cured in the smokehouse, and the rest was either rendered into lard or made into sausage. My mother always canned vegetables in the spring and summer for the winter, and with a new stake, the first winter at Boggy Bottom the family made out very well. It was a long trip to Hugo in the wagon, but there was a small gas station about one-half mile away that also carried basic food essentials. My father kept lines out in Boggy River and usually caught enough catfish or shovel-bill catfish for a change in diet. I was never allowed to fish in the river because the bank was steep and usually slick. To not be allowed to fish in the river seemed, at the time, to be the cruelest form of child abuse. When in Hugo in 1980 visiting my mother, I suddenly decided that a childhood dream would finally be realized. I borrowed a couple of rods, bought some bait, and drove fifteen miles to where the road passed over the Boggy bridge a couple of blocks from where we lived. I noticed the house was gone, but I anxiously baited up and set out my lines. After waiting two hours for a bite, I reeled in the lines and hurriedly drove away, not wanting to get too much reacquainted with the memories associated with this place.

By March 1929 the land was ready to plant. Cotton was still holding well in price, so my father decided to plant every inch of land possible in this cash crop. A few acres were planted in corn for the livestock and cornmeal to use for bread. Cornbread and buttermilk were part of the farm cuisine, and I still at times buy a quart of buttermilk and bake some cornbread, just for old times' sake. That summer a tree in the barnyard was struck by lightning, killing some of the animals. One of the horses later got what we called the "blind staggers" and had to be destroyed. I also contracted malaria.

With malaria I would start to feel ill at around nine a.m.; by ten a.m. my temperature would rise and I would go into a hard chill. By eleven a.m. I would begin vomiting. This would last until around four p.m. when sleep would come because of exhaustion. I would feel washed out for a couple of days and then get better, but in a week another malaria spell would come. Some died of malaria, but I survived by taking quinine, the only medicine available for this virus at the time. Quinine is extremely bitter, and sugar or honey only makes it more bitter. I would take it in a tablespoon of coffee or vinegar, but even this did not help much. I suffered with malaria for three years before it finally left me.

The major news headlines for 1928 were:

January 4: Millions Hear Will Rogers Radio
Broadcasts

January 16: Lindbergh Joins PanAm
February 6: Woman Claims to be Anastasia
March 28: Prices Swing Madly in Record Trading
May 10: Gary Cooper Stars in Adventure Film
May 16: Stock Market Trading Hits Record High
June 18: Earhart First Woman to Fly Over Atlantic
June 25: Jobless Figure Disputed: 2 Million or 4?
July 3: Can You Believe It? A TV Set for $75
August 11: Hoover Says "A Chicken in Every Pot,
   A Car in Every Garage"
August 21: Movie Mogul Says: Talkies Just a Fad
November 10: Hirohito Ascends Japanese Throne

The most relevant headlines as to what was to come in 1929 appeared on December 8—"Major Break Occurs in Market Values":

> Stocks continued their downward tumble yester-day . . . a 72-point decline that clipped more than $83 million from the open market value of shares in Radio Corporation of America. . . . Stocks were dumped on the market for whatever they would bring. . . .

In spite of the uncertainty of the stock market and the price of commodities, my father completed his farming plans for the 1929 crop in April and.May. After all, everyone knew the stock market was un-stable and national economics would stabilize by fall—at least, this is the talk I remember. As futures on farm prices continued to drop, everyone hoped for a recovery. The newspaper headlines continued:

> *January 13:* Wyatt Earp Always Quick on the Trigger
>
> *January 24:* Einstein Reduces Physics to One Law—$E = Mc^2$
>
> *February 11:* Papacy Gets State in Pact with Italy
>
> *February 12:* Lillie Langtry Takes Final Curtain Call
>
> *February 17:* Passengers Watch Movie on Airplane
>
> *April 1:* Billy Sunday Packs 'Em In for Jesus
>
> *May 31:* Ford Will Help Soviets Build Cars
>
> *June 10:* Woman in British Cabinet
>
> *June 27:* Color Television Is Shown by Bell Labs
>
> *August 31:* Arab Revolt as Result of Dispute with Jews
>
> *September 5:* Briand Proposes European Union— A United States of Europe
>
> *October 24:* BLACK THURSDAY: STOCK MARKET CRASH . . .

The byline read: "This is a day that will be known for years as 'Black Thursday.'" Millions and billions of investments in stocks were lost within hours. J. P. Morgan and Company called a meeting of the nation's largest bankers. Morgan issued a statement, "I am still of the opinion that this reaction has badly overrun itself." Other bankers were assuring the nation that the stock market would rebound . . . but it didn't. Hundreds committed suicide as fortunes evaporated overnight.

As financial experts searched for answers, one story pointed out that stock "prices had been pushed too high, and some stocks were selling at 15 to 150 times their earnings." Hidden within a newspaper reporting on the stock market crash aftermath was the following paragraph:

> Thousands of foreign investors have sold their portfolios recently and are reinvesting at home as their countries recover from the war. Domestic speculators have also been probing the market for profits.

Europeans had invested heavily in American stocks, probably to the extent of damaging or undermining the European economy and capital growth. It is hinted that the Rothchilds and the banking establishments of England started the sell-off of stocks to initiate a run on American banks and the stock market itself. Whether planned as an international conspiracy or not, the end result is what counted. The stock market crash began the era in the United States known as the Great Depression that raged unabated until World War II.

The European colonial powers, the outgrowth of the Roman Empire, had never forgiven the United States for winning the War of Independence and subsequently pushing European holdings out of what became the United States. The Europeans profited by the slave trade and England helped the South in order to divide the Union into two lesser powers. Professors John Anthony Hort of Cambridge and Brooke Foss Westcott of Cambridge, whose revisions of the received biblical texts underlie the basis for most contemporary versions of the Bible (NIV, NASB, and others), influenced social and ecclesiastical attitudes in both Europe and America. Fenton John Anthony Hort's letters were published by his son, and on page 458 of volume 2 we find his opinions of both white and black Americans:

> I do not for a moment forget what slavery is, or the frightful effects which Olmstead has shown it to be producing on white society in the South; but I hate it much more for its influence on the whites than on the niggers themselves.... As yet everywhere (not in slavery only) they have surely shown themselves as an immeasurably inferior race, just human and no more, their religion frothy and sensuous, their highest virtues those of a good Newfoundland dog.... I care more for England and for Europe than for America, how much more than for all the niggers in the world! and I contend that the highest morality requires me to do so. Some thirty years ago Niebuhr wrote to this effect: Whatever people may say to the contrary, the American empire is a standing menace to the whole civilization of Europe, and sooner or later one or the other must perish. Ev-

ery year has, I think, brought fresh proof of the entire truth of these words. American doctrine destroys the root of everything vitally precious which man has by painful growth been learning from the earliest times till now, and tends only to reduce us to the gorilla state. The American empire seems to be mainly an embodiment of American doctrine, its leading principle being lawless force. Surely, if ever Babylon or Rome were rightly cursed, it cannot be wrong to desire and pray from the bottom of one's heart that the American Union may be shivered to pieces.

Even though the United States had helped to defeat Germany and restore a measure of peace and stability to Europe, the suspicion and contempt for the United States in Europe was put into graphic descriptions by such intellegencia like Westcott and Hort. How much the thrones of Europe had in bringing about Black Thursday on October 24, 1929, may never be known; however, there appears to have been involvement to the degree that justifies suspicion.

In July, August, and September, cotton prices were unstable and falling. There was not enough to pay off the note and keep enough in the bank to plant another crop in 1930. Cotton and corn prices after the stock market crash fell through the floor. Some of the cotton was bailed and put in storage until the prices would rise again, but they never did. Corn was kept in barns and silos, but as the price per bushel plummeted to ten cents, many turned to converting it to "white lightnin'." On a calm, cool, clear morning we could see tall plumes of smoke rising up and down Boggy River. Distillery was shortened to "still" to mean an illegal process of using corn to make alcohol. One gallon of moonshine sold for one dollar. Many were caught by government agents and sent to prison. Terms usually ran from two to three years.

The winter of 1929–1930 was a most difficult time for the Hutchings family. I can remember at times there was nothing to eat but cornbread and gravy. When early spring arrived, my father somehow got enough money to plant another crop. This time he diversified and planted not only cotton, but potatoes, corn, and peanuts. The market was depressed. Nothing was moving because most people simply had no money. At times our diet was supplemented by wild rabbit or squirrel. Our closest neighbors, the Kazelles, a German immigrant family, also ate possum baked with sweet potatoes, but my mother simply balked at cooking possum. Mr. Kazelle maintained a large flock of guineas. Guineas are a semi-wild fowl, and the hens would fly over our place and lay their eggs in the woods. Often, several hens would lay their eggs in the same nest. My older brother and I would go guinea hen nest hunting. My parents would have considered cooking the eggs, but that would be stealing . . . but us boys had no such restraint. We would each take a glass, along with salt, pepper, and vinegar. On locating a nest, we would break one egg in a glass, season it with salt, pepper, and a dash of vinegar, then down the hatch. The trick was not to break the yoke, and we would often down a dozen or so guinea eggs each.

As spring turned to fall in 1930, economic conditions worsened. There was no market for potatoes, corn, or peanuts, and by the time the picking and ginning of cotton was paid, the farmer was usually out more money than a bale of cotton would bring. I remember on our farm seeing huge piles of cotton out in the field not even taken up to the gin and left to rot. I went to live with my Grandma Askew, who had purchased a farm at the Bearden Springs community five miles southeast of Hugo. Farm owners were practically giving their lands away. Most had borrowed on their land to finance crops, and the option usually was to sell the farm or let the bank foreclose. My grandmother received a pension, as I remember because she was a Civil War survivor. The amount was approximately eighty dollars a month, and in 1930 when most people were flat broke, that was a lot of money. My living with my grandmother left one less to feed and care for at home.

When my father's three hundred dollar note came due, there was no money. Everything went— cows, horses, mules, tools, etc. My parents did keep the furniture, probably because it had no value anyway.

The main news stories in 1930 were:

January 28: Alcoholism Soars in Spite of Dry Law
February 28: New York City Installs Traffic Lights
March 19: Lord Balfour Dies
April 21: World's Great Powers Sign Naval Treaty
August 14: Babe Ruth Makes More Than President
September 14: Nazi Party Grows in Germany
October 23: Hoover Plans Program to Ease
    Depression
December 22: Stalin Justifies Purges in Russia
December 31: Jobless Number Over Four Million

The final headline included the Hutchings' household as our remaining meager items were put on a borrowed wagon to move to a rented farm house that was one-half mile west of Grandma Askew's house. The community was Bearden Springs. The future looked bleak, yet my father was always looking for greener grass on the other side of the fence.

Bearden Springs

The ten years the family lived in the Bearden Springs community southeast of Hugo were mostly a trial of survival. The Great Depression actually did not ease until 1940. While some like my Uncle Tobe had jobs, for most farm families life was extremely hard. My father continued to move from one year to the next. Counting the number of houses we lived in from 1925 to 1941, I can remember twelve. I can especially remember 1933 when the dust from dust storms in western Oklahoma would be driven by winds to southeast Oklahoma. The sky would become red and the sun could scarcely be seen. It was during this period that thousands of families left Oklahoma and made their way to California. The Okie migration continued from 1932 to 1936. Life for urbanites in eastern Oklahoma was just as difficult. Most of the land my father attempted to farm in the Bearden Springs area was poor, and had it not been for the Works Progress Administration of the Franklin Delano Roosevelt Administration, survival would truly have been in question.

When I was in the seventh grade we lived in the

old Graham place. It was a small, four-room house with no well. While there was a creek that ran near the house, in the summer it dried up and we had to carry water from a neighbor's house one-fourth mile away, the Satterfields. The Satterfields were kind and benevolent folks, members of the Church of Christ. They owned their own land and operated a small dairy. In the summer when we had to carry water for washing clothes as well as drinking, the bulk of this chore fell on me. Whether this was a contributing factor or not, I came down with appendicitis.

At that time women did not go to hospitals to have children. Most did not have the money. My oldest sister, Juanita, was at our home to give birth to one of her five children. I was in bed with a severe stomach ache. After Dr. Johnson had attended to my sister, my mother asked him to take a look at me. Dr. Johnson, who was approaching retirement years, poked around on my stomach and remarked, "I will write him a prescription, and if he does not get better in a week, bring him in to see me."

Dr. Johnson happened to bring along an intern just out of medical school. The young doctor asked if he could examine me. He was given permission, and within ten minutes rendered his diagnosis. He told the family that I had acute appendicitis. He said my appendix had ruptured two days ago and peritonitis was already setting in, and that I had a slim chance of recovery, and none at all if I was not operated on immediately. There were no antibiotics or penicillin in those days to fight infection. I was operated on the next day at Hugo Hospital. The appendix could not be removed, but a drainage tube was placed in my side. Almost miraculously I recovered, and a huge scar as a result of the three-month healing period remains to this day. If my sister had not chosen that particular day to have a baby, and if old Doc Johnson had not happened to bring a young doctor just out of medical school along with him, this story would have ended here.

Life on a farm in the early and mid-thirties was not only hard, it was at times brutal. There was no way my father could make a living for the family sharecropping and trying to raise cotton at depressed prices. The Democrats blamed Herbert Hoover for the Great Depression which continued to plague the nation. However, news stories in my possession relate that Hoover time and time again attempted to get Congress to appropriate public relief funds and stimulate the economy. More often than not, the president-elect reaps the blessings and curses left by the preceding administration. Herbert Hoover had the misfortune of being elected president at the beginning of the greatest depression in the history of the world, and a congressional political gridlock prevented him from responding.

The dominant headlines for 1932 read:

February 11: Mussolini Meets Pope
March 2: Lindbergh Baby Kidnapped

July 2: FDR Promises New Deal
August 14: 95,000 Watch Los Angeles Olympics
August 22: Eleven Million Jobless
November 8: Roosevelt Wins 472–59

One of the most positive things I can remember about 1932 was that I could take a quarter with me to town on Saturday, and with ten cents I could get a saucer-sized hamburger, a twelve-ounce Pepsi for five cents, and then get into the theater with the remaining ten cents for an exciting afternoon watching Tom Mix, Hop-a-Long Cassidy, or even Buck Rogers soaring to other planets in his rocket ship. The problem was to get the quarter. I was considered Grandma's pet, so she would usually slip me a quarter along with a wink.

Because times were still hard, my father supplemented his meager income by working two weeks out of the month on the Works Progress Administration (WPA), a public aid program of the new FDR Administration. He would often walk six to eight miles to work, put in eight hours, and then walk back home. My father, until the day he died, never owned or drove a car. He would not even ride a horse—the wagon remained his only method of transportation. WPA workers were paid forty-four dollars a month, and with that money Daddy was able to keep us kids from starving. Mother did everything possible to stretch the meager funds as far as possible, but they would go only so far. The WPA project did keep the unemployed from starving to death, and other good results were also in evidence. Many roads, bridges, and school buildings were built with WPA labor.

Another joint program with the WPA was the NRA, the National Recovery Act. This program was to bring peace and cooperation between management and labor, raise wages, shorten the work week, and prevent overproduction. By August 31, 1933, every company, industry, and place of business were required to display the NRA emblem, an aggressive eagle with a cog in one claw and lightning bolts in the other. There were oppositions as business and industry argued that this was state fascism. However, it was Christians across the country who brought about the death-knell of the NRA. They saw it as the "mark of the Beast." With industry and the church united against the NRA, it was replaced by other FDR welfare programs. One such program was the CCC, Civil Conservation Corp. This program involved enlisting young men between sixteen and twenty years of age for entrance into CCC camps. Enlistment was not mandatory, but with so many upper teens out of work, millions did join. Camps were made up of tents during the spring, summer, and fall months. Each camp had a mess hall. The young men were fed, clothed, and paid thirty dollars a month. However, each CCC enlistee could only keep five dollars; twenty-five dollars was sent back home to help feed the family. My brother Reghal served in a CCC camp at Stringtown in the Kiamichi

Mountains. The town had been originally named "Springtown," but the state sign painter made a mistake and the town entrance sign read "Stringtown." The citizens determined that it was too much trouble to get another sign, so the name remained as painted. The CCC program not only took young men off the streets, but also produced some valuable forest and river conservation work.

The newspaper headlines for 1933 read:

January 22: Xerxes and Darius Palaces Discovered
January 30: Hitler Named German Chancellor
March 20: Nazis Open First Concentration Camp
April 19: FDR Takes Dollar Off Gold Standard
May 10: Nazis Burn Books
June 16: Congress Passes NRA Program
July 26: Nazis Pass Law to Purify German Race
August 29: Nazis Send Jews to Prison Camps
October 27: Arab Rioters Oppose Jewish
    Immigration

In comparison to our contemporary meaning of recreation, there was little of it in the 1930s. Part of the time we did have a radio, when we had the money to buy a two-dollar dry-cell battery. I can remember listening to Jack Armstrong, the All-American Boy; Fibber McGee and Molly; the Red Skelton Hour; Amos and Andy; Jack Benny; Bob Hope; the Grand Ole Opry, and several other radio shows. When there was nothing to keep me in the house, I usually grabbed my .22 rifle or fishing pole and went to the creeks or the woods. My three closest friends were Floyd Satterfield, Harold Henegar, and Roy Wallace. Floyd was my hunting and fishing buddy. From November to February we would light our lanterns as the sun set, get our hound dog named Nig, and we would hunt for possums, coons, skunks, or whatever animal we could catch. Night hunting required a good dog, a .22 rifle, and a strong flashlight. We would walk about one-half mile in the woods or along a creek, and then we would build a fire. The dog would hunt in a circle, and if it treed something, it would bark. We would go to where the dog had something up a tree, shine the flashlight in its eyes, shoot it out of the tree, put the animal in a bag, and continue. If nothing was treed by the dog, then it would come back and let us know it was time to go on to the next area. Hides on the market at that time usually ran from twenty-five cents to four dollars, the price depending on the kind of hide and the quality. By the end of February I usually had forty or fifty dollars worth of hides. This was fairly good money in those days, and I depended on the sale of hides to buy clothes for the coming year.

Harold and I would get together and build crystal radio sets, make telegraph sets, and small electric motors. Roy was simply a good friend. His parents lived in a large, new brick house, and it was a treat for me just to spend the weekend with the Wallace family. After I left Hugo in 1946, I lost track of all three. In 1959 (not sure of the year), I was up at four a.m. taking care of my second daughter, Cheryl, and turned to radio station KOMA in Oklahoma City. A record by the then-young Willie Nelson was on the turntable. When the record stopped, the voice of the announcer came through, "This is Harold Henegar welcoming the listeners to KOMA in Oklahoma City." I looked up the telephone number of KOMA, and Harold and I had an enjoyable conversation recalling old times. I honestly do not remember if Harold and I got together or not, but he must have moved on to another city or other employment, as I lost contact with him once more. In 1995 Floyd was traveling from his home in Amarillo to visit relatives in Hugo and picked up our program on the car radio. Floyd looked up our number and came by to see me at our office located on Beacon Drive, in Oklahoma City, and we also had a good visit recalling events in our lives that had brought us to the present. In 1997 I attended the funeral of my brother-in-law, Fred Boone, and bumped into my old friend Roy.

One avenue of entertainment for teenagers in the 1930s was the community party. Someone would just decide to throw a party. Food would be served, and the boys and girls would play all kinds of games. At the close of the party, which would be well into the night, a boy would ask a girl to go walking. Usually a designated point, a half-mile or so away, would be where the couple was to walk and then return. Sometimes this party closing activity was well chaperoned, and sometimes not. In any event, this was one way young people got to know each other in those days. At one such party at our home, my dad got some whisky somewhere and made a complete fool of himself. We were all terribly embarrassed. I think my mother told him to shape up or ship out, and as far as I knew, he never took a drink of any kind of alcoholic beverage after that.

In 1934 notorious outlaws became modern-day Robin Hoods (just mostly robbing hoods). The newspaper headlines read:

January 1: Prohibition Comes to a Jubilant End

January 31: Jobless Join Civilian Conservation Corps

March 31: Dillinger Shoots Way Out of Trouble

May 23: Bonnie and Clyde Killed in Ambush

June 14: Hitler Stops Paying on Foreign Debts

June 30: Night of Gestapo Murders

July 22: Dillinger Killed in Chicago

July 31: Himmler Takes Over Concentration Camps

November 6: Mao Tse-Tung Marches North to Save Army

November 6: New Deal Wins Big Test at Polls

November 21: Cole Porter Voted Top Composer

November 22: Salvador Dali Shows Erotic and Neurotic Works

November 28: Baby Face Nelson Found Dead in Ditch

December 29: Stalin Purges Rivals
December 31: A Night Out with Claudette,
   Marlene, Greta, Ginger and Fred

One unusual experience I had about the time I entered high school involved what would be explained today as a UFO sighting. The time was at sundown on a clear summer day. I was taking a shortcut across a field to the house, when I noticed a ball of light come over the horizon from the east and stop at a forty-five degree angle, due north from where I was standing. The motion was constant and comparable to a fire ball shot from a Roman candle (type of fireworks), except perhaps a bit faster. The object just stopped in the sky. It did not slow down before it stopped. In about another five seconds another ball of light traversed the same path and stopped by the first; then in another five seconds, a third ball of light lined up with the other two. Helicopters did not even exist in those days; they could not be balloons; they could not be airplanes. From where I was, they appeared to be about the size of a hen egg as viewed from four paces. I sat down on the rocky ground and waited for the objects to move, but they remained motionless. Gradually the light from the setting sun waned and the sky became dark, yet the lights remained motionless. After an hour, I went into the house and my mother had saved some dinner for me. After quickly eating, I ran outside to see if the lights in the sky were still there, but they had disappeared. Whether these were an omen from the Lord, chariots of God as mentioned in Scripture, something from another dimension, fallen angels, I do not know. Even at that time the terminology relating to flying saucers, or UFOs, was unknown. These things that I saw were operated or guided by intelligence; there is no way they could have been man-made machines or operated by humans. Even though I operated a radar system during World War II, I never picked up anything, or saw anything, then or since, that I could not explain. I have no idea if there was a designed purpose in what I saw on that night near Hugo; however, I can empathize with those who say they have seen objects in the sky which they cannot explain.

Newspaper headlines told the story of 1935:

January 16: Ma Barker and Son Fred Gunned Down

February 10: Archaeologists Find Oldest Known City in Chaldea

February 13: Hauptmann Found Guilty of Killing Lindbergh Baby

March 31: Storm Clouds Gathering Over Europe

April 11: U.S. Hit by Dust Storms

May 27: NRA Closing Down

June 10: Japanese Attacking Northern China

June 20: Charles Lindbergh Helps Invent Artificial Heart

July 30: Nazi Repression of Jews Intensified

August 14: Social Security Enacted

August 16: Will Rogers and Wiley Post Die in
  Airplane Crash
August 20: Scientists Discover Vitamin E Crystals
August 25: U.S. Warns Soviets to Stay Out of
  Africa
September 3: Malcolm Campbell Exceeds 300 MPH
September 10: Huey Long Assassinated in Baton
  Rouge
September 15: Howard Hughes' Plane Hits 351
  MPH
October 20: Mao Tse-Tung's Army Reaches Yemen
  After 6,000-Mile Death March
October 28: Mussolini's Army Invades Ethiopia
December 21: DC Airliner Carrying 21 Passengers
  Makes First Flight
December 31: Errol Flynn, Marx Bros., Gable, and
  Hitchcock Offer Escape from Hard Times

High school days for most young men and women
are supposed to be the most pleasant and memorable times of their lives. Mine was mostly the opposite. In order to get enough money to buy my books
and provide for related school needs, my Uncle
Harvey and I cut fireplace wood for fifty cents a rick,
and kitchen stove wood for one dollar a rick. I did
farm work for one dollar a day, and signed up for
FDR's student assistance program. In this federally
sponsored program I swept floors and cleaned toi-
lets after school hours for six dollars a month. I had
no time for sports or band activities. I worked up

until the time I had to catch the school bus, both morning and night. Farm chores still had to be done. I can well remember getting up at five a.m., lighting the lantern, making my way through the snow to the barn, and milking the cows. The cows' tails would become a mass of cockleburrs. Then they would drag their tails through water, and the entire mass would become a frozen lump. To sit down to milk and get slammed in the mouth or on the ears with a flying projectile of a cow's tail full of frozen burrs would certainly wake me up in a hurry, as well as earn the cow a kick in the stomach. After finishing the farm chores, I would still have to get ready for school and walk a mile to catch the school bus. After my three girls got up to be teenagers, when I would repeat my days of hardship on the farm, they would run from the room screaming with their hands over their ears.

The first year I attended Hugo High School the football coach was Os Doenges. Coach Doenges was also the freshman civics teacher. At this period, both the Nazis and Russian communists were committing terrible atrocities, and Coach Doenges believed that the Roosevelt Administration was nothing more than a halfway house to a socialist America. By the end of the first semester, I had become convinced by Coach Doenges that Franklin Roosevelt was Satan incarnate.

Along with the other social welfare programs of the Roosevelt Administration, was a food commodity distribution program. Instead of issuing food stamps to the needy, certain "yellow dog Democrats" were appointed food distributors. (A "yellow dog Democrat" is one who would vote Democrat even if a yellow dog was running on the ticket.) My Uncle Henry was a food distributor in the Cloudy Creek community northeast of Antlers. The commodities (flour, meal, cheese, dried beans, and several other basic items) were kept in the storage house of the distributor, and the distributor doled out the commodities. Knowing my Uncle Henry, it is possible that he played the one-for-you and one-for-me game.

One day a member of the family who had a car drove us up to Cloudy Creek to visit Uncle Henry and family. Lo, and behold, on the front of the porch was a monstrous picture of Franklin Delano Roosevelt. It covered the entire wall of the front porch. By this time, President Roosevelt was ascending to messianic divinity by many, but to demonic possibilities by others. While Uncle Henry was taking the family to view his commodity storage building, I happened to see a box of crayons on a table. Temptation prevailed, and I took a big black crayon and, first, drew a healthy mustache on the face of the president. Then, in an open space, I wrote in bold letters, "THE HAREBRAINED IDIOT."

Sure enough, Uncle Henry and the others came from the storage building to enter the house by the front door. If ever I saw a man about to die of intense anger, it was my Uncle Henry. He ran into the house and rushed back with a double-barreled 12-gauge shotgun. He began yelling, "#@%#! This desecration of our beloved president, the savior of this nation, has just happened. The #@%# person who did this is still around, and when I find him, I will kill this #@%#!" Uncle Henry began running around the house, looking into the outbuilding, then back to the road looking in the ditches. Then he asked me, "Did you see anyone here while we were out back?" I tried to respond while stuttering and gulping for air. "No sir, I did not see anyone else." A strong suspicion, however, prevailed that I had committed this unpardonable sin. I was quite relieved when we were safely in the car heading back to Hugo.

Coach Doenges subsequently became coach at Oklahoma City University. He had an excellent football team in 1946 and 1947. OCU then abandoned its football program because it was not large enough to maintain a competitive football team. I believe that Coach Doenges then went to Tulsa and entered a Ford automobile agency business with his brother. Os came by Southwest Radio Church around 1955 and we talked about the turbulent thirties. He was running for some state office on the Republican ticket, but he was not successful.

The dominant newspaper headlines for 1936 were:

January 17: Germany Looking for Extra Territory
February 26: German Volkswagen Makes Debut

March 7: Nazis Enter Rhineland

April 21: Arabs Resist Jews at Tel Aviv and Jaffa

May 9: Italy Conquers Ethiopia

June 18: Luciano Guilty on 62 Counts

July 31: Civil War Rages in Spain

August 16: Jesse Owens Stars in Berlin Olympics

August 25: Soviets Execute Trotskyites

September 30: Franco's Army Takes Toledo

October 29: Rebels Drive on Madrid

November 3: Roosevelt Elected for Second Term

November 25: Fascist States Form Axis Alliance

December 11: Edward III to Marry Divorcee, Wallis
Simpson

December 30: Seven GM Plants Shut Down by
Strikes

December 31: Keynes Publishes New Economic
Plan

In the summer of 1936, my brother-in-law, Fred Boone, interceded for me in getting a job in one of the Roosevelt Administration's agencies. In 1934 farmers and ranchers were paid to kill beef cattle to reduce overproduction in the meat market. The Administration paid thirteen to seventeen dollars for each cow or steer killed, but the meat could not be sold or eaten. What happened was the sick, the lame, and the scrub beef stock were killed under the program, but the good beef cattle continued to be produced. While this program doubtless helped to improve cattle breeding to the profit of all farmers and ranchers, it did little if anything to influence the beef market. As us usually the case, when the government gets involved in spheres of influence where it should not be, the bureaucracy produces results exactly opposite of what was intended.

The job I landed was with a division of the Agriculture Department. The NRA had been forced out of existence; however, when one political program is eliminated, it simply reappears under a different name or function. The NRA symbol that was offensive to many was eliminated, but the program itself was not only continued, it was enlarged. Farmers could plant only certain designated acres allotted for certain designated crops. For example, if a farmer planted fifteen acres of cotton in 1930, in 1936 he might be allowed to plant only nine acres of cotton. The same rule applied to other crops. And, if the farmer planted more than the program allotted, then he had to plow it up. Of course, someone had to go and tell the farmer how much he may have overplanted and how much he would have to plow up. One of those someones was me. At times, one of those someones would be met at the gate by an angry farmer carrying a shotgun, which was also at times, me.

The way this program was carried out was that I was given allotment sheets with the names of the farmers, their addresses, and how many acres of each crop they were allowed to plant. My territory was from east of Hugo south of Highway 70, to the

Kiamichi River, and south to the Red River. My territory amounted to about one-eighth of Choctaw County. In addition to the allotment sheets of each farmer in my section, I was also given a measuring chain and aerial photographs of every farm in my section. I did not have a car because I didn't have money to buy one. I did have a bicycle, so I put a carrier over the back wheel to carry my papers, chain, and photographs. Some of the farms in my area would be fifteen miles from home, so often I would have to start out at half past five or six a.m. in order to begin work by eight a.m. I usually did not have to use the chain, because crops could easily be plotted on the aerial photographs due to the fact that every creek, tree, brush, and fence row was visible on the photograph. It was then easy for workers in the office to measure each crop plotted with measuring compasses. This job lasted from May to October, and I was paid (as I remember) ten dollars a day, which was great wages for that time when the nation was still struggling to come out of the Great Depression.

As already noted, my social life while I was in high school was practically nonexistent. I was a serious student, made good grades, and girls at that time simply were not in the picture. Even if they had been, there were few families in the Bearden Springs community with girls my age, and in the second place, I had no acceptable transportation. However, on one occasion I was invited to a community party and my mother insisted that I go and get out of the house.

When it came time to go walking, I teamed up with Martha Robinson. Martha's sister, Mary Ann, and another boy accompanied us. Mary Ann later took nurses' training, became a registered nurse, and married Joe Taylor Powell. Joe, Jr. and Joe, Sr. were famous for being the biggest liars in Choctaw County, and I do not believe the marriage lasted very long. At the time, Martha was a scraggly, red-haired, freckle-faced teenager, not exactly the Cleopatra type. After we had gone a few blocks, it was evident that Martha was more interested in Mary Ann's partner than she was in me, and they decided they wanted to walk about ten times farther than our original turnaround point. So I told the three that I had a very hard day, which I had, and that I would have to get up very early in the morning to get to my job assignment, which I would. I told them good night and walked back home. About one week later gossip was going from house to house how Noah Hutchings had tried to violate poor, little Martha Robinson. I got on my bicycle and peddled down to the Robinson home about one mile away and called Mr. and Mrs. Robinson out on the porch. Then I asked for Martha to come out, but I was told she was not at home. But I was able to inform them that their daughter had lied, and that I in no way had untoward intentions toward their daughter. However, it was then that I learned that people believe what they want to believe, especially parents, regardless of the truth.

Nevertheless, this event was trivial and had no import on my life, and I bore the reader with this incident only to make a point. In 1980 I was speaking at an all-day conference in Kansas City. One young man at the meeting introduced himself to me as Martha's son. He said his mother listened to our program every day, and that she planned to come to the evening session. However, if she came I did not recognize her, or she did not introduce herself. It would have been nice to at least see how she may have changed and to obtain closure on this old incident. In every incident in my life the truth of Romans 8:28 has been verified ". . . that all things work together for good to them that love God, to them who are the called according to his purpose."

The economic policies of the Roosevelt Administration drastically changed large areas of the United States. There appeared to be a planned and conscious program to destroy the small farmer. In the 1889 Land Run of Oklahoma, hundreds of thousands of small farms resulted. In the western part of the state these farmers were hurt by the great Dust Bowl disaster. In the southeastern one-third of the state the Great Depression made it impossible for the forty-, eighty-, and one hundred and twenty-acre farmers to make it. The further reduction of farming acreage by the Agriculture Department forced more small farmers to sell their land or let it lie idle. In the years 1937 to 1941, was added the soil-bank program. Farmers were paid from two to three dollars an acre just to put their farming acres in the "Soil Bank." This meant that farmers were paid just to do nothing by letting their farming acres go idle and unplanted. The majority of farmers signed up, because they seemingly were being paid for doing nothing. However, a government check for two or three hundred dollars a year was not enough to keep body and soul together. Subsequently, the small farms were bought by the lawyers, bankers, and out-of-state investors. Banks and lending corporations carried the mortgage notes and the soil-bank allotments made the payments. In other words, taxpayers bought the land for the affluent. In the 1930s, forty to fifty percent of the land was under cultivation in Choctaw County; today, probably not more than one percent is cultivated.

Today, most of the world's cotton is grown in Egypt, Israel, Turkey, and other foreign countries. Basic vegetable and fruit needs for the American family are grown in California, Florida, or the Rio Grande Valley. What happened was actually the capitalistic communization of the United States, or state-run socialism. The system has produced massive immigration of poor and uneducated peoples from the third world. And while the system has adequately produced food for the citizens, no one can foretell the future. If the communication system ever breaks down, then millions will starve to death, because most Americans today do not know how to grow even a hill of beans.

However, the great change in the farming econo-
mies has been environmentally attractive. Deer, wild
turkeys, coyotes, and even wolves are now roaming
the countrysides and woods in far greater numbers
than when I was a boy.

As these urban changes began to take shape in
1937, the main news headlines reported:

January 20: FDR Says Third of Nation
Underprivileged

January 27: Floods on Mississippi and Ohio Make
One Million Homeless

February 5: FDR Restructures Supreme Court

March 4: Benny Goodman Swings

March 18: School Fire in Texas Kills 500
Children

May 6: Hindenburg Dirigible Explodes

May 30: Tallest Dinosaur Found

June 12: Eight Soviet Generals Shot

June 22: Joe Louis Becomes Champ

July 18: Amelia Earhart Lost at Sea

August 22: Japanese Bomb Shanghai

August 28: Buchenwald Becomes Fourth Nazi
Concentration Camp

October 4: Hugo Black, KKK Member, Joins
Supreme Court

October 20: British Restrict Jewish Return to
Palestine

November 29: Nazis Take Children Away from
Parents

December 10: Java Man Shows Humans To Be One Million Years Old

December 20: Disney Produces "Snow White and the Seven Dwarfs"

December 22: Japanese Sink U.S. Ships

December 31: U.S. Census Shows Eight Million Jobless

There were two churches in the Bearden Springs community: a mission from, I believe, a Baptist church in Hugo on the west side, and a lovely little Methodist chapel on the east side. We would often attend the Methodist chapel, and perhaps once a year there would be a well-attended revival service in the summer. However, most of the churchgoing folks went to the Bearden Springs schoolhouse on Sunday morning. Brother Frank Tucker, a kind and saintly man, would teach from outlines he would put on the blackboard. Brother Frank was a Church of Christ layman, as were most of the citizens of the immediate area. My sister and brother-in-law, Juanita and Fred, became members of the Church of Christ in Hugo. One Sunday my mother made a profession of faith in Jesus Christ and joined the Church of Christ. Immediately, those who could convened at the site of Robinson's pool for the baptismal service. In the Church of Christ, baptism is an integral part of salvation, and the preacher wants to get the new convert under the water just as soon as pos-sible. There were no baptismals in the churches, and

I always thought it was strange that no one was converted in the winter when the pools were frozen.

In those days the Church of Christ members were dogmatic and hard-shell in doctrine. The Church of Christ was THE Church of Christ, and if you did not belong to THE Church of Christ, you had only a one-in-a-million chance of making it to heaven. Over the years the Church of Christ has mellowed somewhat until now they will give you one chance in a thousand of making it, even if you might belong to one of those other unnameable groups. Not long afterward my father also joined the Church of Christ.

Although the Great Depression tenaciously continued to hold the United States in its grip, there were signs that better days were ahead. The signs of the coming war, perhaps even greater in scope than World War I, was in the offing. Japanese and Germans were arming and expanding their territories and spheres of influence, and no one knew what the Russian communists were going to do. Plants in the United States making airplanes, tanks, and other weapons of war, were gradually increasing their work force and production. That year I was either working on the government farm program or at a service station, with only one more year left to go in high school. Juanita and Fred owned their own farm, and Geneva had married a good man, Elzie Glaze, who was of an Assembly of God background. Geneva and Elzie operated a service station in Coalgate, Oklahoma. Reghal had a job in Houston,

Texas. My younger sister, Sue, had married some character and they lived in Paris, Texas. I do not remember his name, and just as well, as they divorced after two or three turbulent years.

The only child left at home full-time was the youngest, Harold. Harold had, and at the writing of this lengthy epistle still has, a unique ability of staying in trouble and living by the skin of his teeth. On one occasion he was sent to the barnyard to gather eggs. Some of the hens laid their eggs under the barn, so Harold struck a match to find the nest. I hardly need to mention the result . . . the barn burned down to the ground. Harold, seeing that he had set the barn on fire, ran off and hid in the woods. When we all ran out to helplessly watch the barn burn, there was no Harold. The barn burned down to embers, and still no Harold. Naturally, we thought he had burned in the barn. My mother got a stick and started poking through the ashes and suddenly she cried, "Oh, I found Harold, my precious baby. His insides are on this stick." However, what was on the stick was not Harold, but sweet potatoes that were in a bin in the barn and had been thoroughly cooked in the fire. After a couple of hours Harold sheepishly showed up, and my parents were so happy to see him, he escaped a whipping.

On another occasion Harold went up behind one of my dad's huge grey mares and pulled the short hairs on one of its hind legs. The mare literally kicked Harold over the fence and he landed forty feet away.

He lived, but he still bears the print of two huge horse shoes on his chest. These are just two of the ninety and nine death experiences in Harold's life. I may recount the other ninety-seven, but before I write further I will have to get permission from Harold.

The major news stories for 1938 were:

January 14: NBC Rebuked for Mae West's Show

February 4: Hitler Promotes Himself to Military Chief

March 14: Adolf Hitler Takes Austria

March 18: Mexico Seized 17 American and British Oil Companies

April 10: Otto Hapsburg Warns World Against Hitler

April 12: PanAm Orders 75-Seat Plane

April 15: Dizzy Dean Traded to Cubs

April 19: Franco Says War in Spain Won

June 25: Roosevelt Passes 40¢ Hourly Minimum Wage

September 30: British Prime Minister Chamberlain Hails Pact with Hitler as "Peace in Our Time"

October 5: Hitler Takes Sudetenland

October 9: Yanks Beat Cubs for Third Series in a Row

October 30: National Panic Results from Welles' Martian Invasion

November 9: German Jewish Merchants Experience Nazi Horror

November 12: Kate Smith Sings "God Bless
  America"
December 1: Voted Most Popular Movie Stars:
  Humphrey Bogart, Spencer Tracy, Bette Davis,
  Jimmy Cagney, Pat O'Brien, Mickey Rooney,
  Errol Flynn, Douglas Fairbanks, Henry Fonda

I finished high school in the spring of 1939 and resumed my job with the agriculture management division of the Agriculture Department. At that time
probably no more than one in four high school
graduates continued on to college, so there was no
pressure for me to enter advanced education. However, I did investigate the possibility of enrolling at
Oklahoma State University at Stillwater, which at
that time was known as Oklahoma A&M. Money
was still a problem and there were no government
loans or sponsorships available in the late thirties

An alternate opportunity was presented. Because
I was involved in two federally related agencies, the
invitation came to enroll in a new vo-tech adminis-
tration-funded school in Ardmore, Oklahoma, about
one hundred miles west of Hugo. The airplane industry was being expanded in a quantum leap. Sheet
metal workers, welders, and riveters were needed.
For bright young men entering the program there
would be free schooling, board, and room facilities.
A good paying job was promised upon graduation.

As the summer job ran out, I packed my suitcase
and caught a bus for Ardmore. At first the facilities

were excellent and the teachers and instructors were adequate. However, to me, cutting metal, welding, or riveting all day was the most boring thing in the world. The manager of the institution suggested that I transfer to an office position where typists and file clerks were needed. Had I continued a few more months in sheet metal schooling, a transfer to a larger city along with a good paying job would have been forthcoming. I also would have doubtless escaped the army draft that came later. However, I had already dropped out of the sheet metal school, and there were no permanent job certainties in the clerical division. By the end of the year my funds were running low, so I began considering other possible opportunities.

On the national and international scene the news that made headlines in 1939 was:

January 1: Superman Appears as New Comic Hero

Janaury 28: German Scientist Produces Atomic Explosion of 200 Million Volts

February 22: 22,000 Nazis Rally in New York City

March 15: Hitler Takes Over the Rest of Czechoslovakia

April 1: Britain Signs Mutual Assistance Treaty with Poland

April 8: Albania Invaded by Mussolini

July 30: Hitler Threatens to Occupy the City of Danzig in Poland

August 10: U.S. War Department Places Huge
  Orders for Warplanes
August 18: Judy Garland Stars in New Movie,
  "The Wizard of Oz"
August 23: Hitler and Stalin Surprise World with
  a Mutual Non-Aggression Treaty
September 30: Hitler's 1.2 Million Army with
  Panzer Divisions Quickly Overrun Poland;
  Divides Country with Russia
September 30: Britain and France Declare War on
  Germany
October 14: Battle Ship *Royal Oak* and Liner *Athenia*
  Victims of German U-Boats; Hundreds Go
  Down with Ships
October 20: Britain and France Reject Hitler Peace
  Plan
November 30: Russia Invades Finland
December 18: "Gone With the Wind" Opens in
  Atlanta
December 20: German Battleship *Graf Spee* Forced
  to Scuttle

As the world entered 1940, most Americans were extremely troubled by what was happening in Europe and Asia. The memories of World War I were only twenty-two years in the past. Many had family members who served in the war, and some did not return. Nevertheless, times were generally better due to selling war materials to England and France, as well as preparing for war at home.

One news item that received little attention in 1939 was the release that a German physicist by the name of Otto Hahn had used nuclear fission to produce an explosion that released 200 million volts of energy. The news story, doubtless based on information from Enrico Fermi and other American physicists, stated that it would be twenty years before nuclear fission could be put to practical usage. This was misinformation to possibly mislead the Germans. However, American physicists knew exactly what this meant—that Germany in a few months could have nuclear weapons that would bring a swift end to the war and Hitler would rule the world. Efforts were spurred to a feverish pitch to not only catch up with the Germans in nuclear research, but to beat Germany to the punch. American scientists, and foreign scientists like Albert Einstein, began experiments at Columbia University and the Carnegie Institute. The Manhattan Project then took shape.

After completing my tenure at the federally sponsored vo-tech school in Ardmore, I returned home. While in Ardmore, I can still remember Gene Autry coming to town in a shiny, new, red convertible with the top down. Gene was in his heyday at that time. He wore a large, white, Western-style hat, white and gold-trimmed shirt and pants, a pair of white cowboy boots, and with the top down he would stand up in his convertible on Main Street and favor the locals with a few songs. Gene's ranch was about four miles north of Ardmore in the foothills of the

Arbuckle Mountains. The community changed its name to Gene Autry. The buildings are now so run-down that the town is no credit to the memory of this movie star and entrepreneur. The buildings that contained the vo-tech school were hit by a tornado in the 1980s, but they were repaired or replaced. Each time I go through Ardmore on I-35, I look at the structures and remember the days I spent there.

The major news stories in 1940 were reflected in the newspaper headlines:

January 19: Finns Stall Russians

March 13: Finns Surrender

March 15: U.S. Population Reaches 131 Million

March 16: U.S. Undersecretary of State, Sumner Wells, Tries to Bring Peace in Europe

April 9: Nazis Occupy Scandinavia

May 10: Winston Churchill Becomes England's Prime Minister

May 10: Hitler Launches Blitzkreig in Belgium and Netherlands

June 4: Part of British Army Escapes at Dunkirk

June 6: French Maginot Line Falls

June 14: German Troops Occupy Paris

June 17: Russia Occupies Lithuania, Latvia, and Estonia

June 22: France Officially Surrenders

July 29: Air Wars Over England Begin

August 1: RADAR—New Anti-Aircraft Weapon Used

August 26: British Planes Bomb Berlin

September 27: Japan Joins Axis and Invades French Indo-China

October 29: U.S. Army Draft Begins

November 5: Franklin Roosevelt Elected President for Third Term

November 12: Russia's Molotov Visits Hitler

In spite of tenuous and worsening international dangers and concerns, Hollywood produced its best pictures in 1939 and 1940. Continuing into 1940, *Grapes of Wrath* starred Henry Fonda; *Northwest Passage* featured Spencer Tracy. Others were: Bette Davis in *The Letter;* Jimmy Stewart in *Mr. Smith Goes to Washington;* and Katherine Hepburn in *The Philadelphia Story.*

Along with other young men, I registered for the draft, not knowing when I would be called. Anderson Prichard Oil Company contacted me about taking charge of one of the service stations in Durant, Oklahoma, fifty miles to the west of Hugo.

Durant was twice as large as Hugo in population, and at that time the Texhoma Dam across the Red River was under construction. This dam later formed Lake Texhoma between Oklahoma and Texas. At five a.m. I had to be up and have the station open when scores of workers would be stopping for gas. At one time during the early days of the oil boom in Oklahoma and the development of the east Texas oil fields, gas would cost as little as four or five cents a gallon. But in 1941 gas had risen to seventeen cents a gallon for regular and twenty cents a gallon for ethyl. Mid-sized motor cars were selling for between six and seven hundred dollars.

But this was not an exciting or fulfilling time in my life, as I felt like I was only marking time until I would be drafted. I was sure war was coming, and I tried to volunteer so that I could choose which branch of service I preferred. I was told that so many had volunteered that the draft system was being challenged to keep up with those who were to be drafted. Therefore, I would just have to wait until I was called.

The main headlines in 1941 which indicated the status of the United States and international problems were:

> *January 18:* Roosevelt Submits Lend-Lease Arms
>   Plan
> *February 14:* Bulgaria Accepts Nazi Occupation
> *March 27:* Yugoslavia Repudiates Offered Nazi
>   Occupation
> *April 17:* German Forces Invade
>   Yugoslavia
> *April 27:* Greek Army Capitulates to Axis
> *April 28:* Supreme Court Rules Negros Can Travel
>   in First Class Section
> *May 10:* Hess Lands in Scotland on Mysterious
>   Mission
> *May 19:* British Reclaim East Africa from the Axis
> *May 27: Bismarck* Sinks British *Hood;* Three Days

Later, British Sink the *Bismarck*

June 16: U.S. Stops Selling Oil to Japan

June 30: Germans Launch Massive Attack Against Russia on a Wide Front

August 14: Churchill and Roosevelt Sign Atlantic Charter: Destroy Nazi Regime and Create a Peaceful World

August 27: German Army Advances Deep Into Russia Meeting Light Opposition

September 4 : Germans Encircle Leningrad and Moscow; Say War Is Almost Over

December 5: Germans Suffer Serious Defeat at Moscow as Tanks and Artillery Get Stuck in Mud and Bitter Cold

December 7: Japanese Armada Devastates Pearl Harbor; Bulk of Pacific Fleet Sunk

With Great Britain still under siege and the sad defeat at Pearl Harbor, the question that was on most American's minds was the possible final defeat of England and an invasion by the Japanese. The continued existence of the United States as a sovereign nation was certainly in doubt.

On December 11, my nineteenth birthday, the United States declared war against Germany, Italy, and Japan. There was only one dissenting vote, that of Jeannette Rankin, the Republican representative from Montana.

Most everyone remembers where they were when a momentous event occurred, like the assassination of President Kennedy. On December 7, 1941, I was at home with my parents. At that time they lived on the Robinson place. My birthday fell on the following Thursday, so I was at home that weekend on Sunday because I could not be with them the following week. My dog had found a skunk's den two blocks away from the house in the pasture. I left the dinner table about one p.m. to try to get the dog to leave the skunk's den so that it would not get sprayed and stink up the entire place. When I returned to the house, my parents informed me that they had just heard on the radio that the Japanese had attacked Pearl Harbor. I wondered then how soon I would be drafted, and in which branch of the service I would end up, and on which battlefield I would fight.

Army Years

As the war for the United States progressed in the first months of 1942, the nation marshalled its industry and manpower for a long struggle to be fought on opposite sides

Me at Camp Roberts

of the world. While it appeared that England might survive, at least for a few more months, the war news from the Pacific arena went from bad to worse. The Philippines were lost with an army of approximately 150,000. Hong Kong, Singapore, Malaysia, Burma, and the South Pacific islands were lost to the Japanese juggernaut. The Japanese gamble was first to destroy the United States fleet, which succeeded more than they even hoped for in the attack on Pearl Harbor; then, take the Philippines, the major Allied bases in the lower Pacific; and then keep what remained of the U.S. fleet and the army remnants tied down in a protracted war defending Midway, Guam, Honolulu, and Australia, while Germany won the war in Europe. Then would come an Allied surrender which would leave Japan the master of the Western and Far East hemispheres. For the first year of the war it appeared the Japanese were accomplishing their goals. At first, Japanese victories shocked most Americans, but the war machine of Japan was a well-equipped, trained, and experienced army in all departments—navy, air force, artillery, and infantry. For forty years the Japanese had been fighting Russia, Manchuria, and China. Military plans were well formulated, tested, and carried out.

The waiting period for my draft number to be called seemed forever, so I continued running the Anderson Pritchard service station in Durant. Probably no more than one in a thousand U.S. citizens today realize the unparalleled miracle that occurred in this nation in 1942:

- Thousands of army barracks had to be built.
- Barracks had to be installed with plumbing, electrical wiring, and telephones.
- Millions of miles of roads had to be laid in the army camps.
- The U.S. Navy had to be practically rebuilt.
- Thousands of Navy ships from destroyers to battleships to aircraft carriers were built.
- Thousands of new and better airplanes had to be built—fighters, bombers, and freight units.
- The United States had to help supply English and Russian armies to help keep them afloat.

- Millions of men had to be called up and trained, with limited cadre.
- These millions of men had to be fed and clothed.
- Hundreds of millions of shirts, pants, socks, and underwear had to be made.
- Millions of new carbines, pistols, and rifles must be manufactured.
- Then, there were helmets, helmet covers, forks, knives, spoons, trucks, Jeeps, etc.
- Oil tankers, troop carriers, supply ships, LSTs, and LSMs had to be built.
- Billions of rounds of ammunition had to be made from .30 calibre ammunition to 20mm, to 90mm, to 155mm, to 240mm.
- Then all three branches of the armed services had to be trained to work together to accomplish a single goal—the defeat of two deadly enemies and the preservation of the United States of America.

Whether in retrospect we approve or don't approve of the economic and political policies of the Franklin Roosevelt Administration, it did an excellent job of providing leadership and employing the right people to unite the nation into one dedicated work force. Also, the citizenry had been hardened with eleven years of survival during the Great Depression.

Could the United States duplicate the war effort of World War II today? Probably not, even though the population today is double what it was in 1941.

The American patriotic spirit has been quenched by political corruption, anti-American international psychology, moral degradation, and unlimited immigration by the world's lower classes. However, the special unit army that was developed by the Reagan Administration seems sufficient for the world police action it is equipped to do. Also, there is always the ultimate defense—nuclear missiles. But this greatest war effort put forth by the people of the American Republic will never again be matched, nor has it ever been matched in the annals of human history— even overshadowing Greece under Alexander; Rome under the Caesars; the Mongolians under Genghis Khan; or France under Napoleon.

In the fall of 1942 my call had still not arrived. I was still only nineteen, and the order of the draft, counting down from the twenty-five–year–olds, had not reached me. It took time to build training facilities, train, and equip such a huge army for war. The dam over the Red River south of Durant had been completed and, along with gas rationing, it was no longer profitable for Anderson Pritchard to maintain a station in Durant. I returned home in November just in time to receive my army draft call, giving me one month to get my business and personal affairs in order.

The major news stories in 1942 were:

January 20: Nazis Solve Jew Problem—
    Extermination

January 31: Japanese Take Manila
February 14: Officers at Pearl Harbor Condemned
February 15: Japanese Take Singapore
March 3: U.S. Interns 100,000 Japanese-Americans
May 6: 46,000 Killed or Captured at Bataan and
   Coregidor
May 20: U.S. Navy Challenges Japanese on Coral
   Sea
June 7: U.S. Navy Wins Battle of Midway
August 7: U.S. Invades Solomon Islands
September 21: Germans Execute Hundreds of
   Thousands in Poland
November 11: Allied Forces Land in North Africa
November 25: Russians Encircle Germans at
   Stalingrad
December 2: Atomic Fission Reported by
   Manhattan Project

In later years, Monday morning quarterback jour-
nalists have condemned the United States for putting Japanese-Americans in internment camps. But
no way were Japanese-Americans treated as horribly as American prisoners of the Japanese. The Japanese were unbelievably harsh and cruel, and many
Americans were killed, butchered, and starved to
death in prison camps. When I was in Nanking,
China, in 1996, I investigated the slaughter of the
unarmed and innocent Chinese civilians when the
Japanese took over that city in 1935. Japanese soldiers were given special prizes for killing one hun-

dred Chinese men, women, and children, in one day. Estimates of civilians shot or bayoneted in Nanking ranged from one hundred thousand to a quarter of a million. We are not trying to restart the war with Japan, but critics of U.S. conduct during the war need to know what kind of an enemy the nation was facing at that time. Had the Axis powers won, the critics themselves probably would not have been alive to have the freedom to editorialize. If within the Japanese-American population there had been only one hundred spies or saboteurs, then the internment would have been justified.

A few days before my birthday I took a bus to Fort Sill, Oklahoma, near Lawton, and reported for duty. I observed three other birthdays in the army during World War II—all three on ships either going overseas, or moving from island to island, or returning home.

The first thing was barracks assignment, then to the commissary for clothes. For the first two weeks, along with other new recruits, I was learning how to tell my left foot from my right foot; how to salute without sticking my thumb in my eye; who to say "yes, sir" to; who to say "no, sir" to; and to whom I should just keep my mouth shut. There were IQ tests, educational level tests, and aptitude tests. There were also additional physical exams and vaccinations. After a couple of weeks I received my assignment orders. Along with a few others, I was assigned to a field artillery school at Camp Roberts, near Paso Rob-

les, California, in the mountains, thirty miles northwest of San Luis Obispo. Basic training involved thirteen weeks of army discipline, physical conditioning, and daily classes on survey and artillery fire direction for the 155mm howitzer. During the last three
weeks we went on field exercises to test what we
had learned and get some live experience.

Camp Roberts was only a year or two old. The
barracks were functional and clean, and approximately one hundred men were assigned to each barrack. We were lucky at our barrack in that a regular
army cadre sergeant was in charge. To be under a
"ninety-day wonder" (a short-term noncom) was not
good at all. These commissioned and noncommissioned officers tried to convince their charges they
knew what they were doing, when they really didn't.
Also, they were more strict and hard on the men than
regular army men. Any company or battalion was
really lucky if the officer in charge was a West Point
graduate. Because the armed forces were so rapidly
expanding, regular army officers or experienced officers were just not available. Most of these officers
were already serving in war zones.

Because there was such an immediate need for
officers, officer candidates were sent to a ninety-day
training school. Upon completion they would be
given a gold bar signifying that they were a second
lieutenant. Enlisted men referred to them facetiously
as "ninety-day wonders," but they probably filled a
needed role in the military during the early days of

the United States' entrance into World War II. However, most of the "ninety-day wonders" did not make good frontline combat officers. Noncommissioned officers did not have enough experience and had to pretend they already knew everything and had the necessary leadership qualifications. Therefore, they lacked the respect of those they were supposed to lead.

In the field artillery, most of the survey and fire direction work was done by noncoms. The 155mm howitzer battalion was made up of three batteries composed of four guns in each battery. A headquarters battery, and possibly a supply and ordinance battery, might also be added. On a map of the combat area the position of each gun battery is located. Number one gun in each battery will be fired, with the other three following in dial positions. Several checkpoints will be fired upon until a hit is registered. Then, when enemy targets are sighted, their relation to checkpoints closest to the target is called out by a forward observer or an airplane spotter. The observer calls out, "two hundred yards to the left, one hundred yards over." A fire direction noncom will make the adjustment, and usually get the gun on the target in three shots. Then, the entire battery, or all three batteries, can open up on one target. Today, in field artillery, missile battalions are replacing, or supplementing, the regular 155mm howitzer units. In World War II, there were also 105mm battalions and mortar battalions for closer artillery support. Fire directions would usually be something like this: "Battery adjust . . . shell, high explosive . . . charge five . . . fuse, quick . . . elevation, fifteen hundred mills . . . azmuth, thirty-two hundred mills. Fire ten rounds, on command."

Upon completion of our basic training period, the men in our barracks were split up and sent to different army divisions to fulfill positions in artillery units. About six of us stayed together in a group. My group was sent by train to Camp Howse near Gainsville, Texas. One of the soldiers in the barrack I occupied at Camp Roberts was Stanley Bradley from Boulder, Colorado. Stanley and I were bunkmates, meaning that one of us slept on the top bunk and one slept on the bottom bunk. We had the same farm background, the same habits, and the same recreational affinities. We were both happy that we stayed together as we went to Texas, and it seemed strange to me that I was within ninety miles of Fort Sill where I had been inducted.

Camp Howse (we called it Camp Louse) was a quickly constructed training installation. The buildings were skimpy, two-by-four frames, with thin building boards and tar paper for siding. There were no fans, no air conditioning, no streets—just plain, simple buildings out on the prairie. Camp Howse was to be the location for forming and training a new division to join the American Army in England.

However, the calibre of the officers was deplorable. All the commissioned officers and noncoms were afraid of the division commander, a brigadier general. His only qualification that I could ascertain was that he could fire and install a complete staff of new officers in a twenty-four–hour period. He could also cuss for five minutes without getting his breath. He would speed around the camp between the barracks in a Jeep, acting like a pit bull trying to escape from the city pound. He stopped by the barrack where we were staying to use our latrine, but when completing his mission, found there was no toilet paper. He immediately marched up to the office, demoted the first sergeant to a private, and then stopped a private in front of the barracks and told him that he was now the first sergeant.

After we had been at Camp Howse for ten days, we went with the division on a field trip to the Muskogee area in Oklahoma. Our group from Camp Roberts was supposed to work with a 155mm battalion to help get the infantry and artillery working together. It was, however, an impossibility, because the infantry officers did not know what they were supposed to do. Finally, after five days, the division retreated to Camp Howse. I was extremely pleased when new assignment papers arrived the next week, sending us back to Fort Ord, California, within ninety miles of where we left from Camp Roberts. I felt like a yo-yo. The only thing we accomplished in our month of travels was that I got to visit my parents at Hugo. After we left, the army decided to break up the division forming at Camp Howse and use the men and units there for replacements . . . probably a very wise decision. The camp later became a detention unit for German prisoners, and after the war it was vacated and destroyed. This incident simply illustrated some of the problems encountered in trying to build an instant army.

Fort Ord was a beautiful military installation, situated on the bay eight miles north of Monterey, California. A one-hundred–foot cliff separated from the Pacific Ocean by two hundred feet of deep, white, coarse sand provided an inspiring view from Monterey to Santa Clara. We were told that we would be given six weeks of Ranger training to prepare us for overseas service. The six weeks, however, turned into eight weeks.

Our schedule for Ranger training was:

Monday morning, fall out at five a.m. for roll call. Eat breakfast at half past five. Fall out in formation at seven in full field, thirty-seven pound pack, with M-1 rifle (another ten pounds), and then march eight miles to Monterey in the deep sand along the shore and then march back to be in time for lunch. Fall out again at one p.m. (without pack) with rifle for target practice, hand-to-hand combat practice, run through the obstacle course three times, and then do exercises until half past four. March back to the barracks, shave and change clothes from fatigues to khaki dress, march one mile to the parade ground, march one mile in review before the camp commander, return to mess hall for dinner. Change back into fatigues, and with full field pack and rifle, fall out in formation at seven p.m. March twelve miles into the mountains for night fighting and infiltration practices. Unroll our pack for sleeping (on the hard ground). The mess field truck arrived at six a.m. on Tuesday morning. After eating, we would march back to Fort Ord, arriving at eleven a.m. Then we would shave and change to khaki dress, eat, and fall out at one p.m. in formation for inspection. All who passed inspection would be given a pass to go to Monterey, Santa Clara, Salinas, or some other town nearby, or simply rest in the barracks. No one with a pass had to account for their time until five a.m. the next morning, and then the whole schedule was repeated, over and over, day by day, and week by week.

There were two reasons for Ranger training:

1. To make the soldier physically tough where he could withstand any physical test within human endurance, like the Roman and Grecian soldiers.
2. To make the soldier temperamentally and mentally tough, even to the point of caring for nothing.

Along with the physical training there was psychological training: any infraction of weakness required marching around the parade ground with rifle and full field pack for four hours; cleaning and waxing the barracks floor with a shoe brush, or cleaning the latrine with a toothbrush; instead of getting a pass, report to the kitchen to peel potatoes or wash pots and pans. Our appointed officer and judge of all things was a captain from Virginia. He never exercised with us or went on any field trips or night exercises. The only thing he did was to officiate at evening inspection and lead the evening parade. At the evening formation inspection, he never said but nine words. Every third soldier, he would look at the shoes and then to the head, and say in a loud, southern voice, "I SAY THERE SOLDIER, THERE'S FUZZ ON YOUR FACE." There was never anything wrong except fuzz on the face, but for this, all kinds of unpleasant things might be in store for the unshaven, imagined or real. One of the reasons for fuzz on the face was that when we came off of the day's routine, the latrine facilities were so crowded and with so little time, some did not get to shave. Regardless, if I was one of the third soldiers in the ranks, the captain was going to see some fuzz on my face.

Due to such punishing, physical exercise and treatment, we were always hungry. We never got enough to eat. When we were marching out into the hills and mountains, we would put candy in our socks and then cram them into our mess kit. The socks were to keep the candy quiet while marching. One morning, arriving back in camp after night exercises, the captain called us out in formation. He was absolutely furious. The camp commander had been out in the area in a Jeep and had seen some candy bar wrappers that some soldier had neglected to pick up. According to the captain, we had embarrassed him terribly, perhaps even delayed a much-longed-for promotion to major. We were told that in order to redeem ourselves, the camp commander had ordered that there would be no passes for us. We would have to run obstacle courses that afternoon, and then march back out at night, and our captain was to lead us there and back.

That night we got to the area around eleven. We had taken flashlights so that we could search for the candy wrappers, and then, as instructed, we dug a six-foot-deep hole to bury a few pieces of paper. Shortly after midnight we assembled to march back, and none of us were in a very pleasant mood. The captain had not been training with us, and he barely made it out to the site. So in returning, a few in front began to double-time. We passed the captain up, and we all ran the twelve miles back to camp. We had become that physically tough, and mentally, we did not care what happened once we got back.

We all showered and went to bed for the couple of hours left in the night. We awoke as the wake-up call sounded, but still no captain. As we came out for roll call, we looked down the street to where it turned toward the mountains, and there came the captain limping along. It was obvious that his legs were about to give out and that he must have had blisters on his feet. A couple of us whispered through the ranks to give a special greeting to the captain.

He did not even look at us, but as he ducked to go into the side door, we all shouted: "I *say there, soldier, there is fuzz on your face.*" Revenge was so sweet. We all expected the worst, but the captain never said one word, possibly because he first went to the infirmary for a couple of days to recuperate.

One of the lighter moments while I was at Fort Ord was the building of a beautiful noncommissioned officers club on the edge of the cliffs overlooking the bay. It was one of the most unique and attractive buildings I had ever seen. Bob Hope and Francis Langford gave a performance at the club on opening day. But we did not get to enjoy the club for very long because in the latter part of October we were shipped to Camp Stoneman in Sacramento, California. We were at Stoneman for a couple of weeks getting our final physicals and shots. Then late one evening in the latter part of November (I don't remember the day), we got on a ferry and went down the canal to San Francisco. Alcatraz was just off the port bow as we boarded the huge troop transport that was to take us somewhere, not known at this time.

Getting ten thousand soldiers on a troop transport is something like putting sardines in a can too small to hold them. Bunks were hammocks within a frame. There was about the same room between each bed unit as shelves in a bookcase. There was no escort vessel to defend us in the event the ship ran into a Japanese submarine. We were told that this was a very fast ship that could outrun any submarine. I was glad that we did not get that chance. We were informed one night that an alert was in effect and all cigarettes and lights had to be extinguished, but if our transport was under submarine observation, our ship did outrun it.

Fare on a large troop transport is beans for breakfast, beans for lunch, and beans for dinner. This is all there is, because beans are easily kept, and a hundred pounds of beans will feed a lot of soldiers. Stanley Bradley did spare me a cookie as I observed my twentieth birthday. After a journey of some seven thousand miles, the ship finally docked at Noumea, New Caledonia. It was good to breathe fresh air again after two weeks on a ship of bean-infested soldiers.

I had no idea where we were, but soon learned that New Caledonia was a French possession, an island approximately three hundred miles long and fifty miles wide. Its location was north of New Zealand and east of Australia. Noumea, the capital, was a beautiful little city of approximately ten thousand citizens—mostly French. The natives were of Polynesian stock, huge, and very black for Polynesians. The women had umbrella-style red hair. When I asked how blacks could have red hair, it was explained that they put lime on their heads to kill lice, which in turn changed their hair into a bright scarlet color. Across Noumea Bay on a cliff was a huge white cross. At first I thought this meant a Catholic monastery, but later learned it was a leper colony. In

Africa and other French possessions, there were many lepers. Before 1950 there was no permanent cure for leprosy, so the French government sent all lepers there. I also heard later that some U.S. soldiers had gotten into the colony and fraternized with a few of the women and were forced to permanently stay there. Whether this is true or not could not be confirmed.

After the ship landed at the dock, a column of trucks was waiting to take all the soldiers, sailors, and airmen to a staging area ten miles up in the mountains. The trucks had to make several trips. After our accustomed breakfast of beans, my turn came. The staging area was a maze of tents, a monstrous tent mess hall, and a tent PX. Our tents were assigned and we were given our duffle bags which had been correctly numbered and stenciled. I thought I had seen red earth in Oklahoma, but nothing like this. The dust clung to our clothing and turned everything a rusty red. After sandwiches and tea, the loudspeakers announced that everyone should immediately assemble in an open area inside the camp. The camp commander, a bird colonel, informed us that every soldier, sailor, marine, and airman who had been on our ship should fall out with full field packs and sidearms. Some had sidearms and some M-1 rifles, depending upon the branch of service. Then he turned to a master sergeant and said, "Take these ladies out on a twenty-five–mile hike and let's see what they've got."

It was in the middle of December, but in New Caledonia, it was the middle of summer. It was high noon; the temperature was above one hundred degrees Fahrenheit, and the humidity must have been one hundred percent. We could not walk much more than a block without sweat soaking through our shirts. There was a large contingent of young Air Force personnel on our ship, and they were placed in front of our company. The airmen did not have full field packs, so all they had to carry was a sidearm piece and a water canteen. The airmen started out swinging their arms and singing loudly, "Nothing Can Stop the Army Air Corps." This in itself was an error because they were only wasting energy. To us, their pace was extremely slow, so we began to taunt, "Get these girls out of our way." We did not have long to wait. After five miles, the airmen began to drop out—vomiting and passing out. Before we reached the twelve-and-a-half–mile mark, not one airman was left standing. Trucks had to come out from the camp and the airmen were piled sideboards high as they carried them back. Ranger training had stood us well. Not only was there not one single soldier in our group that did not make the entire twenty-five–mile hike, we did it in record time. We returned to camp with one and a half hours of daylight left. This was how tough we were.

After more physical examinations, we were assigned to our unit. Several in our division were taken another ten miles to the 518 AAA Gun Battalion, a 90mm antiaircraft battalion. Why? I never found out. The unit had already formed, and we were sent in as either replacement or to fill the compliment of personnel needed or required. My army buddy, Stanley Bradley, was also sent to the same unit with me.

At first I was assigned to the optical control squad. To reach high-flying enemy planes, high velocity 90s were required. A person with a certain type of vision could look through the range finder and by matching the images of the plane, or planes, on both ends, firing data could be obtained. But this was not a very good way to determine antiaircraft fire. It was not only inaccurate, and a good guess at best, it was also very slow. Often the plane would be out of sight before the guns could get ready to fire. I was still scratching my head as to just why I had been assigned to this unit when a large van was delivered, approximately thirty feet long and ten feet wide. The operations officer, a second lieutenant, called to me and said, "Here is your machine." I asked, "What is it?" He responded, "You are a trained technician. You are supposed to know what it is."

While there were pitchfork radar units to pick up approaching aircraft, there was never before anything like this. I was given an operations manual for the unit and instructed that I must learn to operate it. The next day three others were assigned to help me, and in another week a radar technician came out to finish orienting us in operation procedure. The unit was a beautiful system. It had a scan scope, a range scope, and an Identification, Friend or Foe (IFF) capability. The range was ninety miles, which at that time was quite adequate. The parabola was retractable and the van was air conditioned, which in the South Pacific was an absolute necessity. A separate unit, about the size of an electric kitchen stove, was mounted on two tires. This unit, called "the computer," could be attached for transit on the back of the van, or to a separate vehicle. No one had ever heard of a computer until the previous year. The function of the computer was to take data from the radar system and convert it into information that could be interpreted by the 90s. The computer did away with the visual system; it fired the guns automatically; it even set the fuses where the shells would explode within feet of the target. The radar and computer were a quantum leap in antiaircraft artillery.

There were, however, two flaws in this earliest radar-computer system. At times it was necessary to communicate with the air force and island defense systems. We could not say exactly how many enemy planes were in a single formation, or their altitude. The range scope could tell us how far the planes were from our location, but for some reason there was no automatic altitude indicator. However, I had three years of geometry, trigonometry, and analytics. I devised an altitude chart with a sliding arm, and it would take only a couple of seconds to compute altitude. The computer knew what the altitude was, but it would not tell us.

Another problem was the IFF system. The response signal was so broad that Japanese planes could come in piggyback on returning air force planes so that the IFF would cover them also. This happened once on Luzon, and the general in charge of Clark Field concluded it was us, not the radar system, that was in error. We had to pull double duty for a month and were confined to the base, which was a small matter since there was no place to go anyway. Most of the time we pulled four hours on and eight hours off. When there was action in the air, we seldom could see it, as we were inside the closed van. We could hear the high velocity 90s, though, blasting away. There were dire predictions that we radar boys would develop cancer, our hair would fall out, and we would become sterile. None of these predictions, as far as I know, were valid.

Being in a separate unit, attached to whoever needed us (air force, Sea Bees, navy, etc.) made us military orphans. If we did not get our mail, no one cared. If we did not receive our requisitions for food, there was no higher authority to appeal to. While the colonel in charge of our battalion was probably a good man, he was a nonentity as far as we were concerned. He never interceded for us, and I do not even remember his name. Regular army officers looked out for their men, but our commander must have been a product of the "ninety-day wonder" system.

The War Department paid the Australian government to supply us with much of our food, especially meat. This would relieve the problem of shipping food from the West Coast when ship cargo space was exceedingly limited. What we got was nothing but goat ribs. The cooks did not know how to cook goat, even though it is questionable that goat can ever be prepared to be edible. What they did was dump goat ribs in a big pot, dump saurkraut over them, and boil them for two hours. It was the most unsavory, pungent, totally inedible mess on the face of the earth. The ritual was the same every day— cook goat ribs and saurkraut, then dig a hole and bury the malodorous concoction. To get away from the smell of goat ribs we had to escape into the jungle for a mile or so. Occasionally we did get a shipment of hams that had been salt cured. These, too, were inedible. The cooks could have boiled the hams for an hour and gotten the salt out so that they could be fried and served, but such a cooking procedure for meat was not in the cook's manual. When we left New Caledonia for New Guinea, the cooks left a hundred boxes of salt hams under a tree. We also received dried, processed food from the States. Again, cooks had not been taught how to prepare dehydrated food. The potatoes came out a bland, tasteless soup; the carrots and peas were hard. Powdered eggs looked and tasted like nothing man nor beast had ever eaten; and C-rations tasted like they had been seasoned with kerosene. K-rations were somewhat acceptable—a small can of Spam, a block of rubber cheese, and two hardtacks. While K-rations were certainly not gourmet cuisine, at least they did not make us sick.

Australia was one of the major beef producers. The Aussie soldiers ate steak, and we got worthless goat ribs. Had it not been for the Americans, Japan would have taken Australia, and we had difficulty suppressing our feelings toward them. The French on New Caledonia were not much better. How we yearned for a steak, fresh potatoes, and especially milk. Once we had reason to go to the dock in Noumea to pick up supplies, and on the way into town we passed a three-story pink house. Sailors were lined up at the house two abreast, two blocks down the street. I thought it was a restaurant, and I suggested to the men that we stop by on the way back and see if we could get a hamburger. A soldier on our detail, who had been on the island longer than I, remarked that this place was not a restaurant. I was careful to never again suggest we stop at the pink house for lunch.

Our mission on the island was, first, to get proficient at shooting down Japanese planes. The second part of the mission was to protect the navy base at Noumea from a sneak attack by Japanese bombers. The lesson from Pearl Harbor had been well learned. We actually had little contact with the French islanders. We did occasionally go into Noumea, but the only French words I learned were, *"Honey, would you like to walk in the park?"*

It should be kept in mind that at this time I was still a pagan or a heathen, whichever word fits. But in my defense, I was still a relatively good person. Except an occasional trip to Noumea for an ice cream cone or a piece of pastry, there was no social life or recreation. One time we did go deep into the jungle for a native luau. I have no idea what we ate or what we drank, but whatever it was, I was sick for two weeks. Just before we left for New Guinea, we were supposed to get a week's R&R on New Zealand. But the marines had preceded us there, and I understood that the population of New Zealand was to expect a sudden increase in six or seven months. Therefore, New Zealand and Australia were both declared off limits to all American personnel.

The Solomon Islands were fairly well secured, and the prospects of the Japanese pushing farther into the South Pacific subsided. Therefore, we were told that we were needed farther north. We loaded our guns, equipment, and members of the 518 AAA Gun Battalion on a couple of ships and sailed for Lae, New Guinea. While at Lae, Mrs. FDR made a "goodwill" trip to bolster the morale of Americans fighting in the South Pacific arena. What she saw was not the spit-and-polish soldiers at the changing of the guard at Arlington Cemetery. She said she was repulsed by the unshaven, dirty bunch of riffraff. There was a sudden conference between the War Department and the White House, and Mrs. Roosevelt was quickly recalled before some GI took a pot shot at her.

Life on New Guinea, on a scale of one to ten in comparison to New Caledonia, was ninety-nine and falling. It rained every day, the jungles held the moisture right on the ground, clothes never dried, and mold and jungle rot were constant problems. The jungle was awesome, the sun never touched the ground, and the massive mahogany trees seemed to reach the sky. We had to wear mosquito netting over our helmets down to our shoulders, heavy gloves to keep the mosquitoes from biting our hands, and two or three loose shirts, with our pants soaked in repellant. Mosquito netting kept the pesky varmints out of our tents, but when we moved from place to place, we would go single file. Each of us would break off a leafy branch. We would hit each other on the back and shoulders, but before we could lift the branch again, the back would be black with mosquitoes again. Living in those conditions, perhaps the reader can appreciate why we were so upset with Mrs. Roosevelt's opinions.

Although I had no personal knowledge of soldiers dying of massive mosquito bites, some claimed that it did happen. If a soldier got drunk and passed out, or became wounded and could not get back to camp, swarming mosquitoes could kill a grown man in short order. With each meal an atibrine tablet was placed in our mess kit. The atibrine was to keep soldiers from getting malaria. Some soldiers threw them away, but not me. I had once contracted malaria, and I certainly did not want it again. But by taking atibrine daily, my fingernails became yellow; my teeth were yellow; my toenails became yellow; and my eyes were yellow. Because of the lack of, and quality of the food we had to eat, I lost weight down to one hundred and ten pounds. With bones showing, yellow teeth, and yellow eyes, I must have looked like something out of a UFO.

The only recreation we had was to swim out to sunken Japanese ships in the bay, but we had to look out for the sharks. The Aussies did build a Bamboo Club where sandwiches, snacks, and drinks could be purchased. Some of us "Yanks," as we were called, decided to patronize the Aussie's establishment, but we were refused entry. That night the club was mysteriously trashed. We tried to blame it on the Japanese, but no one bought the story. Once again we were confined to our area for punishment, but it was no big deal. Again, where were we going to go anyway?

My brother, Reghal, was in Air Force Medical Supply. I got word that on a certain day his plane would be at Nadzab, thirty miles inland from Lae. I managed to catch a ride to Nadzab, but his plane did not make it.

In World War II, as we have already noted, blacks and whites did not serve together. Black soldiers were usually in ordinance or quartermaster. In fact, I remember no Latin-Americans or Asian-Americans in my battalion. There were Jews, Catholics, Protestants, and non-Christians, but only one race. That is just the way it was. I remember one night at Lae that I was assigned a detail to go to an ordinance depot in the jungle and bring back a truck load of 90mm ammo. The ordinance personnel at the camp were all black. We always tried to wait until after dark to go to the ammo dump. However, there was some problem in bringing up the ammunition from another location, so we had to stay all night. We were invited to eat, but we had to go outside. We were not offered a cot, and we could not sleep on the wet ground. I slept on a stack of 105mm shells that had been piled like cord wood. It almost seemed that we were in different armies.

Homosexuals, when discovered, were shipped out immediately, returned to the States, and given a Section Eight discharge. We had a replacement who was shipped out within a week of his arrival. But there was always the possibility that some men pretended to be homosexuals just to get back to the States. Section Eight discharges could also cover other problems, including nervous breakdowns or mental illness. After the Solomons were secured and the Japanese forces were pushed back farther north, we left Lae and by ship sailed to Hollandia. On the way to Hollandia, one member of B-battery suddenly got the delusion that he was Jesus Christ. He went about picking his twelve apostles, and kept trying to get off the ship to walk on water. He was placed in detention, and upon arrival at Hollandia was taken to medical facilities. Serving in the South Pacific was more difficult than serving in Europe. Servicemen were in a different environment, and the loneliness and boredom were at times overbearing. I and four other radar operators bunked in one tent. When one member, Sweeney from Boston, did not replace me at the end of my shift, I went to the tent. Sweeney was gone. He had suddenly snapped and was talking about suicide. He was sent back to the States. At times, it happened that fast. I heard later that Sweeney had gotten better after an extensive stay in a psychiatric ward.

Although New Guinea was only a short distance from Australia, the ecology and animal life forms were entirely different, mainly just monkeys and wild pigs. While these supplemented the aborigines' diet, the natives (who still practiced head hunting and cannibalism) lived mainly on roots, tubers, wild nuts, and grasses. One day while walking through a native village I observed a woman grinding wild maize into flour to make bread paste. The average life span on New Guinea was only about thirty-five years, and the women after bearing children would have very elongated breasts. While both the men and women wore loincloths, neither wore anything above. This poor soul, as she would grind around and around in the stone jar with a wooden mallet, would throw her breasts over her shoulder to keep them out of the way. But slowly, with each round of the mallet, her breasts would gradually slip back down into the jar. I think it was memories like this that later motivated a love for these unloved people, and created a fire in me to share the love of God with them.

There were so many war headlines in 1943 through 1945 it would not be feasible to enumerate them all. As the Japanese became stalled in the South Pacific on their march to Australia, Stalin took a great risk. He gambled that Japan was so threatened by increasing U.S. military power, that he could move the entire Russian army in the east by train to strengthen the defense of Moscow. It worked, and the Germans were turned back, and ultimately retreated to Poland and eastern Europe. In March of 1943 U.S. army and navy planes caught a Japanese convoy carrying a huge Japanese army to reinforce Japanese troops on New Guinea. Every ship, fifty-five in all, was sunk or set on fire. Confident that the Allies would win the war, Roosevelt, Churchill, and Stalin met in Tehran on November 28, 1943, to divide up the world. Here was where Joseph Stalin, perhaps the greatest murderer of men who ever lived, became "Good Old Uncle Joe" to President Roosevelt.

The news stories of 1943 and 1944 relative to the war effort are history. The Germans were defeated in North Africa. The United States got bogged down in Italy. D-Day finally came on June 6, 1944. Much of England and Germany lay in waste as a result of the V-1 and V-2 rocket barrages of Germany and the intensified bombing from air by American and the British bombers.

The U.S. army and air force men in the Pacific greatly admired General Douglas MacArthur, regardless of propaganda to the contrary. His tactics of leaping over, or leaving bypassed Japanese armies to wither on the vine was successful, and thousands of soldier's lives were saved. In 1944, decisions in Washington granted more authority to navy and marine admirals to determine the course of the war in the Pacific. Had General MacArthur remained in total command, it is doubtful that so many thousands of American lives would have been lost on Iwo Jima and Okinawa. At one point in the war for Okinawa, it was decided to retreat from the island because so many ships and lives were being lost.

In November 1944, a massive convoy of ships began to assemble at Hollandia. We knew that something relatively big was up. The Philippine islands of Leyte, Cebu, and Mindoro had already been invaded by American forces, and the next logical island to be invaded would be Luzon. I observed my twenty-second birthday on a ship once more heading for somewhere. We were told our location on a day-to-day basis, but it soon became apparent that our destination would be somewhere on Luzon. As our convoy, which I estimated to be made up of at least one hundred and fifty ships, passed Bataan Peninsula and Corregidor, I saw a flight of about twenty airplanes overhead at about twelve thousand feet. Being in the antiaircraft artillery, we had been trained to identify Japanese planes, and I knew these were Japanese dive bombers. I wondered why there were no navy fighters in the air, or why the antiaircraft guns on the destroyers, cruisers, and convoy ships were not firing. Every convoy ship, freighter, tanker, or troop carrier had 20s, 40s, and higher. The alarm on our ship finally sounded, and all non-navy personnel were ordered off the deck. I had an arm band that I was the noncom in charge of the guard that day, so I was allowed to remain on top.

The Japanese planes flew across the entire width of our convoy, then turned around and started back. They had dropped in altitude to around seven thousand feet, and as they passed over the destroyers, four of the planes flipped over in a perpendicular dive. Every antiaircraft gun on every ship had been following. The order came to fire, and the entire sky became filled with exploding antiaircraft shells. Then, about twenty-five Japanese planes came skimming over the ocean at no more than twenty feet off the water. Others came out of the clouds, and before the kamikaze attack was over, I would estimate that there were probably a hundred planes involved. A huge tanker and ordinance supply ship was fifty yards behind us. One kamikaze evidently decided to try to take it out. There were so many guns firing at it, it just seemed to disintegrate before it hit, and it fell harmlessly in the water between us. Another kamikaze fell in the water fifty yards to our port side. But this was the greatest show I had ever seen. The attack lasted about thirty minutes. I would estimate that fifty of the Japanese planes were lost in the attack, the rest finally withdrew and flew away over Bataan. Several of the ships in the convoy were hit, and I do not know if any of them sank. I could see several burning as night came.

The kamikazes, or divine wind, typified the Japanese psychology. The Japanese serviceman was schooled in the Shinto religion. It was a great honor to die for the emperor and go to be with one's ancestors. Many Japanese soldiers wept in disgrace if they were not chosen for kamikaze or death assignments. It was difficult to comprehend Japanese pilots just flipping their planes over and heading for targets without any thought of pulling out of the dive. But this was the kind of Japanese the Americans fought in World War II—on the ground, on the sea, and in the air.

We landed on the beaches of Lengayan Gulf on Luzon the morning of the second day of the invasion. We got our guns, radar, and all other equipment off our ships as soon as possible, and dug in on the beaches to protect the ships in the harbor and troops on the ground from Japanese air attacks. Bulldozers quickly dug out deep holes for gun emplacements, but we were absolutely amazed that so few

Japanese planes showed up. We were actually disappointed. Evidently, most of the available planes had been used up in kamikaze attacks.

By the third day the beach had been secured, the assault troops, tanks, and infantry had widened the beachhead, and we moved to a position five miles inland. However, the same problem arose again. We were an independent, attached battalion, and we did not have enough food. We stole a quartermaster sign from a truck, put it on one of ours, and lined up at the beach where landing crafts were unloading food supplies. Our truck was filled to the top of the side boards and we returned to our camp, hilarious that we had pulled off the whole thing. But when we opened the cases, we found box after box filled with one-gallon cans of unsweetened cherries. There was simply not much we could do with sour cherries except give them to Filipinos, and I have no idea what they did with them.

After breaking out from the forest line that ringed the beach, there was nothing more between Lengayen Gulf and Manila. It was a one-hundred–mile–long flat valley. There was practically no Japanese air force resistance, so what was to be done with four 90mm antiaircraft batteries? Evidently, the First Cavalry Armored Division could use them. We bypassed Clark Field and in five days we were on the outskirts of Manila. A Japanese division had taken up defensive positions in the old Spanish Wall part of the city. Our 90s, using armor-piercing shells, were to line up about one-half mile away and use direct fire in tearing down the wall. First, we had to get the guns through the city in order to get into position. As our convoy approached the outskirts, there was a roadblock one-half mile ahead that had to be cleared. The Japanese had probably been on the road where we stopped an hour or two earlier, and what happened should only have happened in an R-rated movie. Two blocks away there was a two-story house with lots of windows on the top of a small hill. Filipino women began hanging out of the windows, waving things should not have been waved to our battalion. Trying to stop a bunch of soldiers who had not seen an acceptable female for almost two years, was like trying to stop cattle dying of thirst from reaching a cool stream of water. Whistles blew and we had to move. Many of our men were still putting on their shoes and running to catch up with us as we moved a mile into Manila.

The next day we reached the hub of Manila, which was five streets meeting at one intersection. The city was laid out according to the European plan. Stanley and I were riding at the head of the column, and we were instructed to direct our vehicles and guns right through this intersection. The city was still burning, and bullets were buzzing around our heads. As our trucks and guns sped past, I looked across the main thoroughfare, and there stood a little, old, white-haired woman wearing a dark shawl. I made my way to her and asked if I could help. She pointed across the intersection to where she wanted to go. I took her arm and purposed to do my Boy Scout deed for the day. As we stepped upon the curb, I suggested she find cover, and asked if there was anything further I could do for her. She opened up her shawl, took out a large bottle, and in a brisk British accent asked, "Would you like to buy a liter of Scotch?" There are times in life when there is nothing further to be said. This was one of those times. I simply shook my head, and she tottered on down the street through the smoke and disappeared. I wondered how she had survived years of Japanese occupation.

We did get the guns into position, and after a half-hour bombardment the walls were broken down wide enough for tanks to get through. Shortly afterward all Japanese resistance ceased, but a couple of divisions had escaped to the north and taken up positions along a river with mountains in back.

We moved out of Manila into an abandoned air field. The field had been built for U.S. use. The Japanese had used it during the war, and they had burned the buildings before they left, just before Manila fell. There were five of us in the headquarters section, and we were to set up a fire direction command post. Standard operating procedure (SOP) dictated that we dig fox holes before anything else was done. However, the graveled ground was extremely hard, almost like concrete. The pick axes just bounced back at us. There was one building left. It had holes in the sides and part of the roof was gone. However, to sleep within four walls with even a partial roof was pure luxury.

As we unrolled our packs and took out a box of K-rations, we prepared to live the life of Riley for the next two hours before the sun went down. Suddenly it seemed the banshees of Hades were raining down on our heads. A Japanese artillery battery had zeroed in on the building before we arrived. If you have never been on the receiving end of artillery, and heard the scream of the shells get closer and closer, you have not lived, or died, as the case might be. We barely escaped out of the building, and we dove into a six-inch deep drainage ditch, end to end. After what seemed an eternity, the shelling stopped. The building had more holes in it, and the grass and bushes where we lay had been mowed down by shrapnel to about six inches above the ground.

We moved swiftly several hundred yards away from the building, and before nightfall we all had our own private fox holes. All during that night Japanese soldiers who had been cut off in Manila passed through the area, trying to get back to their units along the river. I could hear, "Hey, Joe," "Hey, John," "Hey, Jack," etc., all night long. The Japanese were attempting to get us to answer in order to either avoid us, or kill us. We all had been through this exercise before, and no one dared to answer.

The next day the guns arrived and we plotted them on the map about one-half mile in front of us along a ridge. We were on high ground and could look over the river where the Japanese were dug in. The colonel in charge of the First Cavalry artillery units, along with two other officers, came out to see us. He asked us who had training and experience in artillery fire direction. I and a first lieutenant, one of the officers who had accompanied him, held up our hands. The colonel handed the first lieutenant a set of field artillery firing tables for 90s. He called on a walkie-talkie to a forward observer for a firing problem over the Japanese lines. The lieutenant figured the problem, and called out the firing order to gun number one of Battery A. The call came back, one thousand yards short. In field artillery you can be one thousand over, and possibly one thousand yards to the left or right of the target, but never one thousand yards short. The colonel then gave me the firing tables and asked me to fire the same problem. With two minor adjustments I was able to get the gun on the target. The colonel said, "I'll take the T-4."

It seemed strange that the First Cavalry was not ordered to pursue the enemy and destroy him. However, General MacArthur was in no big hurry to risk more soldiers lives. In typical MacArthur strategy, the Japanese were left to linger on the side of a mountain until they ran out of food and ammunition.

With some help, a dugout was prepared with a roof over it. I had a cot for a bed and all the comforts of home. I lived in the dugout for a month. I issued regular firing orders to the guns. There was a phone in the dugout. If the First Cavalry wanted me to fire a special problem on the spur of the moment, the telephone would wake me up.

The First Cavalry armored division was an old army outfit. Originally, the division used horses for the mounted soldiers and mules to pull the artillery and wagons. Tanks, mobile artillery, and other armored units had replaced the horses, but the First Cavalry was a beautiful army division. Every order was exact; every piece of information was exact; the location of every piece of equipment, every gun, every soldier, was known at all times. Once a week a firing report was issued. Every firing problem was listed, the firing unit, and the results were given. Every round of artillery shells were counted and identified. For the first time in the army we ate what the other units ate. First Cavalry cooks even knew how to cook dehydrated foods and powdered eggs. Put the powdered eggs in a pot, pour in condensed milk, mix rapidly with a beater, put on a grill, and stir—*voila!* Scrambled eggs like Mama makes at home.

My firing problem one night was to intermittently fire at a bridge over the river. The river was not very big and not very deep. We could hit the bridge, but the Japanese would just repair it. So to keep the Japanese from using the bridge at night, my unit would fire at it throughout the night, changing the length of the time between firings. About midnight I got a call that the Japanese were launching a night counterattack. I was given the coordinates and asked to use all the guns available. I hurriedly figured the problem, and the guns blazed away for about half an hour. A call came to discontinue firing and go back to the assigned mission. When I gave the firing data again to the first lieutenant at the guns, he remarked that there was some bamboo in the way. I replied that bamboo must grow awfully fast because he had been firing there all night. He got some men out to cut down the bamboo and reported back to me. I told him to fire when ready. The entire river bottom lit up with a blast that could be heard all the way back to the gun emplacements. I could hear the fellows on the guns shouting—"We got it; we got it." After checking with our "ninety-day wonder," I determined that he had either taken the firing data down wrong, or I had made a mistake in giving him the data. In any event, inasmuch as it was the assigned mission, he should have caught it. When the weekly artillery report came out from division headquarters, one item was of particular interest. On April 27, 1945, 11:97 a.m., a Japanese ammunition dump was blown up by artillery fire. Firing battery—unknown. I could not bring myself to tell First Cavalry headquarters that we had made a mistake, even though it was for the good. I soothed my conscious with the thought, "all's well that ends well."

The Japanese finally ran out of food and ammunition, and most of them were either killed, starved to death, or surrendered. Since our guns were no longer needed, we moved to Clark Field, the largest U.S. airbase overseas. Our four batteries took position at the four corners of the base for protection against possible air raids, which was fairly remote. However, as I may have already mentioned, one raid was attempted by riding piggyback on our air force's returning planes.

Reghal stopped over at Clark Field for a few days on a medical supply mission, and we got together several times before he had to leave for another base. In spite of the ignorance of some members of the island command regarding IFF problems and procedures, I did get a commendation from the same command for outstanding work in the area of radar surveillance. After we had moved to Clark Field, I reported the presence of several bogies in different areas. They were flying through mountain passes close to the ground, and a general was in the command center when the planes that did not respond to an IFF were being plotted on the immense island map. I was asked if I would like to return to the States for OCS training, but I had refused the offer before. Bars, stripes, degrees, and medals have never meant much to me. It is what I feel about myself inside that counts.

A news report dated February 17 reported the battle for Manila thusly:

U.S. forces liberated Manila and recaptured
Corregidor, the island fortress where the United
States suffered a humiliating defeat nearly three
years ago. General Douglas MacArthur announced on the 6th the fall of Manila and the lib-
eration of 5,000 prisoners of war. The fighting for
control of the Philippine capital, however, continued on for several days more as isolated groups
of Japanese troops clung desperately to strong-
holds in Ft. McKinley and *Intramuros, the walled
city built by the Spaniards.*

On April 12, 1945, President Roosevelt died; on April
28, Mussolini was shot by angry countrymen; and
on April 30, Hitler committed suicide. All three died
in one month. Later I wondered if this had not been
prophesied in Zechariah 11:8: "Three shepherds also
I cut off in one month; and my soul loathed them,
and their soul also abhorred me."

On May 7, 1945, Germany surrendered uncon-
ditionally. The war in Europe was over. Units from
Europe, including a black division, were arriving in
the Philippines by July, and troops under the command of General Douglas MacArthur were angry,
furious, and indignant because of it. We all felt that
troops under MacArthur had fought alone on a shoe-
string and only Japan itself remained. There were
not only hard feelings, there were physical demon-
strations of those feelings. One armored unit, I believe it was from the First Cavalry, ran through a

camp of an incoming European division and tore all the tents down. Some units were moved to the other end of the island to keep down contention.

Japan had reserved four thousand airplanes to use for kamikaze missions when the United States combined armed services invaded Japan. We were all hoping that we could get our 90s on Japanese soil and take part in the big show. But Japanese soldiers on Luzon were still coming out of the mountains and caves as they ran out of food. One morning at Clark Field a squad of Japanese soldiers was seen trying to slip down from a volcanic mountain and make it to the sea. Everyone started to get their rifles and get in on the fight. Once I saw there were only about twelve Japanese and a hundred of us, I turned back. While I hated the Japanese at that time, they were still humans and I was responsible for my own conscious. I hoped they were given a chance to surrender before every one was killed. Some in our battalion came back with swords and other mementos.

As the battle for Okinawa came to an end on June 21, we began getting ready to go to Japan in August. If there was not an invasion in August, then it would have to wait until next April because the winter seas would be rough and the weather cold and bad. But we heard nothing, and we assumed the invasion would have to wait another six months. The reason became obvious on August 6. After my radar shift on that day, I went to the battalions' club house, and I was greeted with the news that an atomic bomb had dropped on Hiroshima, Japan. Three days later an atomic bomb was dropped on Nagasaki, Japan. Japan was given an ultimatum to surrender. On August 15, after six tension filled days, Japan surrendered. It was all over. While we were all happy in a way that the war was over, it was such an enormous letdown. We wondered why all the thousands of Americans killed in Iwo Jima and Okinawa were sacrificed—sacrificed for what?

In late November we went to a staging area at Subic Bay to wait for a ship to take us back home. While walking through camp, I gave a candy bar to a Filipino boy. An angry major barged out from between tents and began to aggressively abuse me for encouraging Filipino kids to come into the camp. I introduced myself to the major and asked him from which unit he was and how long he had served in the Pacific arena. I did learn that he was from Oklahoma City, that his unit was a 240mm field artillery howitzer battalion. His unit had only arrived from the States in July. The guns were so big and unable to move in the mud that they were entirely useless. After I got through telling him what I thought of him, his guns, and his useless trip to the Philippines in the closing days of the war at taxpayer expense, he informed me that he was going to have me court martialled, and he would personally see to it that I remained on the island for at least two more years. I am almost positive the major was Ben McCammon, as later when I talked with Brother McCammon, everything matched. I will have more to say about Brother McCammon later.

I never heard anything further from the major, and at the time, as on December 5, 1945, we boarded a small troop transport for home. On December 11, I observed my twenty-third birthday, again on a ship.

After ten days at sea I knew we were nearing home, because on the ship's radio I heard this jingle: "Super Suds, Super Suds, Lots more suds with Super Suds . . . uds . . . udssssss."

I doubt if anyone today remembers "Super Suds." In fact, I wonder how many citizens of the United States remember World War II. Did it actually happen? Did it really change anything? Do Americans really care, or think about, the millions of young men and women who served and/or died in that war? When will there be a war to really end all wars? Will this next generation be marching our young men and women to Armageddon?

School to Salvation

Our ship docked at San Francisco on December 17, 1945. There were no bands playing or pretty girls waiting to greet us. The war had been over for several months, and Rosie the Riveter, along with a few others, were trying to adjust to the postwar period, which included trying to get to know returning husbands again. One of the greatest concerns was what the millions of workers in defense plants were going to do to make a living, as well as what all these millions of servicemen would do after their discharges. Would wartime marriages hold? Would Mrs. Jones understand why Mr. Jones had fallen in love with Fraulein Schultz? Or, would Mr. Jones understand why Mrs. Jones entertained her assembly-line partner while he was overseas fighting those mean, old Nazis? Or, why was Johnny, Jr., screaming in terror when that strange man charged through the door and began kissing his mommy? Or, what in the world would any of us do next?

Before I could worry about any of the above, I first had to get out of the army. Our unit was taken by bus to Camp Stoneman near Sacramento, the camp from which I had departed. For the next few days we were examined physically, mentally, and psychologically. At each meal we were served everything that we had missed for the past three years: fresh eggs, bacon, ham, cheese, milk, steak, and ice cream. However, we did not get new clothes or a haircut. After all, the army was just trying to fatten us up a bit and then get rid of us. After five days about half of our battalion was notified that we would be sent by train to Ft. Leavenworth, Kansas, for processing and discharge. The rest were sent to other camps for discharge, and with the exception of two or three, I never saw them again.

We had no winter clothes, yet our train went through Las Vegas, Salt Lake City, and up through Wyoming where it was twenty degrees below zero, and there were only lukewarm steam pipes to keep our compartment warm. We had just returned from the Pacific where it was hot, and we almost froze to death. At Cheyenne our train turned southward and stopped at Denver. Some more of our group were dropped off there, including my army buddy, Stanley, who lived in Boulder.

Because our train had to stay in Denver until the next day, and it was bitterly cold, we were taken to an army camp a few miles away to stay the night. We were instructed that we could eat dinner at the USO hall. However, none of us had received a haircut in over two months; we still had on our badly worn battle dress fatigues, including broken down army shoes; we were all sunburned and tanned like charcoal; our eyes, teeth, and fingernails were yellow. Serving food and trying to entertain us were creatures that we had forgotten even existed—beautiful, angelic forms in colorful dresses and high heel shoes with legs in nylon stockings, beautiful glowing and flowing hair like spun gold or glistening sapphires. It all seemed like something we had dreamed long, long ago. With clumsy fingers, we timidly and almost reticently put some food on our plates and tried to hide behind the pillars that separated the dining areas from the game room, meanwhile peeking around the corners with one eye while we tried to retune our hearing to the soprano voices of the nymphs that flittered back and forth.

We did survive the occasion and the next day our train departed for Ft. Leavenworth. Processing and further testing and examinations took another week, and then we were finally given our discharge papers, along with a few hundred dollars severance pay. I caught a bus for Hugo and arrived home on January 6, 1946. Nothing seemed to have changed, except that my parents were a few years older and my hunting dog was gone. My younger brother Harold was still at home, but he had grown up and was attending high school.

Two days later I began to wonder what I was going to do. There were no jobs and my few dollars of severance pay would not last very long. I certainly could not just do nothing and expect my parents to take care of me. In my discharge papers was a notice regarding a GI Bill of Rights, which included a grant for soldiers whose education had been interrupted by serving in the armed forces. I enrolled at Oklahoma A&M (now Oklahoma State University), but discovered I could not attend the university until the fall term, and then certain classes were already full. So many returning servicemen were going back to school that educational opportunities were limited. I withdrew from A&M and enrolled at a small university in Oklahoma City to work for a degree in accounting and business administration. School aid under the GI Bill paid for tuition and an additional ninety dollars a month. Room and board in 1946 was twelve dollars a week, and with working at a supermarket on the weekends, I was able to make ends meet.

By keeping in school without a vacation, I finished my courses and received a degree in early 1949. From 1946 to 1949 I had been busy in school with little money to afford wine, women, or song. While actual fighting between the Allies and the Axis powers had stopped, these three years saw news that changed and shaped the world. At Yalta in February 1945 Roosevelt and "Good Old Joe" Stalin ganged up on Churchill and forced a division of the world. Russia was given a free hand in gobbling up several of Japan's islands, Eastern Europe, and the Balkans. Poor England, along with other Roman Empire pieces, were forced to divulge themselves of their colonies. The United States got the bill for rebuilding Japan and war-torn Europe. Newspaper headlines highlighted major events that transpired in 1946:

January 30: U.N. Holds First Session
March 5: Churchill Warns About the Iron Curtain
March 6: France Recognizes Ho's Vietnam State
March 28: Peron Elected Argentina's President
May 7: Britain and France Leave Syria
May 16: Merman Stars in "Annie Get Your Gun"
June 19: U.S. Offers All Atomic Weapons to U.N.
July 4: Philippines Declare Independence
July 25: U.S. Tests A-Bombs Off Bikini Islands
August 19: Mao Makes All-Out Drive for Victory
August 24: Nehru Heads New India Regime
October 2: Smoking May Cause Cancer
October 16: Nazi War Criminals Hanged
December 28: W. C. Fields Dies on Christmas Day
December 31: Dr. Spock's Book on Child Care
    Voted Most Popular 1946 Book

The major headlines in 1947 were:

January 21: George Marshall Made Secretary of
    State
February 15: Marshall Orders Withdrawal of
    Support for Chiang
March 25: John D. Rockefeller Donates Land in
    Manhattan to U.N.

May 29: Forty Killed in World's Worst Airplane
Accident

June 21: Communists Take Over Hungary

August 15: England Gives India and Pakistan
Independence

August 21: President Truman Sees Budget Surplus

October 23: Robert Taylor Helps Name 79 Movie
Actors as Subversives

October 23: Ronald Reagan Defends Actors Guild

November 25: Ten Movie Stars Blacklisted

December 31: Romania Falls to Communists

December 31: Ancient Scrolls Discovered at Dead
Sea

The pattern of events that was established in 1946
and 1947 continued in 1948:

January 4: Burma Declared Independent Nation

January 12: Truman's Budget Second Largest Ever

January 12: Supreme Court Orders Oklahoma to
Admit Negro to Law School

January 31: Gandhi Assassinated

February 28: U.S. Warplanes Have Difficulty
Breaking Sound Barrier

February 29: Czechoslovakia Falling to
Communists

May 14: Israel Declares an Independent State

June 25: Russia Blockades Berlin

July 26: Truman Orders Racial Integration of
Armed Forces

September 9: North Korea Splits and Becomes
   Communist State
November 2: Truman Beats Odds—Elected
   President
December 1: Madame Chiang Kai-shek in
   Washington to Plead For Help
December 6: Pumpkin Papers Indicate Alger Hiss
   To Be Russian Spy

The next-to-last news item noted for 1948 was perhaps the most important. Madame Chiang was a Christian. She had reportedly led her husband to the Lord, and he became a Christian. Chiang's army had been given U.S. weapons, but when the United States withdrew support, there was no ammunition. The oft-used propaganda theme was put forth that because there was corruption in Chiang's government, then the U.S. should just not support that government This has happened several times since. Some have suggested that the State Department was riddled with communist sympathizers like Harry Dexter White and Alger Hiss. Even George Marshall was accused of being soft on communism, or at best, indecisive in opposing communism. It is also thought that when Roosevelt and Stalin divided up the world at Yalta, part of the deal was to allow Mao to win in China. Chiang and Mao had been both the right and left hand of Sun Yat-sin. Chiang's stated intentions were to make China a republic like the United States. Mao was convinced that communist Russia was the

model government. Had the United States continued supporting Chiang, sixty million lives may have
been spared and China today would be a republic
and a predominantly Christian nation.

After leaving school, it was difficult for someone
who had no inside friends or relatives with business
connections to find a job. I finally did get a position
as bookkeeper for a freight company. However, I
began to have health problems with my teeth and
sinuses. Poor diet in the army may have been a reason for gum and tooth decay, and I had problems
with my sinuses in New Guinea. Nevertheless, the
local VA office would not make these health problems service-related. Finally, I had to take leave of
my job and have expensive dental work done, as well
as an operation on my sinus system. The conse-
quence was that I had to borrow a great deal of
money, and I was out of a job again.

Automobile companies and auto accessory companies were expanding due to a growing car market, so I made application with Firestone Rubber
Company for an accounting position. I was accepted,
but told that the job would not open for two weeks.
In checking the want ads for a part-time job, I noticed an ad for a typist. I was an excellent typist, and
I can still type eighty words per minute.

The job was at the office of Dr. E. F. Webber, a
radio minister. Dr. Webber had been a member of
Paul Rader's evangelistic team, and he had served
as pastor of a Missionary Alliance church in Oregon.

Evidently, while on an evangelistic revival meeting in Oklahoma City, he had met a divorcee with two children and subsequently made her his wife. He started a successful church in Oklahoma City, Calvary Tabernacle, on Northeast Twenty-Third and Kelly. In April 1933 Dr. Webber contracted for time on KTOK, a local radio station, and began a daily, thirty minute, Bible-teaching program. Calvary Tabernacle was his physical church, and Dr. Webber's radio program became his radio church—thus the name Southwest Radio Church.

The office of Southwest Radio Church in 1951 consisted of two rooms over a garage. The staff consisted of only four or five male employees, and I was given a stack of mail to forward contribution receipts. The office manager, Dow Mooney, noticed that I had an accounting degree. Dr. Webber had a problem with the Internal Revenue Service over the designation of offerings—contributions or gifts? I was asked to help get reports ready for the IRS. In communicating with Dr. Webber, I made some uncomplimentary remarks about his entire bookkeeping system, as well as his chances of winning his case. One personality trait of Dr. Webber was that he was quick to anger and made instant decisions. One of those immediate decisions was to separate me from his office. At the moment, this was not an earth-shaking defeat. After all, this was only a temporary job, and in just ten days I would be taking my new position with Firestone.

The weather was still cool on April 3, 1951, so I put on my jacket and went downstairs to catch a bus. At the bottom of the stairs Dr. Webber was waiting for me. He said, "Son, do you like to fish?" I replied that I did, so he invited me to go fishing with him. In those days I was rather pragmatic, so we drove to nearby Lake Hefner and anchored the boat in its middle to fish. After all, I had nothing better to do.

While Lake Hefner is not exactly the Sea of Galilee, Dr. Webber began to tell me about Jesus advising the disciples how and where to catch the most fish. I knew where all this was heading, because I had attended church and read the Bible. In fact, while living with my grandmother, I had read the entire Bible in story form. Also, when I joined the army, included with my gear was a Gideon New Testament. Overseas, I had read through the New Testament several times, and had brought it home with me. I have always since supported the Gideons; I am a Gideon member, and support the organization as time will allow.

As the presentation by Dr. Webber wound from the catching of fish to the crucifixion of Jesus Christ, I heard the simple message of the Gospel explained to me personally—as if it were Jesus Christ taking my place on the cross. Dr. Webber said that God had a plan and purpose for my life, but I must first receive Jesus as my own personal Savior. I bowed my head, prayed the sinner's prayer, and was born again by faith into the family of God. I do not remember how many fish we caught, but it must have been twenty-five or thirty, but this was not now important because the world seemed so different to me as I was let out at a bus stop. With the door of the Buick still open, Dr. Webber asked if I would be back to work in the morning. I replied that I would.

As I waited for the bus I reviewed in my mind the things in the world that had happened in the past two years and their relation to the two prophetic messages I had heard Dr. Webber give, which I had listened to in the office:

1949

February 8: Jet Bomber Crosses Nation in Less Than Four Hours

February 14: Hungarian Cardinal Mindszenty Given Life in Prison

March 2: B-50 Flies Non-Stop Around World

March 18: Allies Give Birth to NATO

May 22: James Forrestal Apparently Commits Suicide

May 24: Communists Sweep Through China

August 7: Vatican Finds Peter's Bones (Again)

August 8: Ecuador Quake Kills 4,600

August 8: X-1 Rocket Plane Flies to 63,000 Feet

September 23: Russians Have A-Bomb

October 1: Mao Forms Communist Government

December 8: Chiang Moves Army to Formosa

December 31: George Orwell's Book Predicts Big Brother Government by 1984

1950

January 6: England Recognizes Communist China

January 31: H-Bomb Added to U.S. Nuclear
Arsenal

February 15: Stalin and Mao Join in Political
Marriage

February 20: Sen. Joseph McCarthy Charges 205
with Communist Affiliations

March 5: TV Bad for Learning Three Rs

March 12: 80 Killed in World's Worst Air Crash

March 29: RCA Makes Color TV Picture Tube

June 24: Another 180 Lost in Plane Crash

June 28: North Korea Invades South Korea

July 21: North Korean Forces Advance Deep Into
South Korea

July 22: Census Finds 150 Million U.S. Citizens

September 15: MacArthur's Landing at Inchon
Scores Big Victory

September 29: Seoul Liberated

November 9: Chinese Army Enters Korean War

December 19: Eisenhower Is NATO Commander

World War II veterans were not being called up to
fight in Korea, so I was safe, at least for the time being. However, as I entered the bus, the radio announced that news from Korea was not good. The
U.N. army (ninety percent American soldiers) had
retreated swiftly back into South Korea to prevent
being encircled by the Chinese army. MacArthur was
wanting to bomb China to slow down the Red Chi-

nese, but Truman was demanding that he not get bogged down into a protracted war against an overwhelming numerically superior enemy.

The next morning I reported back to the office of Southwest Radio Church at eight a.m. As I listened to the broadcast by Dr. Webber the next week, I became intently interested in how what was happening in the world was prophesied in the Bible. When the day came for me to report to my new job, I decided to stay with Dr. Webber. As the days became weeks, Dr. Webber and I became good fishing buddies. He would come up to the office and say, "Hutch, put up your books and typewriter, and let's go fishing." And, although Dr. Webber had an explosive temper, he never yelled at me again. Charles was Dr. Webber's son. David was his stepson, whom Dr. Webber adopted and gave the Webber name. Henry, the oldest son of Mrs. Webber, was not adopted, but David and Charles were still in college and mainly interested in girls and Cadillacs, so it seems that I became the son that Dr. Webber never had.

In 1951 I was twenty-nine years old, deeply in debt, and unable to afford a wife or a mortgage. The first thing I had to do was become solvent. I moved to within four blocks of the office near Northwest Sixteenth and Indiana. The room I rented was in an attic and it had one small window. I paid five dollars a week for the room, and I allowed myself five dollars a week for food. For twenty months I ate out of a paper sack, my diet consisting mostly of peanut butter, cheese, and crackers. Often I would try to save up a dollar to afford a hamburger and fries. I found that a person could live on peanut butter and bread. When I later went on mission trips to China or Russia, I would always take a jar of peanut butter. This was much better than trying to eat the abominable food in China—although the food in China is much better now, and there is a McDonalds, KFC, Wendy's, Burger King, or Pizza Hut on every corner.

However, toward the end of 1951 I was becoming a permanent fixture at the ministry, my debt was almost liquidated, and I had proven it was possible to live on ten dollars a week.

The dominant headlines in 1951 were:

January 28: Viet Minh Attack Hanoi

January 28: Atomic Tests Shake Las Vegas

February 17: U.S. Forces Fight Reds Over 38th Parallel

February 26: 22nd Amendment Limits President to Two Terms

March 30: Rosenbergs Found Guilty of Spying for Russia

April 11: Truman Fires MacArthur

May 12: Hydrogen Bomb Tested

May 27: China Annexes Tibet

June 20: 21 Communists Indicted in New York

August 18: Average American Annual Pay—$1,436

August 23: 90 West Point Cadets Dismissed for Cheating

December 24: Libya Gains Independence

In 1952 I finally got out of debt and purchased a house near Northwest Twenty-Third and Portland. My mother and father, who had moved to Lubbock, Texas, came to live with me. My younger brother Harold finished his army service and joined us.

The program and mission format that Dr. E. F. Webber established for the ministry never changed. Programs were evangelistic, Bible teaching, lots of guests, with continuing news of what God was doing today to fulfill His plan and purpose. There was also a mission base. The first month I was at Southwest Radio Church I wrote checks to missions in the amount of $110,000. This was just for one month, and Dr. Webber never took even one dollar for mission fund-raising costs. Just a few of the missions were: Sudan Interior Mission, African Inland Mission, Korean Orphan Home, Nepal Border Mission, Vallore Eye Clinic, China Inland Mission, and others.

One of the regular guests on the program was Dr. J. Vernon McGee. Dr. McGee had been born at Durant, just fifty miles west of Hugo where I was born. Dr. McGee did not have a radio ministry at that time, but he was gaining a reputation in California as a Bible expositor. However, Dr. McGee was not a good pulpit presenter. Dr. Webber rented the Civic Auditorium and featured Dr. McGee in an evangelistic endeavor. To add hype and color Roy Rogers,

Dale Evans, and other Hollywood stars were brought in to help draw a crowd. However, after three nights the attendance had dropped to no more than two or three hundred, and Dr. Webber had to close the Old Time Revival venture. Evidently, from being a guest on Southwest Radio Church, Dr. McGee got the idea of starting his own radio ministry.

Another guest on the program was Dr. Carl McIntire, who was gaining a reputation at that time by fighting the World Council of Churches, the National Council of Churches, and the apostates and communists who were taking over most of the mainline denominations. I even marched with Dr. McIntire in Tulsa to oppose the appearance of the communist clergyman Nikidim from the Russian Orthodox Church. At that time a Carl McIntire was needed, and he expanded his ministry over radio stations in every state.

In 1996 I had lunch with Dr. McIntire in Collingswood, New Jersey. Even at ninety-one, Dr. McIntire is still fighting to save the church from what was the ravaging wolves, but his voice barely reaches across the street from his home now. He is still trying to ride a horse that has already escaped from the corral. Pride goes before a fall, and Dr. McIntire got to a point where he considered himself above those who were trying to help him. He took huge sums contributed to his ministry to invest in projects like the tabernacle complex at Cape Canaveral in Florida. When he could not pay his radio bills and stations were forced to cancel his program, he would threaten to sue. Soon, few stations would carry his ministry.

Another regular visitor to Southwest Radio Church was Homer Rodeheaver, Billy Sunday's song director. Dr. Rodeheaver would come to Oklahoma City, bring his trombone, and be on the program. Southwest Radio Church helped him raise the funds to establish Rainbow Ranch for Boys at Palatka, Florida. The name has now been changed to Rodeheaver's Home for Boys.

Perhaps the most frequent guest on the program was Dr. Herbert Lockyer. Dr. Lockyer, although British, spent much of his time in the United States. He must have written over two hundred titles—*All the Men of the Bible, All the Queens of the Bible, All the Women of the Bible, All the Kings of the Bible, All the Children of the Bible, All the Prayers of the Bible,* etc. Southwest Radio Church published some of his smaller books. I remember one incident when one of the employees, a rather rotund gentleman by the name of Henry Fowler, was making his way to the office with a bushel basket. Dr. Lockyer asked, "I say, Henry, is that your lunch? Ho, ho, ho!" Henry put his basket down, took off the newspaper cover, and proceeded to show Dr. Lockyer what he was indeed having for lunch. Dr. Lockyer, startled, responded, "By jove, it is your lunch!"

Billy James Hargis also appeared on the program. Dr. Webber also took Billy James out on meetings with him where he became acquainted with some of the ministry's more affluent listeners. Dr. Webber also helped Dr. Hargis to raise funds for the Russian balloon project. The object of this project was to send balloons with scriptures attached over the Soviet Union from Eastern Europe. If any good was accomplished by this project, it would have been to keep Americans aware that Russian borders were closed to the gospel by this atheistic nation. After Dr. Webber was called home to be with the Lord, I tried to steer David and Charles away from Dr. Hargis as I felt this was not the direction the ministry should go.

Southwest Radio Church continued to have guest ministers who had information that needed to be shared with others. There are at least a dozen ministers I could name today, who have extensive ministries, that got their initial start at Southwest Radio Church. At a conference of pre-millennial ministers sponsored by Dallas Theological University, one pastor came up to me to shake my hand. He said that he just wanted me to know that half of the delegates would not be here if it were not for Southwest Radio Church. However, if the majority of these men and women have anything to say at all about the hand that pulled them up, it is usually bad. Like the ungrateful pig, they just eat the acorns and never bother to look up and thank the tree that grew them.

The Korean War (called a U.N. "police action") continued to plague the nations in 1952. There was rising concern about communist revolutions in Southeast Asia, and Marilyn Monroe was the nation's newest sex symbol. Other headlines in 1952 were:

January 5: Nationwide Dragnet Catches 500 Drug
   Dealers
February 15: King George Is Dead, Long Live
   Queen Elizabeth
February 26: England Has Bomb and Nuclear Plant
June 1: John Dewey Dies
June 14: U.S. Launches First Atomic Submarine
November 5: Eisenhower and Nixon Elected by
   Landslide
November 5: John F. Kennedy Elected Senator from
   Massachusetts
December 15: Operation Changes George
   Jorgenson to Christine Jorgenson

The last important event that I remember in 1952
was that Dr. Webber presented me with a brand-new
1952 Royal typewriter. It was on this typewriter that
I was to write approximately eight thousand radio
scripts, over one hundred books, tens of thousands
of pages for other publications, and thousands upon
thousands of letters. It is on this typewriter that I am
writing this book. This typewriter has traveled with
me around the world, as well as to almost every state.
In 1996 the *Daily Oklahoman* devoted an entire page
to my typewriter. In 1977, while I was out of town,
my assistant got my typewriter cleaned and a new
platen installed. This is the only service done on this
typewriter in forty-six years, yet never has a screw

come loose or been replaced; it operates today as well as it did in 1952, and the type is just as plain and straight as it ever was. While I am somewhat dubious about God watching over soulless machinery, I cannot help but believe He is watching over my typewriter. After all, I should be entitled to a little superstition.

In early 1953 I received a call from Janet Bradley. Janet was the wife of my army buddy, Stanley Bradley. Stanley had married his childhood sweetheart, and I remember him showing me her picture. They had one child, a boy, who was at that time four years old. Janet related that in 1948 Stan had started showing signs of a neurological disorder, but ignored it for about a year. When he finally did go to a doctor, it was diagnosed as multiple sclerosis. Stanley had reached a plateau in this dreaded disease of young adults where care was becoming expensive, and Janet could no longer take care of him. She asked me to help her get his condition service related, which I did, and Stan was admitted to the Veterans Administration Hospital in Denver. When I got my vacation in the summer, I bought a new car, a sporty two-tone Plymouth, and drove to Denver to see him. Stan's condition was worse than I had anticipated. While he knew me, he remembered little of our years together in the South Pacific. I stayed in Denver a couple of days, and then left to visit my sister Geneva and my brother Reghal in Lubbock. A few months later Stanley died. I kept in touch with Janet for a year and then lost contact with her.

The Webber family had their church membership in the First Methodist Church of Oklahoma City. While Dr. Webber was obviously a Baptist in doctrine, he simply did not fit into a Baptist-type church structure, and it did not seem to bother the Methodists that he contradicted basic Methodist beliefs. Also, the Gaylord organization, which published the *Oklahoma City Times* and *Daily Oklahoman* had an ongoing war with him. They never failed to give him a swift kick on both the front page and the editorial page. It seems that Gaylord had attempted to get a city ordinance passed that would prevent oil wells from being drilled inside the city limits. Dr. Webber went to bat for the homeowner's cause and won. So the Webber family was pretty much ostracized within the social and church community of Oklahoma City, except for a reluctant nod by the Methodists. Dr. Webber used his influence to get his son, Charles, and his adopted son, David, licensed to preach on the Methodist circuit. However, at that stage in their lives it is doubtful if either one of them got much beyond the Lord's Prayer, homiletically speaking.

The Korean War was still going on in early 1953 and both Charles and David had to register for the draft. It was doubtful that David would pass the physical tests because of poor eyesight; however, Charles was definitely a draft possibility. Dr. Webber bought an old, dilapidated Pentecostal church building at 1813 Northwest Second Street in Oklahoma City. A considerable amount of work had to be done on the structure before it could be ready for church services. Dr. Webber's old church on Northeast Twenty-Third and Kelly had moved to Nichols Hills and changed its name to Metropolitan Baptist, so the church on Northwest Second Street was also named Calvary Tabernacle, the name of his first church.

As I remember, Charles was appointed either pastor or associate pastor, and many thought that Dr. Webber had started this church only to keep Charles out of the draft. Whether this was the real reason or not the Lord will have to judge. I had not joined a church at that time, but I had attended on a semi-regular basis at First Baptist Church where Dr. Herschel Hobbs was pastor. The wild bunch at First Methodist were a little too much for me. So at the first service of the new Calvary Tabernacle, I joined, mainly because I was expected to do so. Even though Charles and David were expected to be the spiritual leaders in the church, Dr. Webber did almost all the preaching and pastoral duties. Dr. Webber would get his two boys at the podium, put his arms around them, and let the audience know what fine sons he had, and then he would tell them to go sit down. However, the attendance at Calvary Tabernacle never exceeded one hundred and usually ran between forty and fifty. While Dr. Webber had tremendous influence in the southwest and maintained a large listening audience, few wanted to come to this poor section of town to a rundown church building. This was just the way it was.

Another interesting footnote to Dr. Webber's ministry is that he was a thirty-second degree Mason. All I knew about the Masons at that time was that they must have something to do with brick laying, and if Dr. Webber wanted to lay a few bricks on the side, that was all right with me. I soon learned that contemporary Masonry had little, if anything, to do with any type of building construction. However, even though there may have been some glitches in Dr. Webber's personality and ministry, I had tremendous respect for him. He was a powerful preacher. No one, as far as I know, has done more for the cause of Christian communications than Dr. Webber, even though he never got the credit. Dr. Webber nurtured new radio ministers and led the way to take the Gospel around the world by radio and television. I still meet many of our senior citizens who say they were led to saving faith in Jesus Christ by the ministry of Southwest Radio Church and Dr. Webber. The thousands who were saved through Dr. Webber's mission efforts will remain unnamed until the Judgment Seat of Christ.

In 1953 Russia extended its empire and relentlessly pursued the goal of world domination, while economics nationally continued to rebound from World War II. Science, especially medical science, also made remarkable new discoveries. The headlines in

the newspapers for the year again signified the signs
of the time:

March 5: Stalin Dies From Stroke
March 26: Salk Vaccine a Success
April 15: Pope Pius Approves Psychoanalysis for
  Catholics
April 18: Birth Control for Wives Debated
April 25: DNA Secrets Revealed
April 28: French Evacuate Northern Laos
June 2: Hillary Climbs Mt. Everest
June 19: Rosenburgs Executed
June 29: Army Takes Over in Cambodia
September 12: John F. Kennedy Marries
November 29: French Paratroops Land at Dien
  Bien Phu
December 3: Pregnancy Accomplished by Frozen
  Sperm
December 23: Lavrenti Beria Executed as Accused
  U.S. Spy

My duties at Southwest Radio Church in 1954 remained clerical in nature—keeping a set of books for
the ministry, doing the payroll, and filing necessary
tax reports. However, Christian program production
was changing. New techniques were emerging, including saving the on-line charges by sending the
messages recorded on tape. Also, denominations like
the Southern Baptists developed cooperative mission programs that diverted much of the funds and

attention to united church efforts rather than to individual missions. More radio ministers like Theodore Epp of "Back to the Bible" were emerging. New television ministries were also appearing, and it was becoming more difficult to pay the radio bills. More attention had to be given to programming and fund raising through books and literature dissemination. We wondered if the days of Gospel radio broadcasting might be numbered.

I was now over thirty years of age with no marriage possibilities in sight, even though I thought it was time to settle down. In June I attended an American Legion affair. I happened to sit down at a table next to a rather attractive girl. I introduced myself and she replied that she was Jean Pierce. In the following conversation as we munched on *hors d'oeuvres,* I learned that she was a farm girl. Her parents were divorced. Jean had graduated from a business college, and worked as a secretary for a paint company. Jean liked to fish, bowl, and enjoyed pretty much the things that I liked to do. She was down to earth, realistic, and very talented. When I asked her for a dinner date the following Saturday, to my surprise, she accepted. It did turn out that we were most compatible, and we had a terrific time that summer simply doing what we wanted to do. Come November, I asked Jean to marry me. She accepted, and we set the date for February 5, 1955. In thinking back on the hard times during the Great Depression, my struggle to get through school, my years in the South

Pacific, it seemed suddenly that the Lord had made His countenance to shine upon me.

Looking forward to next February, I began to save money for rings and a honeymoon. The newspaper headlines for 1954 were:

January 1: Search Starts for Abominable Snowman
January 14: Joe Dimaggio Weds Marilyn Monroe
January 21: Nautilus, First Atomic Sub Launched
March 1: Puerto Ricans Shoot Five Congressmen
March 17: Eleven Israelis Slain in Beersheba
March 25: Sinatra Wins Oscar
May 6: Bannister Breaks Four-Minute Mile
May 7: Dien Bien Phu Taken by North Vietnam
May 17: Supreme Court Orders School
   Integration
July 19: First Boeing 707 Flies
July 21: Vietnam Divided Into Two Nations
July 27: British Leave Egypt
October 2: West Germany Joins NATO
October 10: Ho Chi Minh Rules North from Hanoi
November 30: Lassie Stars on TV
December 2: Senate Condemns McCarthy
December 27: Astronomers Say Universe Created
   in Big Bang

The month of January in 1955 passed rapidly. I traded my Plymouth in on a new red and white Chevy. The weather cooperated as February 5 was an unusually, beautiful day for a winter month. There was no wind, not a cloud in the sky, and the temperature rose to seventy degrees. We did not have a large wedding, just a few friends. Dr. Webber performed the ceremony in the living room of his home near the state capitol building. Jean wore an appropriate navy blue suit for the occasion. After the ceremony Mrs. Webber served cake and punch.

We had decided to take a week off from our jobs and honeymoon in New Orleans. We did not get out of Oklahoma City until after three in the afternoon, and as fate would have it, we spent our first night together in Hugo. Hugo was on the road to New Orleans. Neither of us had been to New Orleans. The city was getting ready for Mardi Gras, and the weather turned damp and cool. As we did not go to nightclubs, or care for Bourbon Street, there really was not much to do. We did visit the parks and historical sites and went to a stage show. After a few days, we started back home. As we passed through Hugo we stopped to spend the night with my sister and brother-in-law, Juanita and Fred. Juanita insisted that we spend the night because it was getting late, and she said that a fabulous new singer was going to be on the "Ed Sullivan Show" that evening. While we enjoyed our visit with my sister, I really did not care for the new singer. As far as I was concerned, you could get the same sounds and motions by placing a boy, barefoot, on a hot stove with a snake in his pants. The new so-called sensation was Elvis Presley.

We read in the Bible that after six days of creation, God said that everything He had created was very good, except one thing—that it was not good that man should be alone. Jean and I set up housekeeping in a very nice apartment near Northwest Twelfth and May Avenue. We got along great, we loved to do the same things together, and both of us with a farm background adjusted to whatever problems came our way and we just went with the flow. Jean had accepted Jesus Christ as her Lord and Savior in the fall of 1954 at Calvary Tabernacle, and we attended church and Sunday school regularly. We entered a bowling league, and we often went fishing. In April Jean became pregnant. The apartment owner did not allow couples with children, so we moved to a duplex at Northwest Thirtieth and Shartel.

As the year drew to a close, I continued to work at Southwest Radio Church, but Jean took leave of her job the first of December to await the birth of our first child. World events continued to paint a gloomy prophetic picture. Nation after nation was getting the A-bomb, the H-bomb, and seemingly arming for Armageddon. The beginning of the moral decline of the social order was upon the nation, and the cold war with Russia kept getting hotter and hotter. It appeared that a world nuclear holocaust could erupt at any time.

One of the main missions of the Southwest Radio Church had always been to serve as a Watchman on the Wall and declare the signs of the times.

Many had criticized Dr. Webber for associating the events of World War II with the prophecies of Daniel, the Olivet Discourse, and the book of Revelation relating to the Antichrist and the Tribulation period. However, every time the Watchman blew the trumpet an enemy did not always assault the city. In World War II Hitler rose up out of the boundary of the old Roman Empire. He was dedicated to killing every Jew in the world. Pope Pius had made a covenant with both Hitler and Mussolini. Hitler was sending his German Panzer divisions down through the Balkans and across North Africa to claim Jerusalem and the Holy Land, and World War II lasted for seven years. So all the signs were there, and these signs were becoming more evident in 1955.

February 22: Missile with Atomic Warhead Tested
February 28: Israel Attacks in Gaza Area
March 17: Yalta Secrets Are Published
April 18: Einstein Dies
May 14: European Eastern Bloc Signs Military
    Compact
July 6: U.S. Employs 100 Germans to
    Make Rockets
November 26: U.S.S.R. Has H-Bomb

The Swamp of Mental Illness

Jean gave birth to Carol on January 8, 1966. The delivery was normal and Carol was a beautiful baby. Neither Jean nor I were really comfortable living in the city, so I finally located an acreage on the outskirts of Nicoma Park, a development ten miles east of Oklahoma City. The pumice stone, five-room house and five acres was purchased for fifty-six hundred dollars. I immediately started breaking ground and we planted ten times more vegetables than we could possibly eat and freeze. We could not even give them all away.

In July I noticed a change in Jean. She began to remove herself from the living room and sit in the bedroom looking out the window. Her conversation became strained and disconnected. I started to worry when she would hold the baby for hours without feeding or changing her. One morning Jean was so incoherent I did not go to work. I had never had any experience with a mentally ill person before, and I was at a total loss to know what to do. I called her mother, but she had no suggestions. I called the family doctor, but he was busy and out on a call. I had to get the baby away from Jean to feed her and change her diaper, but when I forcefully took Carol from her, Jean went into a spasm and fell into a catatonic state. I called my neighbor, Mr. Shell, and he informed me that the best sanitarium in Oklahoma was only three miles away on Jones Road, Coyne Campbell Sanitarium. He told me to stay with Jean and he would call them. In twenty minutes an ambulance pulled up in the driveway. Two men in white tied Jean on a stretcher and I followed to fill out the necessary papers for admittance. After getting Jean into the sanitarium, I retrieved Carol from Mrs. Shell and took her to my mother.

I was not allowed to see Jean for three days, and then only because I demanded it. I was taken to a steel door with a small six inch square window. The blind was pulled back and I looked inside. There sat Jean on a bench, in a padded cell, with her hands tied to prevent her from scratching her face, and a look of terror on her face. I loved Jean so very much. I would have given my life for her, and to see her in such a desperate situation was almost more than I could bear, but I had always been taught that strong men don't cry, and I hid all my feelings under a cover of stoicism.

Jean remained at the sanitarium for two months. During this time she was given a series of electric shock treatments, alternating with insulin shock treatments. This was the accepted treatment for mental illness at that time, and is still used at times.

After Jean had been in the sanitarium for a week, I finally got to see Dr. Campbell. He was recognized as one of the very best psychiatrists and neurologists in the southwest. The diagnosis was schizophrenia and manic depression. I asked, "Why?" Dr. Campbell asked me if I knew anything about Jean's family history, and I had to admit that I knew very little. He suggested that I find out. As I subsequently learned, then and later, Jeans' mother could not live with her dad because of manic behavior, even to the point of constantly threatening her with a butcher knife. Her father was also, the majority of the time, a hermit in the sense that he lived in the backwoods and could not stand being around people. At times he would open up a barber shop for six months, but then he would disappear. I would trace him down and usually find him in a hut, cut off from civilization. I would take him to town, stock up his supply of groceries, and he would be so glad to see me. But then two or three days later I would receive the most hateful, vengeful, abusive letter from him. Jean had two sisters living in other states, and both of them also had to spend considerable time in psychiatric wards.

For the next year Jean was under psychiatric examination and treatment, and slowly resumed normal behavior. We were happy once more, but I retained an uneasy feeling going to work and leaving her with the baby. In 1958 Jean became pregnant a second time, and nine months later another girl was born. We named her Cheryl. Six months later the same abnormal behavior returned. We could not go back to Dr. Campbell, because one day as he was having dinner with his family, he stood up and held up a cyanide pill. He said, "If I take this pill, I can be dead in three minutes." As his family watched in horror, Dr. Campbell swallowed the pill and he did, indeed, die in three minutes. It is reported that psychiatrists have the largest suicide rate of any other profession or group.

We were assigned to another neurologist, Dr. Prosser, an elderly and more kindly person, and a Christian. However, Campbell Sanitarium encouraged patient spiritual help and devotional periods. In fact, I brought two devotionals while Jean was there, but this time I did not take Jean to Coyne Campbell Sanitarium. Dr. Prosser suggested Baptist Hospital. By this time, treatment for mental illness was changing. Mind altering and chemical balancing drugs were mostly used. Jean was released once more in six weeks.

We were more cautious this time. During her latest hospital stay, I had to get another neighbor, Mrs. Shoate, to stay with the girls. And, as Jean's normal behavior returned again, I felt it was needful to get her out of the house. So, she would work at the office two or three days a week. Jean was a terrific worker. She typed more than one hundred words a minute; she could put out more work than any three people at Southwest Radio Church. Later she installed and ran our first computer system. In the years that she was well enough to work, she helped Southwest Radio Church greatly.

Carol, Cheryl, and Cathy

In 1961 Dr. Prosser thought it was safe for Jean to have one more child. We both wanted a boy to carry on the family name. Our third daughter, Cathy was born. One year later I came home from work and no one was in the house. I checked with the neighbors and my wife and family were nowhere to be found; no one had seen them leave. In the back of the acreage was a grove of trees, and as a last resort I looked there and found them. They were all standing next to the fence, and I rushed up to Jean and asked her if there was a problem. She replied, "Me and the girls are waiting here for the Rapture."

Jean was once more taken to the psychiatric ward of Baptist Hospital. And several times in the coming years I would take Jean in for a checkup at Dr. Prosser's office, and he would say to her, "Jean, for your own good, you will have to go to the hospital again for a few days. I am going to call the ambulance, and your husband will go home and get your clothes." Jean would cry, beg, and plead with me to take her home, but I couldn't.

There were a few good years in my marriage to

Jean, but mostly they were a living hell. Cathy and Carol both took piano and band. I had to take them to weekly lessons and wait up for them until midnight when the band played at school sports events. I had to go to PTA, see the teachers about their grades—I was both mother and father to them. At times Jean would go into temper tantrums and rage for days. Her treatment of the girls, both mental and physical, was beyond cruelty. Often I would just have to get in between Jean and Cheryl. One day we came home and there was no Cathy. Cathy had just turned sixteen and gotten her license. Cathy had planned ahead and sold all her records. She had drawn what money she had out of her savings account, got in the 1972 Chrysler, and drove down into central Texas. I had the police, the pastor of First Baptist of Nicoma Park, and all the membership out looking for her. Finally, about dawn, Cathy came driving the car into the driveway. She said she just couldn't bear the home situation any longer, but she didn't have any place to go. After Carol left home she never returned, as far as I know, to see her mother.

I taught Sunday school and training union at church, and the members might not notice anything abnormal about Jean, but once we got home she would begin yelling and screaming at me. At times I would find my clothes out in the yard, and when I came home there would probably be a forty-page mean and hateful letter under my plate or pillow. Often when going to work in the morning I would turn to the right on the interstate with the intention of driving off into the sunset and never going back, but then I would remember the girls and turn around. Later, the girls told me the only thing they blamed me for was not getting them out of the home. But at that time, I was checkmated. The state mental facility would not take Jean. I was told that she was under a doctor's care and she was my responsibility. If I left, what would happen to Jean? After all, she was my wife and my responsibility. As the years progressed, Jean got worse.

One incident I remember in 1978 was leading a tour from Southwest Radio Church on a Mediterranean cruise through the Greek islands. As we passed through the airport on the way to our gate, I saw a unique appearing individual in overalls, a long beard, smoking a pipe. His wife, with long stringy hair and wearing 1960s looking clothes, was carrying a baby papoose-style. I thought, "Sure hope these hippies are not on our ship." When I got to my stateroom on the ship, there was the unique individual—Zola Levitt. We were to share the same suite. We became friends and Zola asked me about my wife and home situation, and I related to him the status of my marriage. He asked if I had remained faithful to my marriage vows. I told him that if and when I could not, I would have to resign from Southwest Radio Church. As long as I lived with Jean as husband and wife, that was something that a Christian simply did not do. But often a divorce comes long before the legal separation papers are granted. A husband and wife are to be one flesh, so a married couple may still be united legally, but with no spiritual or moral bonds between them that related to the biblical definition of a husband-wife relationship.

In 1982 the state legislature of Oklahoma passed a law that no one could force another person, even members of the same family, to enter a hospital without their consent. I am sure the men and women in the Oklahoma State House and Senate thought they were passing a good law, and in some respects it was. But no longer could Dr. Prosser say, "Jean, you are going to have to go to the hospital, and your husband will go home and get your clothes." To get Jean back into the hospital I had to have the sheriff or a deputy come out and handcuff her, take her to jail where she would be examined by three psychiatrists, and then go before a judge for a hearing, and then I could take her to the hospital. This was an impossibility for me, as I had to work and travel.

The last time I was able to get Jean psychiatric attention was in 1980 for a month's treatment at St. Anthony Hospital's psychiatric ward. In the 1970s so-called miracle drugs appeared like Lithium and later Prozac. The problem was that Jean simply would not take the drugs.

Now I know what some of the readers are thinking: "All psychiatric treatments are of the Devil; all mental drugs are of the Devil. You should have prayed with her, loved her, and read the Bible together." But when a loved one is hallucinating and threatening harm to themselves or others, there is no way they can be reached. They are not capable of mentally coming to any conclusion. No one has more love and sympathy for the mentally ill than I. Those who suffer mental problems and illness suffer infinitely more than anyone with the worst kind of physical problem. They are in a deep, dark hole with no way out; frightened, scared, not knowing who they are or what they are supposed to do. Even in her periods of insane rage, I still loved Jean and wanted to help her more than anything else in the world, but I just could not reach her.

One night I came in late from an out-of-town meeting and was sleeping late the next morning. Cathy came by the house and found every gas jet in the house wide open, and Jean was gone. Had Cathy not come by for another ten minutes, I probably would have died. All three girls kept telling me that I had to leave or Jean would kill me. A few weeks later I came home after a church service. My body and nerves were crying for peace and rest. Jean knew that I hated rock-and-roll music with a passion, so she turned up every radio in the house to heavy metal, just as loud as possible. When I tried to turn the sound down she would throw pots and pans at me. So, I packed a few clothes and got in my car and never went back. The girls would go by the house to be sure she had enough food to eat and clean up the place. Jean got a lawyer and sued for a divorce on the grounds of desertion. I did not contest it. I did meet Jean a year later to see how she was getting along, and at least check on her from time to time. But we were not together more than ten minutes until she was yelling and shouting, so I gave up.

When the sperm from the male enters the egg of the female, forty-six chromosomes carrying three billion genes instantly merge and unite to form an architectural pattern of the individual that is to be formed, as King David said, "in continuance" (Ps. 139). Our genes go through Ham, Shem, and Japheth, all the way back to Adam and Eve. Adam and Eve had two feet, two hands, one mouth, one nose, etc., and so do we. Some of us are white, some are black, some are brown, because our genes go all the way back to the three sons of Noah. But in all these three billion genes, if there is just one flaw in one gene, an abnormality will show up, either at birth, in elementary years, in teenage years, and no later than adult years. In the ancestral lineage of Jean, there was a flaw in one of the genes that control mental activity. This flaw did not show up until Jean was in her late twenties.

My daughter Cheryl was a go-getter, a real business whiz. When she was just barely twenty she had her own shop and employed a dozen people. One day when Cheryl was in her early thirties, Chris, her husband, called me. There was something wrong with Cheryl. She was talking strangely, had thrown his clothes out in the yard, and had asked him to leave. I went by to see Cheryl. She greeted me warmly and continued on her treadmill as if nothing had happened. Since that day Cheryl has been in and out of mental illness wards and psychiatrist's offices. A dozen times she has changed medicines. But Cheryl realized that she was much like her mother and needed help. While Cheryl is no longer able to pursue her occupation except on a limited basis, she is able to live a fairly normal life. Cathy, my youngest, has worked in computer science in two large international corporations. She and Bill have two children, but within the past two years she has developed behavior patterns as a warning signal. However, mild medications so far have been adequate. Carol has a strong will and she is a survivor; however, she too has a tendency to hide from past associations and responsibilities.

I am sure that in the early stages of Jean's mental illness new methods of treatment that are employed now could have been useful. As already noted, there were a few good years in our marriage, but as time passed the illness became more pronounced and uncontrollable. Before 1977 Jean was able to use her tremendous skills productively at certain intervals. Also, in no way do I even infer that psychiatry is a substitute for spiritual growth or Christian counseling. To depend upon psychiatry as an answer is like depending upon the scalpel rather than the physician. Nevertheless, there are times when those who suffer from mental illness need a psychiatrist or neurologist, not only for the patient's sake, but also for the husband, wife, or family.

I have gone into considerable detail in discussing the effect of mental illness on myself and our children so that others may be on guard and benefit from reading the account of my experience. I know that Paul wrote in 2 Timothy 1:7, "For God hath not given us the spirit of fear; but of power, and of love, and of a sound mind." We should keep in mind that Paul here was referencing himself and Timothy. I don't know why the rain falls on both the just and the unjust in the same amount. I wish I did. I do know, however, that God is sovereign and that all things do ". . . work together for good to them that love God, to them who are the called according to his purpose" (Rom. 8:28).

I have often wondered what my marriage to Jean would have been like had she not had this grievous mental deficiency. But what is, is, and we must deal with life's circumstances as they are. In my own tribulations I gained patience, hope, faith, strength, and knowledge, and God's grace to help and give comfort to others. Above all, I have learned to love others who have fallen short or just need to be loved. As Romans 5:5 admonishes us to do, "the love of God is shed abroad in our hearts by the Holy Ghost which is given unto us."

Death of a Legend

Dr. E. F. Webber

Since its beginning, South-west Radio Church had been aired over a rela-tively small network of ra-dio stations, never more than nine or ten in number. The main outlets were KBYE in Oklahoma City and KWFT in Wichita Falls. In 1956 Dr. Webber did make a serious attempt to enlarge the outreach to a nationwide ministry. A thir-teen-week contract was signed to air a special pro-gram over most cities in the United States with a population of over 250,000. The initial response was most encouraging. Dr. McGee had also encouraged Dr. Webber to schedule the program over a new Christian station in Long Beach, California—KGER.

Previously, Dr. Webber's passion for missions would take him away from the office. In the early fifties he could claim traveling more than one mil-lion miles by air to foreign mission fields. This was quite an accomplishment in those early days of passenger air travel. The planes were all props, passenger space was limited to thirty or forty, and ground support, especially abroad, was practically nonexistent. However, this did not keep Dr. Webber from visiting mission stations in India, Ethiopia, Belgium Congo, China, and other nations. He caught the last passenger flight out of Beijing before the communist army of Mao took over the city. Before leaving on a mission effort, Dr. Webber would announce to the listening constituents, as well as those on the mailing list, that he would be gone a month to two months. The contributors, though, would simply hold their offerings to the ministry until he returned. Upon returning, Dr. Webber would find there was no money in the bank.

While he was a great personality and preacher, his conception of finances was extremely deficient. Instead of mailing a letter to the supporters telling them he was back and needed funds to pay the radio bills, he would cancel the program over stations. Such was the case in 1956 with the national network and KGER. Perhaps it was God's will to confine Southwest Radio Church to a regional ministry at that time.

Some of the dominant newspaper headlines in 1956 were:

March 15: "My Fair Lady" Released
March 22: Martin Luther King, Jr. Guilty of
  Ordering Illegal Boycotts

April 19: Prince Ranier of Monaco Marries Grace
 Kelly

June 29: Anti-Communist Rebellions in Poland
 and Hungary

September 9: Elvis Presley Greatest Recording Star
 Ever

October 31: Egypt Takes Over Suez Canal; U.N.
 Moves to Avert Middle East War

November 6: Eisenhower and Nixon Win

December 2: Castro-Led Revolution in Cuba
 Grows

Between 1955 and 1959 both David and Charles married. Charles married Dorothy, a petite blond who was both beautiful and intelligent. David married a tall and attractive brunette, Madge. Charles took God's instruction to Adam and Eve that they should have children and replenish the earth quite seriously. As I remember, for the next four or five years the Charles Webber family was blessed with an increase. Madge was unable to have children. Later, Dr. Lubrett Hargrove, a trustee of Southwest Radio Church, did locate a newborn baby for David and Madge to adopt. One weekend Dr. Hargrove flew the baby up to Oklahoma City in his airplane. The new edition was christened Edward.

It was in one of these years, as I remember, there was quite a crisis in the Webber family. No one had bothered to tell Charles that David was his adopted half-brother. He was not the son of Dr. E. F. Webber.

Either someone told Charles, someone told Dorothy, or Charles found out for himself. Dr. Webber's health was deteriorating. He increasingly took long naps during the day in his rocker, and his color was often pale. He had had a series of heart problems in 1947 and 1948, which was the reason he relinquished his church on Northeast Twenty-Third. If David and/or Charles were to be groomed for future leadership of Southwest Radio Church, it was time to have them, at least intermittently, on the program. While David, Charles, and Mrs. Webber did have a part on the "Sunday Revival in Song" program, they were never allowed on the daily program. During 1957 and 1958 previously recorded programs were played. The problem with these programs was that they were, for the most part, dated, prophetic, what God is doing today-type programs. They were not like Dr. McGee's messages on strictly biblical exegesis that could be run and rerun. It is doubtless that the ministry could have continued beyond 1960 unless a change occurred.

The period between 1957 and 1958 was a most interesting time in the history of the United States, as well as what occurred in the area of foreign missions. No missionaries were allowed in Russia. Churches in Russia had been closed and millions of Christians died before the firing squads, or as slave laborers on such projects as the Volga Waterway. The church in China existed only as an agent of the communist, atheistic government. Later, during the so-called "Cultural Revolution" in China, churches were closed and Christians were slaughtered. In India, Angola, Sudan, and all across Africa and Southeast Asia, Christian missions were either closed or missionaries persecuted. Communist-led revolutions were occurring in the Caribbean, Central America, and South America. Christianity seemed to be in retreat, and there were serious concerns about the entire world falling to communism. Could this be the prelude to the Tribulation? This period was certainly a time when God's prophetic timetable needed to be consulted. Paul said in his letter to the church at Thessalonica that that day should not take Christians by surprise.

It was in this period of concern and uncertainty that the John Birch Society was born and grew into a national information organization. John Birch was a missionary in China who was sentenced to death by the Mao government. Oscar Wells was a fellow missionary and friend of John Birch. Mr. Wells' daughter, Shannon, served in the U.S. space program and spent several months on the Russian space station *Mir* in 1995. Mr. Wells now lives in Bethany, Oklahoma, close to the offices of Southwest Radio Church. I meet with him on occasion for breakfast at a local McDonalds.

I belonged to the John Birch Society in the late fifties and early sixties. I withdrew from the organization for two reasons: the founder and president of the organization promoted evolution; and it was not that I did not agree with the Society's anticommunist program, it was just that I could not stand someone telling me what I had to believe. The liberal press vigorously attacked the John Birch Society and finally destroyed its effectiveness. The media perceived it to be a revival of McCarthyism.

The newspaper headlines for these years captured the signs of the times:

1957

January 21: Ike Warns Russia to Stay Out of Mideast

January 23: Israel Refuses U.N. Demand to Give Up Gaza

March 22: Smoking Scientifically Proven to Cause Cancer

March 28: Six European Nations Sign Common Market Agreement

April 22: U.S. Installs Intercontinental Atomic Missiles

April 27: Mao Invites 100 Flowers to Bloom in China

May 2: Joseph McCarthy Dies at Age 48

July 20: 100,000 Hear Billy Graham in Yankee Stadium

August 14: Youth Crime Growing Problem

August 31: Malaya Gains Independence

October 4: Russia Beats U.S.; Launches *Sputnik,* First Earth Satellite

November 3: Russia Puts Dog, Laika, in Orbit

December 19: U.S. Installs Atomic Weapons in
Europe

1958

January 24: Atomic Fusion Experiment Successful

February 1: U.S. Puts First Space Satellite in Orbit

March 24: Elvis Is in the Army Now

April 13: Van Cliburn Wins Piano Contest in
Moscow

July 31: Army in Iraq Takes Over; Kills King

August 3: Mao and Khrushchev Meet to Unite
Against U.S.

December 1: Drug Thalidomide Causes 7,000 Birth
Defects

December 18: Five New African Nations Declare
Independence

The new element in the Cold War that was introduced in 1957 was the space race. In spite of the fact
that the United States had brought over some of the
best German rocket scientists, Russia beat the United
States to the punch. Evidently, Russia had taken the
best of the crop of German rocket scientists. The concern at the time was that if Russia had better rockets
and better rocket science than the United States,
wasn't the United States in danger of a nuclear rocket
attack? The United States did finally get a thirty-
pound ball in orbit, but it was small in comparison
to the thousand-pound craft that was needed to sustain a live dog in space. On January 5, 1959, Russia

launched a 3,238-pound satellite that would pass the moon and orbit the sun. Later that year, Russia launched other satellites to photograph the moon, and declared that it was so far ahead in the space race that the United States was now a second-rate nation, and the world belonged to them.

It was in the midst of these daily rash of news reports about the space race that I came to the office as usual in August. I knew something was wrong, as David's and Charles' cars were in the driveway. I learned within a few minutes that Dr. Webber had died of a heart attack during the night.

In addition to family arrangements relative to the forthcoming funeral, there were a host of things we had to do in the office. Stations that carried the program had to be notified. They were instructed to play hymns with announcements about the death of Dr. Webber every few minutes. After the memorial service, we had to prepare special programs by the Webber family expressing appreciation for the support and love extended by friends and listeners during this period.

Cards and letters poured in by the thousands from those who were either saved or blessed by Dr. Webber's ministry. Most of the letters and cards also contained offerings. I met with David, Charles, and Mrs. Webber about whether to try to continue or not continue the ministry. Sufficient offerings had come in to keep the program on the air for several months, so we all decided to give it our best try.

One of the first things we did was to contact all the ministers who had been on Southwest Radio Church programs or who had benefited from the ministry of Dr. Webber. We hoped to include these memorial letters in a memorial book for Dr. Webber, and to have the ministers record a message for the program in which they would express what his ministry had meant to them. To our amazement, very few even responded with an acknowledgment. Dr. Theodore Epp of "Back to the Bible" had listened to Dr. Webber over KWFT, and from the Southwest Radio Church ministry Dr. Epp had received a calling to start his own ministry. His refusal was curt, short, and to the point—no! This was also typical of some others. Here was a man who had pioneered Christian communications and led the way; thousands were saved by hearing the Gospel over his broadcasts; he had supported missions around the world; many had gotten their start in Christian communications through help extended by Dr. Webber, yet in his death they turned their faces from him. And, it was such a little thing we were asking. It was then I learned that most men in full-time ministry— church, missions, or communications—are often the most selfish, greedy, un-Christian people in the world. And not only that, many will cut your throat or stab you in the back if it is to their gain. Not all, but many. That is just the way it is. Paul mourned that all the churches in Asia had turned against him; the church of Galatia refuted him as an apostle; and several of his epistles record the treachery of false brethren. The three epistles of John stress the importance of love and honesty among Christians, but seldom do Christians leaders read these letters.

In continuing the radio program, we really never considered using the recorded messages of Dr. Webber. In the first place, not very many had been saved, and those that were saved contained dated references. Later, we did edit some of the old tapes and replay them, but at that time we did not have the needed technology. Charles and David did have a few sermon outlines from messages given at rural Methodist churches. After a couple of weeks their materials were exhausted, and they were really not very good anyway. Both were inexperienced and naive to believe that light, sugarcoated sermons were going to hold a radio audience. By the end of 1959 the mail had dropped to a trickle. Not only were the programs weak, but many had felt their connection to the ministry ended with the death of Dr. Webber.

I had never attended one class at a seminary, nor written anything longer than a two-page letter, but I had listened to Dr. Webber for eight years and studied books on doctrine and eschatology. It was apparent that the type of programs being presented were not sufficient. I suggested putting the three Webbers into a single program format, and present them as "The Webber Family." I wrote the scripts for the programs, and as I remember, Mrs. Webber mortgaged her home to get funds to see the ministry through the summer. While the programs were not great, they did have a certain appeal. Even so, there was still not sufficient funds coming in to maintain three households, pay the radio bills, and pay the salaries for an office staff. At Thanksgiving in 1960 we sent a letter to the people on our mailing list stating that it appeared we would have to close down the ministry of twenty-seven years at the end of the year. There was a large response in contributions, and many pledged support if "The Webber Family" would continue.

The program format was strengthened by making Monday the prophecy and current events day; Wednesday was the day to teach the international Sunday school lesson; and Friday became question and answer day. Tuesdays and Thursdays became chapel days with the Webber Family. With these changes, and my going out on meetings with David and Charles, support increased and the future of the ministry became brighter. Also, due to the strong pro-America and anti-U.N. theme established by Dr. Webber, we received some support from members of the John Birch Society.

The headline news stories these years were:

1959

January 3: Alaska Becomes 49th State
January 16: Fidel Castro New Cuban Dictator
March 20: China Annexes Tibet
May 28: 2 Monkeys Survive U.S. Space Venture

August 21: Hawaii Becomes 50th State
August 26: Communists Attack Laos
November 19: Ford Deserts Edsel
December 31: Rock-and-Roll Keeps Rolling

1960

January 29: Doctors Install Artificial Kidney
February 27: Negroes Initiate Nationwide Cafe
Sit-In
April 25: Race Riot at Biloxi, Miss.
May 28: Downing of U.S. U-2 Over Russia Scuttles
Paris Peace Conference
August 7: Castro Nationalizes American Property
August 16: Cyprus Becomes Independent State
August 17: Eleven Colonies in Africa Become
Nations
September 26: Castro Speaks Four Hours Before
U.N.
October 12: Khrushchev Bangs Desk at U.N. with
Shoe
November 9: Kennedy Defeats Nixon
November 16: Clark Gable Dies

As a closing note for 1960, and perhaps a sign of the times, in 1960 Lucille Ball and Desi Arnez, the perfect couple, filed for divorce.

The Lean Years
and the Good Years

In my own personal affairs as well as the ministry, the years from 1960 to 1965 were perhaps the most difficult. From 1961 through 1962, the ministry was still confined to no more than ten or twelve radio stations, and with three Webber families being supported, there was not enough money to hire sufficient help. I still kept the books, managed the office, answered the mail, and wrote a thirty-minute radio script every day. Because the work load was so heavy, I had to type the scripts at home. I would usually work until midnight, and get only five or six hours sleep. When Jean was in a manic-depressive state, she would stay in bed for days, and I would have to do the cooking, get the girls ready for school, and clean the house. Charles and David were never taught or trained to know what work really was. Never once during those years do I remember either of them thanking me for working an extra six hours a day without extra pay. In looking back, I now wonder why I did it. I guess it was because I accepted it as the lot in life that God had cast me to fulfill. Had I felt sorry for myself, or complained, I would have been lost.

As I remember, my weekly salary in those days was ninety dollars, and it still amazes me how I could have managed. However, I did make a few dollars on the weekend filling out income tax returns and, then as always, there seemed to be enough money. We never went hungry and never had to go in debt. The little meal in the barrel was always just barely sufficient.

While the ministry programming remained mostly Bible teaching, a strong prophetic base was maintained. There was always something in the news that indicated the world was being prepared for the return of Jesus Christ. The headlines for the two years were:

1961

February 24: Leakey Finds "Earliest" Human Remains

March 1: Peace Corps Ready to Go

March 21: Kennedy Increases Aid to Vietnam

April 2: 40 More Dead Sea Scrolls Found

April 12: U.S.S.R. Puts First Man in Space

April 25: Invasion at Cuba's Bay of Pigs Ends in Disaster

July 2: Hemingway Commits Suicide

July 17: Ty Cobb Dies

July 21: Grissom Second U.S. Man in Space

August 31: Berlin Wall Divides City

October 30: Stalin's Body Not Welcome in Lenin's Tomb

1962

January 1: Landslide Kills 3,000 in Peru

January 4: U.S. Unites Land at Saigon

February 4: JFK Bans Cuban Imports

February 26: John Glenn First American to Orbit Earth

February 28: Kennedy Vows Victory in Vietnam

March 2: Wilt Chamberlain Scores 100 Points

March 15: 312 Die in Air Crashes

April 14: 1,179 Bay of Pigs Prisoners Sentenced to Thirty Years

May 29: U.S. Sends Army Units to Thailand and Laos

June 3: Air Crash in France Kills 121

July 11: Satellite Sends First TV Production Internationally

August 5: Marilyn Monroe Commits Suicide

October 28: Cuban Missile Crisis Threatens Nuclear War

November 10: Eleanor Roosevelt Dies

November 20: U.S.S.R. Removes Missiles from Cuba

November 27: First Boeing 727 Flies

As I remember, it was in July 1962, on a Saturday, that Billy James Hargis was supposed to pick up

Charles to go to a meeting in Enid, Oklahoma. As already noted, I was against either David or Charles associating the ministry with Dr. Hargis. I had gone fishing at Lake Hefner that afternoon, and when I returned home Carol informed me that David had called and said that Charles had died. Upon calling David, it appeared that just before Dr. Hargis arrived at Charles' home, he started shaking, turned white, and died within a span of two or three minutes. Charles had issued some rather strange instructions in the event he should die—that no autopsy was to be performed. His wife, Dorothy, respected his wish. There are times when in young or middle-aged adults, the heart begins to beat uncontrollably, or fibrillate, and the person dies within a few minutes. My neighbor, Dick Shell, who was only forty-five, was using an electric saw to cut wood. His heart suddenly began beating rapidly and he died before the ambulance could arrive. I do not know if that is what killed Charles, but it is possible.

With Charles gone, it was easier for me to write for one person than for two or three. The script had to be written differently for Charles than for David. Charles was most expressive, but David was almost deadpan. One listener called and asked why David didn't just read the dictionary. But with Charles gone I also began to occasionally take part on the program. One of the program series I wrote was a commentary on the Song of Solomon. Pat Zondervan, who came to the office on occasion, liked the copy and

Zondervan Publishing Company published it. Although I wrote the book, it came out under David's name and, of course, David got the royalty check which, probably, was only three or four hundred dollars. Later, other books that I wrote were published through Nelson Publishing, Zondervan, or Huntington House.

It was not until after 1975 that my name appeared on any of the books. This might seem strange to the reader, but I never sought recognition, fame, or money for anything I ever did. If someone else wanted the royalty or the recognition, that was fine with me. I always felt it was my responsibility to fulfill my obligation regardless of what others did or did not do.

In 1961 the three Webbers (David, Charles, and Mrs. Webber) had filed for a nonprofit organizational status. Because of Dr. E. F. Webber's past problems with the IRS, recognition did not come until 1964. This recognition helped to attract larger contributions, and the books kept coming from my typewriter from program scripts. By 1965 the ministry was on more than twenty stations, and an invitation came from the National Religious Organization for the ministry to apply for membership. While this was a sign that Southwest Radio Church had arrived as a credible Christian communications organization, we were still tentative about all the big-shot liberals and compromisers. So in January 1966 David and I boarded a train to attend the National Religious

Broadcasters convention which was being held that year in the Palmer Hotel in Chicago. I remember the trip because a record snow fall of over three feet blanketed the Midwest, including Chicago.

In 1966 the National Religious Broadcasters organization was run by the program producers, which is not the case now. Dr. Rudy Berterman was president that year, and we quizzed him and the steering committee about doctrine and the possibility of WCC and NCC influence, including Pentecostals and Charismatics. While we were still somewhat guarded, we allowed the ministry to be voted on for membership and the ministry was accepted.

With the expanding outreach of the ministry, financial problems decreased. I was able to hire another employee or two to relieve my burden in working nights at home. Also, valuable members like Dorsey Buttram of Oklahoma City and Dr. Lubrett Hargrove of Corpus Christi were added to the board. The main headlines for 1963 through 1966 were:

1963

January 14: Kennedy Promises Tax Cut

February 28: Deal with Khrushchev—Missiles Out, Troops In

April 17: Betting Scandal Rocks NFL

June 20: Pope John XXIII Dies; Pope Paul VI New Pope

July 26: Yugoslav Quake Kills 1,000

August 28: King Says He Has a Dream

August 30: Hot Line to Moscow to Help Avert
Sudden War

September: Border Dispute Between Russia and
China Erupts

October 9: U.S. Sells $250 Million Wheat to Russia

November 22: Kennedy Assassinated in Dallas

November 24: Oswald Killed on TV

1964

February 24: Beatles Say They Are Greater Than
Jesus

April 5: Gen. Douglas MacArthur Dies

April 12: Palmer Wins Fourth Masters

May 11: B-70 Flies Three Times Speed of Sound

July 2: Johnson Signs Civil Rights Act

August 30: World Census Finds 3.1 Billion People

September 2: Sergeant York Dies

November 3: Johnson Big Winner Over Goldwater

December 10: King Wins Peace Prize

1965

January 30: Winston Churchill Dies

February 11: War in Vietnam Heats Up

July 28: LBJ Sends 50,000 More Troops to Vietnam

July 30: LBJ Signs Medicare Bill

August 2: Americans Seeing UFOs

August 15: Race Riots Rage in Watts

1966

January 8: U.S. Forces Launch Offensive in
Vietnam

March 13: Sukarno Kills 100,000 Communists in
   Indonesia
April 26: Artificial Heart Pump Implanted
April 30: Mao Launches Cultural Revolution in
   China
May 28: Opposition to Vietnam War Grows
June 8: U.S. Space Probe Lands on Moon
November 6: Ronald Reagan Elected California
   Governor
November 8: First Negro Senator Elected
November 20: New Fashions Unveil Miniskirts

The first half of the sixties in the United States saw a
departure from traditional patriotism. The Vietnam
War and the Negro's fight for equality caused serious repercussions and divisions within the country.
The Beatles introduced a new psychological attack
against music, the heart of the world. A new drug
culture, accompanied by the hippie dropout generation, was something that Americans had never experienced before. As the Cold War heated up, the
deployment of more and larger intercontinental
nuclear missiles foreshadowed a possible atomic
world war with the demise of the entire human race.
The Supreme Court, leaving its constitutional role
of judging, made laws in the area of religious freedom in public schools, accompanied by advocates
of so-called free love. Divorce rates began to spiral
along with the rise in the number of children born
out of marriage, and Johnson's new welfare state

only served to add fuel to the fires of immorality. However, at the same time, more Americans began to search the Scriptures for answers, and at the ministry we pointed to all these things as signs of the last days—the days of Noah and the days of Lot as Jesus foretold. The need for such a prophetic forum as Southwest Radio Church was more evident than ever, and the ministry continued to expand in outreach.

In the spring of 1966 the requests for Southwest Radio Church literature had increased to the degree that we converted the part of the garage apartment where the office was located into a printing shop and bought our first press. A young man by the name of Marco Rambin answered our want ad for a press operator. Marco seemed to have sufficient references and experience. He introduced a young woman with him as his wife. Marco, like the rest of the small office staff, listened to the daily broadcast for a couple of days. As I opened the office door on the third morning, I noticed that several items were missing, including my 1952 Royal typewriter. I was devastated because I loved this typewriter. As one would guess, Marco did not show up for work. The rest of the day passed, but no Marco. However, as I arrived at the office the next morning, there was Marco waiting with my typewriter and the other items he had stolen. It seems that Marco was not a Christian as he had said he was. The young woman with him was not his wife, but a fellow hippie dropout. They both were on drugs and had simply stopped in Oklahoma City to get some money to continue on to California. However, after stealing my typewriter and the other items, on the way to the pawn shop Marco evidently developed a conscience pain for the first time in his life. He stopped by a church, went in, and confessed his deed to a minister he had never seen before. This pastor explained the Gospel to him and his girlfriend, and they were miraculously saved. Marco continued to work at Southwest Radio Church for fifteen years, off and on. He went to law school and received a degree in criminal justice. The typewriter that Marco stole from me is the same one I am using to write this story. God certainly does work in mysterious ways His wonders to perform.

Prophets from Moses to Malachi foretold that Israel would be scattered into all the world, but in the end of the age a remnant would begin returning to the land promised to the seed of Abraham through Isaac. When in 1948 Israel became a nation and defeated five Arab armies, although outnumbered thirty to one, this was a dominant prophetic sign that the messianic age was dawning. But the old city of Jerusalem where Mt. Moriah is located is the Jerusalem recognized by God, and Jesus said that Jerusalem would be trodden down of the Gentiles until the times of the Gentiles expired (Luke 21:24). On June 22, 1967, the combined Russian trained and equipped armies of Syria, Jordan, and Egypt suddenly attacked Israel. The small Israeli army, supplied by the United States, was again overwhelmingly outnumbered. But in the Sinai Desert alone the Israeli army and air force destroyed over two hundred tanks and four hundred airplanes. In just six days the Israeli army was knocking on the doors of Cairo and Damascus, and only the threat of Russia entering the war on behalf of the Arab nations stopped the Israelis. But the occupation of the old city of Jerusalem seemingly fulfilled the prophecy of Jesus, indicating to many that His Second Coming was at hand. However, there was one small factor overlooked. The Israeli army could have demolished both the Dome of the Rock and El Aqsa Mosque on the Temple Mount, and at that time no Arab nation could have intervened. But the Israeli *kibbutz* system had been established by socialistic, nonreligious Jews. The majority of the Israeli leadership at that time were secular agnostics. To claim the Temple Mount would throw the political, theocratic leadership in Israel to the orthodox who would immediately rebuild the Temple. So the military and the political leaderships left the Moslem buildings untouched and let the Temple Mount remain under the control of the Jordanians. So there is a part, the main part, of old Jerusalem still being trodden down of the Gentiles. Evidently, the time for the return of Jesus Christ was to be delayed.

Nevertheless, Christians and Bible scholars across the United States began clamoring for information about Bible prophecy. Was the reclaiming of old

Jerusalem a sign that the end of the age was near? A question being asked even by the press. A pastor in Tulsa received nationwide attention for his explanation of the Olivet Discourse, but David Webber, the leader of the oldest and foremost prophetic ministry, went unnoticed. So David made a decision to concentrate on Bible prophecy as the primary objective mission. I objected, but David, who was president, overruled me, and this resulted in a major change in programming. I felt we were painting ourselves into a corner, but I still tried to maintain a balance in programming.

With our three girls in school and Jean enjoying one of her better periods of mental stability, she came to work in the office in 1968 and 1969. Jean was a great help during these two years that she worked, and the ministry continued to expand. The world marched on to the following headlines these three years:

1967

January 23: Bloody Battles Rage Through China in the Cultural Revolution

January 27: Three Astronauts Die in Mishap

March 9: Stalin's Daughter Defects

May 1: Elvis Marries

June 28: Israel Smashes Enemies in Six-Day War

July 8: Vivian Leigh Dies of Tuberculosis

August 30: First Black Supreme Court Judge

October 10: Che Guevara Killed in Bolivia

November 14: Dean Rusk Sees Bigger War in
Vietnam

December 21: First Heart Transplant

1968

January 5: Benjamin Spock Indicted for Anti-Draft
Advice

January 31: Viet Cong Launch Tet Offensive

March 31: Johnson Won't Seek Another Term

April 8: Martin Luther King, Jr. Assassinated

April 9: Negroes Riot in Major Cities

June 1: Helen Keller Dies

June 8: Bobby Kennedy Killed in Los Angeles

November 6: Nixon Wins

December 27: Three U.S. Astronauts Orbit Moon
and Return

1969

March 2: Concorde Flies

June 22: Judy Garland Dies, Suicide Suspected

July 20: Armstrong and Aldrin Land on the
Moon

July 20: Woman Drowns in Edward Kennedy's
Car

August 9: Five Found Brutally Slain in Sharon
Tate's Home

August 17: Woodstock Rock Festival Brings Tens
of Thousands

September 7: Bishop Pike Dies in Judean Desert

November 14: Solzhenitsyn Calls U.S.S.R. a Cruel
Society

November 15: War Protesters March on Capital
December 24: Charles Manson Arrested in
   Hollywood Murders

In 1970 I was gone from the office for eight days while undergoing a gall bladder operation, the first time I had to take a leave of absence for any cause. David and I continued to hold meetings across the country in conjunction with the expanding radio coverage. The mail continued to grow as we edited the radio scripts into books and publications. We had to hire more employees and purchase more equipment, but David and Mrs. Webber wanted to keep the office in the garage apartment, as it was adjacent to Mrs. Webber's home. David was very close to his mother, and every time we would stop on the road he would have to call her.

A hippy rock band moved into the house next door, and I simply could not concentrate on my work. Nothing can unravel me more than rock music. I finally issued an ultimatum to the Webbers that unless we could get a bigger office and move away from the hippies, I was through. Reluctantly they agreed, and so in 1972 we moved to a property located at Northwest Seventeenth and May Avenue. There was a duplex and two smaller buildings on the property. We converted one building into a print shop; one building into an office for me to work so that I could have some peace and quiet; and the duplex into a working office for the staff.

Because my work load had greatly increased, an accountant, Mrs. Dortha Harvey, was hired to relieve me of this responsibility. The first year at the new offices a publishing firm in Dallas published my book *Prophecy In Stone*, but although several hundred thousand copies were sold, I never received one dollar in royalties. I was told the firm went bankrupt, but I suspect this was a scam to cover up theft. I was beginning to learn that under the label of Christian ministries and promotions some of the most unsavory crooks in the world operate. The signs of the times reflected in headlines for 1970–72 were:

1970

April 30: U.S. and North Vietnamese Troops Battle in Cambodia

May 16: Twelve Student War Protestors Shot at Kent State

June 28: Thousands of Homosexuals March in N.Y.

July 21: Russia Builds Aswan Dam on Nile

September 14: Arabs Hijack Five Planes, Blow Up Three

1971

February 10: Earthquake Kills 51 in L.A.

February 13: North Vietnamese Occupy Laos

February 13: Vice President Agnew Hits Three Spectators on Golf Course

June 14: Women Committing More Crimes Than Men

September 11: Nikita Khrushchev Dies
October 28: England Joins Common Market
November 18: China Joins U.N.

1972

January 22: Ireland, Denmark, and Norway Join
   Common Market
February 28: Nixon Visits China
March 3: U.S. Space Probe Heads for Jupiter
May 2: J. Edgar Hoover Dies
May 28: Duke of Windsor Dies
May 30: Japanese Terrorists Kill 25, Wound 72,
   at Tel Aviv Airport
June 17: Five Ex-CIA Men Caught in Watergate
   Offices
September 8: Arab Terrorists Kill 11 Israeli
   Olympians in Munich
October 26: Henry Kissinger at Paris Peace Table
November 1: 500 Americans Get Sex
   Change
November 8: Nixon by Landslide
December 10: Astronauts Tour Moon in Land Rover
December 26: Harry Truman Dies

On a hot summer day in 1971 I received a call that my father had suffered a heart attack. He had been taken to Hugo Memorial Hospital. I immediately left for Hugo. When I arrived he seemed to be resting comfortably. I picked up the shirt he was wearing that was still in the room and shook it to straighten out the wrinkles before folding it to place it on a shelf. Salt covered the floor. My father had been roofing a house in 103 degree temperatures when he suffered the attack, even though he was nearly eighty years of age.

My dad was released from the hospital, but in a couple of months he had another heart attack, and this one was fatal. He was a hard worker, honest and truthful, with a good reputation in the community. At his funeral, the church was packed with others standing or listening at the windows. This was the greatest compliment to his life that could possibly be given. We should all ask ourselves, "If I were to die today, how many would come to my funeral?"

The years between 1972 and 1975 at the new offices of Southwest Radio Church were rather pleasant and productive ones. Jean had a serious mental setback in 1974 that required another stay in the hospital, but at the office things were much better. My two works on Henry Kissinger and the Jupiter Effect received national attention and probably a couple of million copies were disseminated. This not only produced funds for the ministry, but more Christians became aware of Southwest Radio Church. The broadcast was expanded to Los Angeles, San Francisco, Portland, and Seattle. By 1975 more than sixty stations were carrying the program. During this period David and Madge got a divorce, but the court decided that David was without blame and he received full guardianship of their son, Edward.

There were a couple of other problems in the Webber family that caused me grave concern, but there is no need to address these. Peter had a weakness in his spirit, and Paul had a weakness in his flesh, and Satan always attacks God's children at their weakest points.

By the spring of 1975 the ministry had grown to such an extent that more presses and more employees were needed. In just two years the ministry had outgrown its new quarters. Also, some new and important members were added to the general board. New members were nominated by David to active board members for approval by vote. From the board, five trustees were appointed. The only way to overturn the will of the trustees was by a general or special full board meeting. Some organizations have a limited board with only family members or rubber stamp employees in a limited number, sometimes no more than three. Such boards leave the head man free to do whatever he wills without any restraint. Such was not the case at Southwest Radio Church. David and I had to submit a yearly financial report for approval, and give an account of our ministry as demanded by the trustees or the board. It will be important to remember this when we get to a later chapter on the "Shootout at the OKC Corral."

After the Jim Bakker scandal the National Religious Broadcasters held a meeting in Chicago to establish a related entity to govern the financial accountability of the membership. There were approximately forty delegates from the larger communications ministries in the United States. The organization that was established was called EFICOM, and when the moderator asked for a contribution from each member to help pay for the meeting and expenses to get the new department off the ground, guess who stepped forward to pay for the entire bill: Jimmy Swaggert's son, who made a pretty speech about how the Swaggert ministry was going to help restore honesty and credibility to Christian communications. It was only a few weeks after this that Jimmy Swaggert himself fell from grace and became an anathema to the entire NRB membership. So just belonging to an organization, even one that polices financial accountability, does not mean that is what will happen. A strong board and an independent CPA audit is the best assurance that contributions given by the supporting Christians will be used for their intended purpose. In the fall of 1997, two IRS agents from Oklahoma City came out for an audit of the publishing arm of Southwest Radio Church. After one week they called me to meet for consultation. They found nothing amiss and told us to just keep doing what we were doing. One of the agents came to my office and thanked me for what the Southwest Radio Church ministry meant to him personally.

As the office space at the new location just off Northwest Seventeenth and May became crowded after only two years, Ben McCammon, a new board member who was also a real estate agent, suggested a building at Northwest Sixth and Classen. This building was the old First Nazarene Church of Oklahoma City. Due to downtown blight, plus the fact that the congregation had moved to new development areas, the church relocated. The building itself needed extensive repairs and it was much too large for our needs. However, the ministry was growing so rapidly it was concluded that we might need the entire space within a few years.

One of the almost paranormal mysteries about the location was that just south across the street was a long, two-story building where I had received room and board while attending the university twenty-three years previously; and, just across the street east was the building where Jean lived when we were dating twenty years previously. It seemed that something kept bringing me back to this very spot.

At that time the entire area was in deep depreciation, and it was a high drug and crime area. After two or three break-ins we had to hire a guard to keep watch at night. We moved into the new location in late August, and by the beginning of 1976 the building had been refurbished sufficiently to locate the staff comfortably and move the printing operation into one of the wings. The primary news stories while moving from the garage apartment to the huge building complex on Northwest Sixth Street were:

1973

January 21: Supreme Court OKs Abortion During First Three Months

January 22: Lyndon Johnson Dies

January 27: U.S. Signs Cease-Fire in Vietnam

February 28: Indians Occupy Wounded Knee

August 22: Henry Kissinger Named Secretary of State

October 22: Egypt and Syria Suddenly Invade Israel on Yom Kippur

December 16: O. J. Simpson Sets New Football Rushing Record

1974

January 20: Women Increase Role in Business

February 23: Patty Hearst Abducted

March 3: 345 Killed in Turkish Airliner Crash

March 31: Kinsey Report Says More Americans Gay

April 8: Hank Aaron's 715th Homer Passes Ruth

August 8: Nixon Resigns Over Watergate

August 9: Ford Becomes President

September 12: Communists Take Over Ethiopia

November: Arafat, with Gun, Speaks at U.N.

1975

April 5: Chiang Kai-shek Dies

April 27: Pol Pot's Army Captures Cambodia

May 7: Ford Declares End to Vietnam War

July 19: U.S. and Russian Space Vehicles Join in Space

September 29: Casey Stengel Dies
November 10: U.N. Condemns Zionist Racists
November 24: Franco Dies—Juan Carlos King
December 7: Cuban Army Fights in Angola for
   Communism

As 1976 dawned upon Southwest Radio Church, the ministry was being well received as the need for a continuing major religious and prophetic report forum increased. In order to keep up with the mounting work load and produce new publications, Dr. Emil Gaverluk and Dr. Hugh Moreton were added to the staff. With the mailing list now approaching one hundred thousand, we were still using old addressing systems. Jean was enjoying one of her more mentally stable periods, so she returned and installed our first computer system. There was no definite plan to make Southwest Radio Church a major international ministry. We were only responding to the call for additional programming and publications from constituents. By January 1976 the program was carried by approximately eighty radio stations from the West Coast to the East Coast. David and I decided to work out of one office in order to be in constant communication and present a united leadership; however, this was soon to change.

Problems in Paradise

When Jesus hung on the cross dying, He was crucified between two thieves. One of the thieves mocked Him and charged Him angrily of being a false Messiah. The other thief defended Jesus and asked the Lord to remember him in His kingdom. It took absolute faith for this thief to place his hope for a future life in an accused criminal dying on a cross beside him. But Jesus looked at the believing thief and remarked, "Today shalt thou be with me in paradise." I believe the angry thief was a Jew and the believing thief was a Gentile. Had the believing thief been a Jew, Jesus would have said, "Today shalt thou be with me in Abraham's bosom." *Paradise* is a Persian word meaning a peaceful, beautiful park. The believing thief would know what Jesus meant; the unbelieving thief would not know what Jesus meant.

In 1976 Southwest Radio Church was a wonderful and inspiring place to serve the Lord, and it is in such paradises that Satan does his most effective work. David and I, for the most part, worked together in perfect harmony. We served together, bowled together, went fishing together, and with both of us in the same office, we worked together in all phases of the ministry.

One of the problems that arose was that as the program began to be carried on more and more stations, the daily interchanges between the stations took much of our time. The smart thing to do, at the time, was what other major ministries were doing: hire an agency. So, David and I talked with John Boyd and Ed Steele, operators of Creative Communications from the Los Angeles area. While the legal percentage of the radio bill due an agency was fifteen percent, I believe we paid the agency somewhere around ten percent of the gross bill. The agency wants to see the client succeed, because the more stations the programming gets on, the higher the commission to the agency will be. I do not say this was the case with CCA, but the board thought so a few years later as the debt began to pile up and the agency received more and more monies in commissions. This was one of the problems that later developed between David and the board, and I am sure it has become a problem with other ministries as program producers have departed from the large agency corporations and gone independent.

Another problem that developed was that as the mail increased, additional secretaries had to help open and code the mail. David liked to oversee this daily procedure personally, but I could not work in the room with David, or even in that area, with all the talking and confusion. So it was decided that I should move on the other side of the building to the southwest wing. Of course, if I moved I had to take several employees with me to help in research, proof-reading, and other duties. Previously, David had hired Cathy and John High. Cathy was an excellent secretary and office coordinator. However, she had become used to consulting with me on everything, and after I moved she would run over to my office every two or three hours to check with me. This took my time and irritated David. Also, because I was an accountant and still filled out the required tax records, Mrs. Harvey, with the accounting records, moved down the hall in the same wing.

This was in 1978 when David and I did a few programs with Vendyl Jones on efforts to find the ashes remaining from the last red heifer sacrificed in Israel. Of course, at that time everyone thought we were crazy, talking about ashes from a cow burned over two thousand years ago. However, in 1997 the whole world was excited about a suitable red heifer being born in Israel that would make possible the resumption of sacrificial Temple worship. At the time, my secretary happened to be redheaded. She was dedicated to seeing that I was not disturbed at work. Because in this respect she was rather aggressive, the rest of the office called her "the red heifer."

Because the office staff had become so spread out, to see that the work was better coordinated, David gave Cathy High supervision over the east side, and

Dortha Harvey, who was a very hard worker and efficient supervisor, was given charge over the west side. Subsequently, over the next couple of years, competition arose over who had the most employees and the most authority. Consequently, the ministry had more employees doing the same work and the number rose to seventy-five. Some girls were doing nothing more than running up and down the hall gossiping. When I could not resolve this problem with David, I called for a trustee's investigation.

I know some of the readers will shudder in horror that such a thing could happen in a ministry, but it happens at times in all ministries and churches. When it happens and those responsible do not challenge the system, then there is something wrong. I have been in other mission ministries overseas, and in like ministries in the States, and seen the same situation with nothing being done.

After considering the situation and consulting for a couple of days, the trustees decided to appoint an independent council from the general board. They selected Mr. John Stowe, of Norman, an attorney. Mr. Stowe was given a six-month contract. On his first day he fired thirteen secretaries. David had fired Dortha Harvey, so there was no one to figure the payroll or keep the books. Mr. Stowe rehired her so that the employees would get paid. Again, some may shudder that thirteen employees could be let go in one day, but we have to consider that larger ministries have hundreds of secretaries, and I wonder how many of them could be dismissed without hurting work procedures. Again, it is a good thing that Southwest Radio Church had made provisions for such action in the bylaws.

John Stowe and I got along just fine, although he was exceedingly authoritative and unforgiving. I had served in the army and strict discipline did not disturb me, but it disturbed David greatly. It was the war of "David and Goliath Stowe" every day. David would throw stones, but Stowe would hurl back boulders. When the six months were up, Mr. Stowe wanted to continue as general manager or CEO. Had I continued to back Mr. Stowe, this would have happened, but without David, and this I could not do. So, exit John Stowe, but I still think highly of him and appreciate the service he rendered the ministry. During the tenure of Mr. Stowe, other employees were fired and replaced by what he considered better workers. Inasmuch as I worked with Mr. Stowe, I usually got the blame.

To add a footnote to the John High family, not only was Cathy an excellent secretary, she was a wonderful Christian. John was also a terrific announcer and worker in the recording department. However, John was one of those persons who could never accept the security of salvation by faith. They were members of Sunnylane Baptist Church, one of the larger churches in the convention, and often when a new evangelist would come John would get saved again and rebaptized. This was an embarrassment to Cathy and their two boys. John was always trying to prove to himself that he was saved. After a mission tour to the Middle East in 1980 on which I visited a radio station in Lebanon that carried our program, John said that the Lord had called him to serve in that radio station. I oriented John on what to expect. I informed him that this station was in PLO territory, that there were machine gun emplacements around it with barb wire restraints and guards on duty, that the location was near Hizbullah territory and beneath the Beaufort Castle, a PLO stronghold. But, John responded that he did not care; the calling was from God, and he was going.

John made all the arrangements and we even, I think, paid his airline ticket over. But, after John had been in Israel for twenty-four hours and made a quick trip to the station, Cathy got an international call. John was coming home. It seems the Lord had made a mistake. Not long after that Hizbullah did overrun the station and killed every staff member. We owe those brave native Christians a debt for being faithful unto death.

Not long after this incident, Cathy and John left Oklahoma City and moved to Lake Charles, Louisiana. I heard they were employed at a combination Christian TV and radio station. I later received a report from the pastor of a church they attended in Lake Charles that John had denied the faith, converted to Judaism, and forced Cathy and the boys to follow him. I pray this is not true. They were such a wonderful family for something like this to happen.

In 1977 David and I decided to increase the missionary outreach of the ministry and start a separate program in Spanish to be aired in Mexico, Central America, and South America. The program was to be called "Profecías Bíblicas." John Barela, who had been released as pastor from an independent Baptist church in Fairfax, Oklahoma, was hired to be the speaker. John spoke a Tex-Mex brand of Spanish. Although John's Spanish was far from perfect, he was able to communicate the Gospel to the nations south of the border. Rev. Barela is one of the best one-on-one evangelists I have ever met but, he just had trouble following scriptural guidelines. John moved to Tulsa and started his own ministry, which from all reports has been moderately successful. Jose Holowaty from Argentina took over as host of "Profecías Bíblicas."

Another matter that I reluctantly refer to was a second marriage by David in 1979. It was an unfortunate happening that was later annulled.

But we read again in Romans 8:28 that all things do work together for good to those who love God and who are called to fulfill God's plan and purpose. So, the ministry survived and continued to increase to approximately one hundred and twenty stations by the end of 1980. In the meantime, these other events were happening in the world:

1976

January 23: World War II Records Indicate Pope's
Relations with Nazi Germany

February 29: World Spends $300 Billion a Year on
Armaments

April 5: Howard Hughes Dies

April 20: Barbara Walters First Woman News
Anchor at NBC

June 19: Racial Violence Erupts in South
Africa

June 20: U.S. Turns Lebanon Over to Syria

June 29: Enormous 8.2 Quake May Have Killed
One Million at Tangshan, China

July 4: Israel's Daring Raid at Entebbe Frees 105
Hostages

July 4: U.S. Observes 200th Anniversary

August 26: 28 Die of Mysterious Legionnaires
Disease in Philadelphia

September 19: Mao Tse-tung Dies

October 23: Gang of Four Tried in China for Crimes
Against People

November 2: Carter Elected President

November 23: O. J. Simpson Rushes for 273 Yards

November 24: Quake in Turkey Kills 3,000

December 10: Nobel Prize Goes to Milton
Friedman

1977

January 7: Rupert Murdock Increases Empire

February 1: Movie "Roots" Draws 80 Million

February 18: First Space Shuttle Vehicle Readied
for Mission

March 28: Two 747s Crash; Kill 574 in Canary
Islands

April 16: Army Tests Women Cadets at West
Point

April 23: Ethiopia Expels All Missionaries

May 18: Begin New Israeli Prime Minister

August 16: Elvis Presley Dies

August 30: Son of Sam, Berkowitz, Caught

September 7: Treaty Gives Panama Future
Canal Control

October 14: Bing Crosby Dies

December 25: Charlie Chaplin Dies

1978

January 15: Cowboys Win Super Bowl

April 7: Neutron Bomb Put on Hold

May 18: Abortion Legalized in Italy

June 9: Mormon Church Admits Negroes

July 25: First Test Tube Baby Born in London

August 26: Pope Paul VI Dies; John Paul I, New
Pope

September 18: Sadat, Begin, Carter Meet at Camp
David

September 20: John Paul I Dies

September 28: San Diego Crash Kills 150

October 23: Polish Pope John Paul II Chosen

November 29: 909 Commit Suicide at Jonestown,
Guyana

December 7: Army Reconsidering Gays for Service

1979

January 26: Nelson Rockefeller Dies

January 30: Shah Forced to Abdicate in Iran

January 31: U.S. and China Resume Diplomatic Relations

February 26: Ayatollah Khomeini New Strong Man in Iran

March 31: Egypt Gets Back Sinai in Return for Peace Treaty

May 3: Margaret Thatcher First British Woman Premier

May 29: 273 Die in DC-10 Chicago Crash

June 10: European Parliament Members Chosen

June 11: John Wayne Dies

July 2: Supreme Court Rules Teen Abortions Without Parents Consent OK

October 6: Pope Pays First Visit to U.S.

November 26: Iran Seizes U.S. Embassy Staff

From 1975 through 1979 the world had witnessed many earth-shaking events and changes that pointed to a New World Order. At Southwest Radio Church the problems that arose within the ministry would return to haunt us in the next decade.

The Tour of a Lifetime

Dome of the Rock—Jerusalem, Israel

It was not until 1976 that Southwest Radio Church began to organize and sponsor tours to the Middle East and other parts of the world. David led the first tour to Israel and Jordan, and I led the following tour comprised of approximately one hundred and fifty members. My tour was a Mediterranean cruise and Israeli tour. We left from Greece, and our ports of call were Venice, a port in Yugoslavia, Alexandria, Ashdod, Kusadasi, and five or six of the Greek islands (Rhodes, Crete, Santorini, Delos, and Patmos). My first tour was rather uneventful, with the exception that about half the tour group became ill from eating at an Arab hotel on Mt. Olivet. After 1976 David would usually lead two groups a year and I would also lead two. About half of David's tours went to places like Alaska, Hawaii, Scandanavia, etc. Mine were mostly to more Bible-centered lands and mission tours. One of my most memorable tours was one to five Middle Eastern countries and England in 1978: Iraq, Syria, Jordan, Egypt, and Israel. This tour group was comprised of eighty women and twenty-five men. John Barela went from the office to help with logistics and Dortha Harvey was also included to help take care of logistics and personal matters for women members.

Our first stop was London. We had a very nice stay in London. The night we were to depart there was a dress-up dinner affair, and we went straight from dinner to board the airplane for Amman, Jordan. That day the Israelis had chosen to initiate an invasion of the Bekaa Valley in Lebanon. When we landed in Jordan, Amman was blacked out, there were tanks on the runways, and armed soldiers with machine guns hurriedly escorted us from the plane to the small terminal. There we were searched and rudely told to open our suitcases and packs. After an hour's delay we were hustled back on board a new 727, which took off immediately for Baghdad. About twenty minutes after we took off the plane ran into a vicious storm. There was constant lightning, and hail hammered so hard against the plane I thought it would surely break up. At the same time I swore it was going backward. I had never before, or since, gone through such turbulence in an airplane. Two-thirds of the passengers were from my tour, and about one-third were Muslims. The Muslims were out in the aisle bowing up and down toward what they thought was Mecca, and John Barela at the same time was leading our people in "Nearer My God to Thee."

The Arab pilots have a saying, "What Will Be, Will Be." I guess it was not our time to go because miraculously the plane plopped down at the Baghdad airport at midnight. There were three buses and drivers to meet us.

After a fifteen-minute ride, we arrived at our hotel quarters, but instead of a hotel, it was a long string of what looked like fourth grade fishing cabins in the middle of a field. As in Amman, Baghdad was blacked out. We were given some small flashlights and our cabin numbers. There were no carts or porters. We had eighty women dressed in dinner wear, with high-heel shoes and nylon stockings, dragging their suitcases through the mud in the dark while trying to locate their cabins. I was already beginning to fear for my life.

Somehow, after an hour, all the round pegs found their round holes, which is more truth than fiction. The only toilet in the cabin was a round hole in the corner. When I laid down on my bunk the mattress sagged all the way down to the floor . . . and I was supposed to have the best room. I shuddered to think what the others were like. Life became even more precious.

The next morning a horn blew to wake us up, which was probably not needed as few went to sleep anyway. We were all herded into a large dining room area with crude wooden tables. Boys came out with baskets of boiled eggs, fried Iraqi bread, and fig jam— that was it. If you have ever seen eighty women with old makeup and uncombed hair early in the morn- ing—well, it is a horrible sight. We were given only fifteen minutes to eat, and those who did not get an egg or a piece of bread were just out of luck.

We were told by our national guide, Aziz, that we would have thirty minutes to go to our cabins to get ready to leave on tour. Our tour director was Louis Baxter, half Egyptian and half Italian—he was tall, mean, cruel, and foulmouthed. Dr. Hugh Moreton and Dr. and Mrs. Emil Gaverluk were also on the tour. Baxter only went as my tour director one more time. He was such a degenerate that I told him he would not be needed any more. Dr. Moreton went with me three more times, but I refused to take him any longer because he wanted to take his bossy wife, and he would somehow gather a few older ad- mirers and form a clique. I never allowed cliques within a tour to develop, nor would I pander to tour grinches. A tour grinch is someone on the tour who gets pleasure by being negative and making every- one else miserable. I always got the best accommo- dations possible, but if a tour member can't stand a little sand in their oatmeal or a few cockroaches, then they should stay at home. However, over the years I have gained the reputation of being the best Chris- tian tour leader available. I finally got to the place on tour that I would just go alone, or perhaps take my wife Kim and one photographer.

Ishtar Gate

After the thirty minutes had elapsed, the whistle sounded to alert us to get on the buses. We were scheduled to visit the Babylon of Nebuchadnezzar. Baghdad is on the Tigris River and Babylon is on the Euphrates, sixty miles to the southwest. There was a four-lane divided highway between the two sites. Along the highway were dozens of brick factories which were making bricks for the rebuilding of Babylon. According to Isaiah 13 and Jeremiah 50–52, the city of Babylon was to have been destroyed like Sodom and Gomorrah. However, this has not happened yet. There were twenty-five thousand Jews still in Babylon at the birth of Jesus Christ. As the city declined in importance it was deserted, and over the course of two millennia it became buried by windblown sand and the Euphrates River. German and English archaeologists also pillaged it for artifacts. One-half of the beautiful Ishtar Gate is now in the Pergamon Museum in Berlin.

Nevertheless, Babylon was so huge (fifteen miles square) it was impossible to remove all the bricks, even for building. We read in Genesis 11 that in those days they burned the bricks throughly, and the bricks of Babylon, though three to four thousand years old, are still perfect. The new bricks being used have

Nebuchadnezzar's name on one side and Saddam Hussein's name on the other side. Saddam believes he is the reincarnation of Nebuchadnezzar. Much of Babylon had been restored and some temples rebuilt when we were there, and the rebuilding has continued to this present time. Iraq held a universal month-long festival in Babylon in 1987 and invited Madonna to be the queen of the ball, because Saddam believes Madonna lives in the hearts of the Iraqi people. The reason is that Madonna is a contraction of the Latin *Mia Donna*, which in the Chaldean means "Semiramis, wife of Nimrod."

After touring the ruins and efforts to restore Babylon, we returned to Baghdad. The next morning we went to the museum and were scheduled to take a sleeper train to Nineveh near the Russian border that evening. We went to the train station, which was blacked out, but instead of a sleeper train, there were two day coaches reserved for us. It seems that our train was being used to take men and ammunition to the PLO forces in Syria and Lebanon, and we were hooked to an ammunition train going through Russia and Syria to Beirut. We were told to take our seats and to not even think about moving. All night long as the train traveled northward, Iraqi military police walked up and down the isles beating clubs into the palms of their hands.

We arrived at Mosul, or Nineveh, about daylight. We traveled around part of the walls and visited the palace of Ashurbanapal. The cuneiform writings on the walls relating to the exploits of the Assyrian victories are still very much in evidence on the walls. We returned to our cottages in Baghdad and arrived about dark. In order to go to Iraq none of us could have an Israeli stamp in our passport, nor were we supposed to go to Israel after we had gone to Iraq. However, a tour member had left a tour brochure in his room showing the complete itinerary, so we were hauled down to talk with the secret police. To be found out of the will of Saddam Hussein at that time was a dangerous thing. Hussein made his appearance in Baghdad in 1969 by hanging nine Jews on the streets of Baghdad with a warning on their bodies for all Jews to get out of Iraq.

We were finally let go after questioning. We pleaded ignorance and it was fairly easy for the police to agree that we Yankees were indeed ignorant. But this experience upset the tour group and general war possibilities in the Middle East were looking more grim. Dr. Gaverluk got the shakes and began to stir up the tour members to get me to fly them back to the States by way of India. In the first place, I would have had to come up with two hundred thousand dollars, and we would have been sued for millions for getting the tour members into such a jam and not completing the tour. After that, I did not take Dr. Gaverluk on tour again either.

We continued on the tour schedule and left the next morning on a six-hour bus ride to Ur in southern Iraq near Kuwait. Ur was also a very large city. It had also been buried under about twelve feet of sand, but we did get to see the ancient tomb of a queen who had been buried with her chariots, horses, and servants. The rebuilt ziggurat was also impressive, and we got to walk through the streets of Ur that had been cleared of sand. We visited what is said to be the house of Abraham and Sarah. The doorpost with Abraham's name on it is supposed to be in a British museum; however, I have never been able to find it. The British are excellent pillagers, but poor cataloguers.

Coming out of the Ur area we turned onto the highway back to Baghdad. The buses stopped to gas up at a service station, and hallelujah, this station had a bathroom. Bathrooms are at a premium in Iraq. We usually had to avail ourselves of weed or reed cover, and to find a real bathroom was pure luxury. So zoom . . . one hundred and five tour members line up at the restroom. Two went in and came out with no problem, but the third participant was the largest person on tour. She was a female weighing somewhere around three hundred and fifty pounds, take or leave a hundred pounds or so. And, it so happened that the door to this restroom was a steel door. So this dear woman took her turn, but in attempting to exit, the door would not open. Somehow the lock had become jammed. We kicked, banged, prayed, and tried everything but cursing . . . and I am not sure that some did not try this. Finally we noticed that there was a transom over the door. We got the transom open, found a stepladder, and handed it to the imprisoned person. She got on the stepladder and finally got her head and shoulders through up to her breasts. These posed a problem, but finally, one at a time, progress was being made. But then it seemed we came to an impasse . . . the stomach seemed to fill the entire space. We would push her stomach in at one place, but there would be a bulge show up in another place. Not to be out-done, two of the men got hold of her arms and tried to pull her through. Clothes and skin began to tear, and we thought about putting some oil on her to make her egression easier, but she flatly vetoed this plan. There was nothing else to do but push her back inside the restroom. I had noticed some poles out by the road when we came in, so I sent two of the men out to get one. Four or five of the more husky members took hold of the pole and bashed the privy in. Our caged lady was finally released. However, the proprietor of the establishment along with a couple of dozen other male Iraqis who had stopped and were watching the proceedings, began to mutter and look at us threateningly. I hastily got the tour members on the buses and we sped northward along the Euphrates River looking for a friendly patch of reeds.

The next morning we gladly left Baghdad on a 727. Aziz, our Iraqi guide, said good-bye and hoped to see us again, as he intended to go live with his brother in Detroit. We landed again in Amman and hurriedly boarded buses for Syria. We stopped to tour the Roman city of Jerash, one of the cities of the decathlon. This city is wonderfully preserved and visitors to Jordan should go to this site if possible.

The highway we took to Damascus ran just to the east of the Golan Heights. The Israeli army was on the volcanic hills and high ground just over the border. The Syrian army, including tanks and artillery, was dug in along the highway in assault formations. Our buses passed right through the entire length of the Syrian armed forces. When we got to Damascus our fearless tour arranger, Mr. Baxter, was so scared he went into his room, locked the door, and would not come out.

The next morning we visited the "traditional" house of Ananias, walked down the street called Straight, and saw the place in the wall where Paul escaped in a basket. The only one of the three places that we could accept as the true site was the street called Straight. We also went northward to Masoula, the little city were Aramaic is still spoken by some, and then on to Homs. We were at Homs at noontime. We parked near a high school, and the students were overjoyed to meet Americans and they tried out their English on us. A few weeks later Assad sent his army into Homs and slaughtered fifteen thousand, and not one word was said in protest by the United Nations or the United States. Had Israel killed even fifteen Arabs without cause, there would have been a world upheaval. This is the double standard that exists in the Middle East.

On the way back to Damascus our guide took us to the Castle of the Knights on the edge of the Bekaa Valley. This castle was built by Richard the Lion-hearted and housed knights from England, France, and Germany. It was never taken by Saladin, and the knights departed under a safe passage guarantee and went to Rhodes. The castle itself is an impressive bastion, looking just as it did when Richard and the brave knights of Europe were there to take the holy land from the infidels. The Syrian chefs had prepared a barbecue for us in the castle, which was a real treat for our tour members.

The next morning we were to leave at seven a.m. and head for Petra in Jordan, but our guide had heard that the PLO was going to machine-gun our buses as we left Damascus, so we got our tour group up at two a.m. and headed south. We roared out of Damascus as fast as seventy miles per hour. Dr. Lubrett Hargrove, a board member, was also on this tour. Mrs. Harvey had become seriously ill, so Dr. Hargrove and I made a stop at the border and placed her in a taxi. Lubrett and I took her to Amman where she could get medical attention while the buses and the rest of the tour continued down the King's Highway to Petra.

After leaving Mrs. Harvey in good care at a hospital in Amman, Lubrett and I went on to Petra, and went back a couple of days later and put her on a plane to the States. We joined the rest of the tour for a flight to Cairo. In Egypt we saw the usual sites in the Cairo area, but we were also unpopular in Egypt. There were strong anti-American feelings, and guards with machine guns at the airport would take billfolds from men's pockets and take the money. There was nothing we could do about it. The last day in Cairo I was interviewing our guide for a radio program, and within five minutes after I had finished I became very ill. In just a few minutes my temperature shot up to one hundred and four. Dr. Hargrove gave me what antibiotics he had, and with aspirin to keep my fever down I made the night. I would not stay in Cairo, so some of the men literally carried me to the bus. I laid on a bench at the airport until we got on a plane. That night in Amman Dr. Hargrove stayed in my room with me to check on my condition. Sometime during the night I awoke and heard a strange noise in my room. It was like nothing I had ever heard. After getting my head cleared and my hearing oriented, I determined that this noise was coming from Dr. Hargrove. I was able to pick up a pillow and throw it at him. He awoke with a snort and wanted to know what was going on. I replied that I had finally figured out what he sounded like: a rooster, a boar hog, and a hound dog in a fight, with the hog gradually winning. I do not think Lubrett has ever forgiven me.

From Jordan we went to Israel, and while I continued with the tour group I was still very sick and my high fever continued. After I got back to States it took me three months to get over the combined virus and pneumonia. After that I was always careful about what I ate and did in Egypt. There are germs there that are left over from the ten plagues.

While on this tour I was cursed, threatened with lawsuits, pleaded with to end the tour, and challenged by some in the ministry who went with me. Yet since that time I have met dozens of those who were with me on that tour, and without exception all have said that it was the greatest experience of their lives. As in all phases of life, tribulations and dangers are never pleasant at the moment, but once we triumph over them, they become badges of honor. Such is life and such is human nature.

More About Tours and Tourists

In having led dozens of tours, I have made thousands of friends. These friends become the most faithful and generous supporters of the radio ministry. Without tours, Southwest Radio Church may not have survived. In the tours I have led, no tour member can accuse me of improper behavior or failing to conduct myself as becoming a Christian who put the safety and welfare of the members first. While one or two may have had to return home because of illness, I have never lost a tour member, and the most serious injuries have been a broken leg and a broken arm. I have to admit that on several occasions I have come close to sending a few back home.

On one tour a lady from either Portland or Seattle, I do not remember which, did not read her final instructions about changing hotels in Tel Aviv, so when we arrived from the airport she did not understand why we were not at the correct hotel. As I remember, her first name was Penny, and she kept crying and yelling as I was trying to get everyone in their room and oriented about touring the first day. I sent a member of the ministry over to try to quiet her, but she would not shut up. Next, I asked our guide to try to explain to her why the hotel was changed, but she would not be placated. Finally, I asked our agent, Yehuda Levy, to speak with her, but her wails became louder. The rest of the tour members became impatient and uneasy, so I had to do something to take charge. I approached Penny, shook my finger in her face, and shouted: "You will shut up, and you will shut up right now, or I will take you back out to the airport and personally put you on a plane and send you back home." That did the trick. Penny quieted down, went to her room, showed up in a good mood at dinner, and enjoyed the rest of the tour.

Penny went with me on two more tours, and as our staff can verify, I am usually the most patient and understanding person in the world, but there are times assertive measures are required. I remember on another trip to Israel and Jordan there was a tour member whose first name was Bill. Bill was a businessman and a bachelor. He listened to our program over a Baltimore station, but why he went on a Christian tour was difficult to understand. Bill was a party-person deluxe. He liked to smoke, he liked to drink, and he liked women. Finally, the second day, I told Bill that a Christian tour was not his thing. What he should do was go back to the Baltimore-Washington area and party all he wanted to, because he was not going to find what he wanted on my tour. I instructed him to have his bags packed and be in his room at four p.m.; Yehuda and I would take him to the airport. We went to Bill's room, but no Bill. I don't know where he stayed that night, but when we got on the bus the next morning there he was in the back. I did not say anything, and neither did Bill. However, he was quiet that day, and on the remaining ten days of the tour Bill was a perfect gentleman. Since that time Bill has become one of the best friends I have ever had. He will meet me at Washington National Airport in his limousine and take me wherever I want to go. He has been on many subsequent tours. If we hold a meeting in his area he always comes, and he became a faithful supporter of the ministry.

Like the example of the dear lady who got stuck in a restroom at Ur, there have been dozens of unusual and humorous things that have occurred on tours. These may not seem funny at the time, but in retrospect they take on a humorous afterglow the further the incident is removed in time and space.

In 1982 I led a large group on a ten-nation tour. We started in the Netherlands, flew to Portugal, and then went into Spain by bus. We were a couple of days in southern Spain, and then our bus took the ferry over to Morocco. On the way back to Madrid, Spain, we had to catch the ferry back over. However, there was a severe storm that frequently occurs in the Mediterranean called a *euroclydon* (Acts 27:14). After we arrived at the port from Rabat, the wind blew the rest of the day, all that night, and the rest of the next day. Finally, about dark the second day of the storm, the wind abated sufficiently to get back over to Spain. But while we were at the port city waiting for the ferry, an announcement was run that Prime Minister Begin of Israel and his chief army general had been assassinated in a street café in Jerusalem. The announcement kept running over and over on the state television network. I was very concerned because we were going to Egypt next and then to Israel, and I did not want to get caught in a Middle East war with a large tour on my hands.

Going back to Spain on the ferry, I asked everyone I could find who could speak English about this report, but no one seemed to know anything about it. After we landed I inquired, and as we drove to Cordova I asked at every stop, but I could find out nothing. Finally we got to Cordova. Our hotel was on the side of a mountain at least a hundred steps about street level. I bounded out of the bus, ran as quickly as I could up the stairs, and bolted into the lobby. A distinguished looking clerk with a trim mustache wearing a bow tie was waiting on a guest. At the first opportunity I broke in and asked, gasping, "Have you heard anything about Prime Minister Begin being assassinated?" He looked at me rather coldly, and in a crisp English accent replied, *"Which room is he in?"* As I have noted before, there are times when there is absolutely nothing more to be said. This was one of those times. Stunned, I simply turned and went back down to the bus to get my vouchers so I could check the sleepy tour members into the hotel at two o'clock in the morning. The next morning I learned that Prime Minister Begin was well and hearty, so we continued on the tour to the next country, Egypt.

Another rather unusual human interest story occurred on one of my tours to the Middle East in the middle eighties. I do not remember anything unusual about this tour until we were nearing the Dead Sea. There was a tour member from Dallas whose last name was Duckworth. Mrs. Duckworth confided in me that the real reason she joined my tour was so that she could swim in the Dead Sea. The Dead Sea has such a high salt and mineral concentration that it is impossible to sink. Josephus reported that in his day (about the time of Jesus' ministry) this sea was called the Asphaltic Sea because of the thick oil pools on the water. He also noted that Romans would play tricks on prisoners by tying their arms and legs and throwing them from cliffs into the water.

It seems that as a girl Mrs. Duckworth never learned to swim. She tried and tried and would always sink like a rock. She joined the YWCA, but neither the swimming instructors or any of her fellow members could teach her to swim. There was a young man in town whose last name was Duckworth. She reasoned that if she got her name changed to Duckworth, perhaps this would help. So, she married young Mr. Duckworth, but it did not help. Her husband could not teach her to swim, and later, neither could her children. Finally, a grandson said to her, "Grandma, there is one place in the world that you can swim. It is the Dead Sea, because no one can sink there."

In late afternoon we checked in at a hotel on the shore of the Dead Sea. However, for those who do choose to swim (and many don't because it is almost like swimming in motor oil), I tell them that although they can't sink this does not necessarily mean that they can swim. I warn them to take it easy and slowly edge into the water, because all at once the feet will come off the bottom and the head might go under while the legs go straight up. This is dangerous because should water be swallowed, it is poisonous. Also, the eyes will feel like a cup of salt has been dashed into them. And, if someone gets too aggressive in attempting to swim, like a bottle with a cork thrown into the water, there is one chance in two that the wrong end will come up.

After getting the tour group checked in, I went down to the beach and reclined in a chair, waiting for those who opted to take a swim in the Dead Sea. Soon, about a dozen came down, and Mrs. Duckworth was leading the pack. As they went into the water, a tour member stopped to discuss something with me, which took my eyes off of Mrs. Duckworth for a couple of minutes. When I looked back, there about one hundred and fifty feet out in the water was Mrs. Duckworth with her head under the water and her feet and legs waving aimlessly like an egg beater. I yelled for a hotel employee to help me. We rushed out and pulled Mrs. Duckworth back to land. She had swallowed a lot of Dead Sea water, so we called for a doctor, who pumped her stomach out and gave her an antidote.

I did not go to bed until I was assured that Mrs. Duckworth would be all right. The next morning I went to her room, and although not feeling the best, she thought she could continue on the tour. In the lobby she confided in me that it was just not in the cards for her to swim, and that for some reason God had withheld this life's ambition from her. I assured her that God was saving her for the real thing—a beautiful lake in Heaven where she could swim for a thousand miles without ever getting tired. She smiled weakly, patted me on the shoulder, and got on the bus.

After leading the tours for fifteen or twenty years, they seem to run together, and only the members, individually or collectively, identify the more interesting or unusual tours. One such tour was again to Israel and the Middle East in 1986. This was the year there was considerable terrorist activity in that region. Airplanes were being seized, ships were being pirated, and passengers were even being killed in airports. The U.S. State Department issued a warning against U.S. citizens going to the Middle East. That year I had a rather large tour signed up, but the month before departure many became concerned and cancelled. I ended up with only thirty-three members, and twenty-seven of these were either Pentecostals, charismatics, or both. On tours, members are usually divided in doctrinal and church identifications, and I never allow doctrinal differences to disrupt the flow and purpose of the tour. I instruct members that we are there for one purpose—to see the biblical sites and study the relevance of what we see to biblical history and eschatology. On mission tours I keep the members intent directed to the dissemination of the Word of God. There are exceptions, and the 1986 tour was one of these exceptions.

When I heard that I had thirty-three remaining, in spite of the dangers, and twenty-seven were either Pentecostals or charismatics, I remarked: "Either the Pentecostals and charismatics have no sense, or they have an awful lot of faith." I later decided it was a little of both. On that tour we began in southern Israel at Eilat on the Gulf of Aqaba, an extension of the Red Sea. The very first night I got a call from the hotel manager. It seems that some members of my tour group were having a prayer meeting on the beach, and this was not just another prayer meeting. They were praying specifically that God open the Red Sea as He had done for Moses. The next day I attempted to teach a little hermeneutics by telling them that God instructed Noah to build an ark, but that does not mean that He wants Christians to build a literal ark; that God instructed Moses to go up on Mt. Sinai and receive the law, but that did not mean

He wanted us to go upon Mt. Sinai and receive the law; and that Moses led the children of Israel through the Red Sea, but that did not mean He wanted me to lead them through the Red Sea. I do not think my lesson was really understood or appreciated, because when we went to Jerusalem one of our first stops was at the Garden of Gethsemane. Half of the tour group got their packs and instead of going into the site, they took off in the opposite direction to the old city. I ran after them waving my arms and asked where in the world they were going. They responded that they were going to do what Jesus and the apostles did. When I asked what that was, they replied, "Go throughout Jerusalem and cast out demons!" I do not know how many demons they cast out that day, but they returned to the hotel that evening worn out from resisting Arab peddlers and pickpockets.

Throughout this tour in 1986 the Pentecostals and charismatics were complaining to the Israeli tour agent, Yehuda Levy, that they had come to Israel to get a spiritual experience and they simply were not getting it. I called them together and informed them that I had obtained the best lodgings, food, and guides possible; I had taken them to every biblical site I promised and had a historical teaching at every site, including any prophetic application. I told them further that if they wanted an experience, they could go into their closet at home and have one, and it would not cost them three thousand dollars.

On the last day of a tour to the Middle East we usually have a farewell dinner. As I remember, on this tour in 1986 the dinner was at the Hilton Hotel in Jerusalem. The spokesman for the Pentecostals and charismatics was a millionaire from New Jersey. As we were recounting events on the tour and having a few testimonials, this spokesman for most of the group stood and said that he and some of the brethren had been to Caesarea that day, and as they were praying, his left leg, which had always been shorter than his right leg, began to grow and ended up the same length as his right leg. He continued, "Brother Hutchings, will you now come and offer a prayer in thanks to God for this miracle."

I was in somewhat of a spot, because I had never noticed the man limping or having a built-up left shoe, and I certainly did not want to thank God for something that might not be true. So I came into the middle of the tables, bowed my head, and prayed: "Thank God for whatever He has done in this man's life this day." After I returned from leading this tour, someone sent me a copy of a New Jersey newspaper with a front-page story about this millionaire who had been on my tour having a calling to sell all his properties and establish a foundation for Christian missions. I prayed that the funds would be invested wisely in the Lord's work and not in building another ark or tabernacle in the wilderness.

Another unusual tour was in 1993. Kim and I had just finished a two-week Bible distribution tour in

Russia. We ended up at St. Petersburg, but that week there were forty thousand Jehovah's Witness missionaries in St. Petersburg. Each Jehovah's Witness had a copy of their bible, and it was their mission to individually convert a Russian to become a Jehovah's Witness that week and then give them a Jehovah's Witness bible. We had scheduled our airline tickets to get back home from this tour and in four days lead another tour to Israel and the Middle East. The problem was that the Jehovah's Witness people had tied up all the airlines in St. Petersburg. Our tickets were no good, and in Russia there is not a lot that can be done about such matters. We finally did catch an Al-Italia flight to Milan, and then from Milan we had to catch a flight to Kennedy Airport in New York. To make a long story even longer, we finally did get to New York, but time was running short. We actually tried to fly from St. Petersburg to Tel Aviv, and meet the tour group there, but the cost was something like twenty thousand dollars.

As we landed we were told we only had one hour to catch our rescheduled flight to Oklahoma City, and that included going through immigration and customs. We finally got to the TWA domestic terminal, and we were told our departure gate. But as we were running to the gate, I heard over the terminal intercom that the gate had been changed. Kim was extremely tired, sleepy, and desperate to get home. She did not hear the announcement, and just kept running. I was seventy years old at the time, and I put out every ounce of energy I had left to run and catch her, but she kept pulling away and pointing toward the gate. Finally, I had to throw her against the wall and shake her to get her attention. She was hurt, but there was nothing else I could do. I did get her to listen then, and we turned around and just barely made our flight. We landed in Oklahoma City thirty-six hours before we had to leave again for Israel. These are times when I thought seriously about a sanity check for scheduling two tours back-to-back.

It was Friday when we checked in at a hotel in New York in downtown Manhattan, as we were scheduled to depart the next morning. When in Manhattan I always try to eat dinner at Mama Lou's, as the Italian cuisine there is excellent.

Kim was carrying the money we would need for tour airport taxes, etc., as well as our passports. Kim did not trust me with valuables, as I have been known for losing a bowling ball while standing in my tracks. But somewhere between our hotel room, the restaurant, and the return to our room, a pickpocket picked her purse. When and where it happened we have no idea, as the purse was with her all the time. Missing from the purse was about half of the tour money and my passport, which was the most important item taken. Had they taken Kim's passport I could have sent her back home and taken the tour group on to Israel. But there was no way I could get on the airplane. Buddy Harvey from the office was on the tour to take pictures, so I put him in charge and told the tour members at the airport that our agent in Israel would take care of them, and our guide Gila Tribech knew what to do. With the assurance I would join them in a couple of days, Kim and I returned to the hotel.

It was July 4 weekend, which meant I could not see about getting a passport until Tuesday. On Tuesday morning Kim suggested we get to the passport office at seven a.m., but I thought that the office didn't open until nine a.m. and that eight a.m. would be soon enough to get there. Imagine my horror when we arrived at the immigration building and thousands of blacks and Latins were pouring out of the structure, lining the streets for blocks. It looked like another biblical plague of the locusts. In typical bureaucratic fashion, there were no separate lines for those who wanted passports, those who wanted visas, renewals, extensions, etc. Everyone went into the office through one door. When inside, we would then be asked what we wanted. We got through the first door at one p.m., then stood in line for two hours to get through the second door where we could apply for another passport. We had rescheduled our flight for five p.m., so it did not look like we would make it. Finally at three p.m. an announcement was made that all who needed passports to make evening overseas flights should move to another line. By four p.m. I finally had a new passport. We rushed outside and caught a cab to go back to the hotel to pick up our luggage. We had forty-five minutes to get to the airport. Everyone who has attempted to move in drive-time traffic in New York understands the problem. I gave the taxi driver forty dollars to get us to the airport on time. The poor man did everything he could—went through alleys, cut through lines of traffic, broke every known traffic law in the jurisprudence system of the Western world. He drove up to the Al-Italia check-in section at five p.m. I told Kim that we would make it because overseas flights are always at least thirty minutes to one hour late taking off. I rushed up to the counter, threw out our passports and tickets, but we were told the doors to the airplane had already closed and it was out on the runway waiting for takeoff. I looked at Kim and suggested that we go back home and sit this one out. But as we turned to leave the check-in counter, the employee at the airline looked at the screen and said that we were scheduled to leave at seven p.m. instead of five p.m. Someone had made a mistake. Our tickets said five; but the computer said seven. The agent said she had no way of knowing how this could have happened, but we made the later flight and landed in Israel twelve hours later. It was getting dark when we arrived at the airport near Tel Aviv, and we had to pay a cab one hundred and fifty dollars to take us to where the tour group was at a *kibbutz* near Kireyot Shimona, as far north in Israel as is possible to go, on the border with Lebanon. This is the town that Hizbullah terrorists shell from time to time.

It was eleven p.m. when we walked into the *kibbutz* to check in. A dear pastor from Hawaii who had been on my tour before, had taken up a collection from the tour members and presented me with a hat full of money, more than enough to replace what had been stolen. There also came up to the counter a very strange looking man in an old beat-up felt hat with chicken feathers in it. I prayed, "Oh Lord, tell me this person is not on my tour." When the Lord did not answer, I knew I had been had. His name was Kenny from Nebraska. He had brought no suitcase. What he had done was put on several shirts, several pairs of pants, and several pieces of underclothes. When one shirt or pants would get dirty, he would simply take them off and throw them away. Kenny roomed with Buddy Harvey, and I asked Buddy how he could stand the smell. Buddy replied, "Shucks, it's not so bad until he takes off his shoes." This was one of those tours that included Egypt, and while we isolated Kenny as much as possible, and encouraged him to go on his own, he must have found something of interest in Egypt. He returned a year later and married an Egyptian woman.

It is possible to continue for years and books about unusual people and situations that occurred on tours I have led to different parts of the world, but before being forced to terminate this section I must mention irrepressible Debra Devito. On a tour to Turkey in 1997 while in the royal museum in Istanbul, we were viewing displays containing a piece of Mohammed's hair, and bones of various saints and historical characters, I casually remarked that if all the bones of Peter were put in one place it would take a freight train to carry them. Debra in innocent surprise responded, "Why, I didn't know Peter was such a big man."

Oops!

There have been times when local city or national agencies have used their own imaginations and initiatives in arranging the tour schedule. I remember leading one large tour where the local Cairo agent arranged for our group to eat lunch at the Mena House Hotel in Giza, where the diners have a clear and close view of the pyramids. Only millionaires, and preferably billionaires, can afford a night at the Mena House, so I was delighted, of course, that my tour would be so privileged.

The Mena House presents entertainment for diners, and for us was arranged a very long table adjacent to the stage. As the tour leader, my chair was placed actually touching the stage. After our beverage and salad had arrived, out came the entertainment in the form of a bevy of belly dancers. I have seen belly dancers, or what I thought were belly dancers, shown on television or in movies, but I had never witnessed anything like this. At times there may have been one girl performing, then two, three, six, or even a dozen. They wiggled and bumped continuously so near me that I did not need a fan. All at once every eye of every tour member was fastened on me. They all wanted to see my reaction, and they were waiting for a sign from me if it would be proper for them to look, or would I just get up and leave.

In foreign countries we have to be careful not to offend our host. Also, on this occasion we had no other place to eat, and the tour members had already paid for lunch in their tour cost. So I just waved a hand to the group, signalling they should go ahead and eat, and turned and watched the performance. Then the tour members became more at ease, enjoyed their lunch, and no one mentioned the incident after we left.

Once while leading a tour to the Far East, one of our stops was in Tokyo. The local agent had included in the schedule dinner at a cabaret. I really had no idea what a Japanese cabaret was, and after all, in England tour groups have lunch at pubs. When our group arrived at the cabaret we were taken and seated on the balcony where dinner would be served. In looking down on the floor, a few couples began to dance, which was not in itself offensive. However, as our meal was being brought in, two bird cages appeared on either side of the balcony. And sure enough, there were birds in the cages—or on second look, it was Japanese lovelies made to imitate birds. I knew they were supposed to represent birds because they had wings. Then, on a third look, I perceived that that was all they had on—just wings.

I sat frozen as the two cages were lowered down

the sides of the walls, and then turned and crossed right in front of my group as they traveled along the banister. One tour member made a shrill, indignant squeak, grabbed the arm of her husband, and headed down the stairs toward the doors. Then, a dozen or more ladies, leading their husbands, followed. The remainder of the tour group refused to budge, contending that they had paid for this and they were going to stay. Our bus was to pick us up in an hour, so I had to stay at the cabaret. And we were scheduled to go to a geisha show next, about which I developed extreme trepidations. If this was a Japanese cabaret, what would a geisha show be like? As it turned out, the geisha show was extremely boring. The actors were men dressed in heavy padded clothing and made to look like girls. I was relieved when the show ended and we could finally leave.

The next day I had a most difficult time in professing my innocence in the whole affair at the cabaret and mending the offended feelings of the wives.

The Lord has blessed me more than I can possibly put into words by allowing me to go see the pyramids and either the remains or sites of the other six ancient wonders of the world, and Petra, Karnack, Luxor, the Valley of the Kings, Guilin, the Volga River, London, Paris, Thailand, Singapore, and thousands of other marvelous places I could mention. But the people on my tours have been far more interesting and wonderful than the most exciting places in the world.

Jesus referred to those who have eyes to see but do not see, and ears to hear but do not hear. The ability to find beauty in the ugliest of places, the discernment to find humor within the scope of people agonizing in serious circumstances and laugh about it later, or marvel at the gift of sight, feeling, sound, taste, and above all to love, is indeed having eyes and seeing, having ears and hearing. While the Great Wall of China was erected before the time of Christ and is a marvelous work of construction and engineering by an ancient people, it is as nothing to the miracle that occurs at the conception of a new soul as three billion genes unite to preprogram a human being and even number the hairs on their head. I feel sorry for those who are unable to stand in awe of God's marvelous creation, or shed a tear as even a sparrow falls to the ground.

To Russia with God's Love

Russian women on a park bench in Moscow

In 1988 and 1989 it seemed almost beyond reason that after forty-five years of the Cold War with Russia, never knowing from one day to the next whether a global nuclear war would erupt or not, suddenly the Soviet Union seemed to be disintegrating from within. Communism from a humanistic viewpoint is a good idea; the only problem is that it neglects to accept the self aggrandizement of human nature and the call of liberty by the human spirit. When I visited Russia in 1991 there was no evidence that there had been any new construction, except on a limited basis, since 1917. Waterways had been improved and the military establishment maintained, but the infrastructure of cities and communes was rotting away. The same was true in China until Western capitalism rescued that nation in 1980.

In 1990 Sergei Nikolov, director of the Baptist Churches of northwest Russia, came to Oklahoma City. He presented two programs over Southwest Radio Church and then preached on Sunday at the First Baptist Church. Rev. Nikolov was pleading for funds to build evangelical churches and for fundamental evangelists to come to Russia and help in the revival of Christianity in this atheistic land. I got Dr. Robert Lindsted of Wichita, Kansas, interested in joining with me in planning a crusade to Russia. Although at first we were tentative, not knowing what to expect, we raised funds for Bibles and Christian literature. A few others, some of which were experienced missionaries, joined us. The following is an account of my first missionary effort in Russia, written in August 1991.

On June 19, 1991, Dr. Robert Lindsted and I led a tour of thirty-eight on a Bible distribution mission to Russia. Our objective was: (1) appraise the degree of religious liberty under *glasnost*; (2) determine the church situation in Russia; (3) witness and distribute Bibles, salvation booklets, and tracts; (4) gain insight into the predictable political course of a nation whose leaders had set themselves against God.

Neither Dr. Lindsted nor I had been to Russia, so we went with no preconceptions except media coverage and reports by other Christians who had gone before us. We discovered to our amazement that what we experienced firsthand was almost beyond belief.

Meeting in Moscow

Constituents of Southwest Radio Church had contributed funds to purchase twenty-five thousand New Testaments; Dr. Lindsted and Bible Truth of Wichita, Kansas, provided five thousand entire Bibles, and in addition, approximately seventy-five thousand salvation tracts and booklets were included. The total weight of Bibles, New Testaments, and tracts was almost twenty tons; eighteen hundred cartons and boxes. It was an impossibility to just load all of this material on a bus and take off across Russia. Therefore, we had booked passage on a vacation passenger ship with intentions of visiting as many cities as possible along the Volga waterway.

I led the first contingent of six members. We left via Finnish Airlines in a DC-10 from Kennedy Airport, flying over Greenland and skirting the Arctic Circle. The seven-hour flight was uneventful, but we missed our connecting flight in Helsinki by thirty minutes. Not wanting to wait another seven hours for the next Finnish Air flight to Moscow, we caught a small Russian Aeroflot plane. Seated around me on the flight were six Russian males, probably business men or bureaucrats. In spite of "no smoking" signs, all six puffed incessantly on cigarettes. The most popular brands in Russia are Camel and Winston. However, on the small plane, Winstons certainly did not "taste good," and if possible I would have "walked a mile" to get away from the Camel stench. Also, as we found to be typical, the Russians consumed one alcoholic drink after another on the ninety-minute flight. I noticed they were spending dollars instead of rubles. Russians today prefer dollars because inflation is so bad that a ruble is worth only about three-and-a-half cents officially or two-and-a-half cents on the black market.

My relief upon approaching Moscow to get away from the boozers and nicotine smog was short-lived because a thunderstorm was in progress over the city. Plunging through thirty thousand feet of turbulence in a small plane was unsettling; however, I found some comfort in the assurance that surely God had not brought us almost halfway around the world to smash us to bits at the steps to the center of atheistic communism.

After landing we muddled our way through customs, but found no one to meet us. We were able to locate a tourist aid booth and obtained the use of a van and driver to escort us about twenty miles to our ship for a modest fee of twenty dollars. I was shown my quarters by a guide who was a student at Moscow University, of Chinese racial characteristics. Her father and mother were nuclear physicists, and she offered that her family had voted for Yeltsen in the recent elections. My cabin mate was Rev. Ray Edwards, a Presbyterian minister from the Birmingham, Alabama, area. Four hours later the other thirty-two members of the tour arrived.

(I was supposed to have bunked with Dr. Lindsted in a stateroom, but Gale Baxter [not Louis Baxter], who was in charge of logistics and a member of Dr. Lindsted's church, had reassigned me to room with Rev. Edwards on the pretext that he needed to be in a larger area to do his job. Five minutes after I turned the cabin lights out I understood why "Brother" Baxter needed more room. The Reverend snored like five 747s taking off at Kennedy Airport. I thought then that I was going to have to watch "Brother" Baxter. In any event, I did not get any sleep at night and I was exhausted the entire tour.)

The Power of Prayer

Our first dinner aboard ship was a foretaste of the food we were to expect for the entire tour—quite adequate, but nothing to write home about. Most of the packaged food came from France, with breads and meats from local Russian supply. Vegetables were limited to potatoes and carrots; chicken was limited to one meal; practically no pork; beef, though obviously not grain-fed, was provided in some form at almost every meal.

Coffee, tea, or milk, if not served at the meal, were available upon request.

Our Bibles and New Testaments were to arrive at the ship sometime during the first day before we sailed at six p.m. Moscow time. Dr. Lindsted had brought along with his group several Russian New Testaments, and we had the tracts. So the first day we traveled by bus through Moscow to Red Square, and we established our freedom to distribute God's Word in Russia and bear witness of Jesus Christ by passing out the New Testaments and tracts before the walls of the Kremlin. The Russians were friendly, happy to see us, and above all, pleased to receive the New Testaments and tracts.

In our group were pastors, seasoned missionaries, and Christians on fire for the Lord who would not be intimidated. We not only passed out New Testaments and tracts to the Russian workers, but also to the police, the guards, and communist officials. Most took New Testaments with a smile, but some guards did cautiously hold them behind their backs until they could slip them into their pockets. While passing out Bibles in front of a government building, two high government officials stopped to visit and inquire about what I was doing. They both spoke good English and remarked they were glad to see me. I gave them a tract and a Bible. They gave me their cards and offered that if we had trouble in

Russia to just call them and they would take care of it. Fortunately, we experienced little difficulty in carrying out our mission. But what a thrill it was to stand in front of the gates to the Kremlin, where leaders and conspirators of world communism have plotted to take over the world and erase the name of God, and freely pass out Bibles and bear witness that Jesus Christ came to save all, including Russians, who would believe on Him as Lord and Savior.

Upon returning to the ship we discovered that our Bibles and tracts had not arrived. To sail without them would be a disaster. Dr. Lindsted obtained a promise from the ship's captain to delay departure for another hour, until seven p.m., then he led a prayer meeting. Ten minutes before departure the first truck arrived, and by the time it was unloaded, the second truck came. The crew, members of the tour, and even Russian passengers, joined in to get the Bibles on deck. The power of prayer had prevailed, and we were now prepared for the most exciting and blessed adventure that any Christian could ever hope for in a lifetime.

Our First Stop

All night we traveled through a canal, wide enough for two ships to pass. This canal was built in the early thirties, as we were informed by our guides, by political and religious prisoners. It was eighty miles long with eleven locks, and again according to our guides, half a million laborers died during its construction and were buried along its banks.

During June in the Moscow region, night is only about four hours long, so we were able to see much of the countryside. Few houses or people were in evidence, practically no land was in cultivation, the area was flat and covered with forests of small pine, spruce, aspen, and maple. Early morning the ship passed from the canal into the Volga waterway, an extensive navigational system composed of a series of reservoirs connected by locks. Freighters and tankers from all over the world enter the waterway through the Don River, which leads into the Black Sea, or the Volga River, which empties into the Caspian Sea.

Our first stop, reached by early afternoon, was Kalinin, a city of 360,000 population. *We were informed by the Russian Bible Society, our guides, and everyone we talked with that the Southwest Radio Church/Bible Truth group were the first Christians who had gone into Russia personally giving out Bibles and witnessing.* We were not under the official sanction of the government; neither did we have association with any church or organization in Russia. We were on our own, and we were the first Christians as a group to enter Kalinin. How would we be received? Inasmuch as Russia and the United States had been Cold War enemies, what would be the attitude of the people? Would the inhabitants of Kalinin even take our Bibles?

We loaded approximately five thousand New Testaments and Bibles, along with thousands of tracts and booklets, on the bus and stopped at a park in downtown Kalinin. When the people found out who we were and what our mission was, they welcomed us with open arms. As far as we could determine, there was no church of any kind in Kalinin, yet the people by the hundreds came by to hug and kiss Christians from America and rejoice as they eagerly clasped Bibles to their breasts. We had to leave Kalinin with many still wanting Bibles; some cried when they were told we had no more Bibles on the bus.

A Thirst in the Land

"Behold, the days come, saith the Lord GOD, that I will send a famine in the land, not a famine of bread, nor a thirst for water, but of hearing the words of the LORD" (Amos 8:11).

Our next stop was Kostrama, a city of 450,000, and our reception here was even greater than at Kalinin. At times we had to seek refuge on the bus to keep from being smothered by the crowd. From Kostrama we traveled to Uglich, a historic Russian city where Demetri, the epileptic son of Ivan the Terrible, was killed or died under mysterious circumstances.

At Uglich there was no bus available to us, so

we had runners bringing Bibles into the town. The army felt sorry for us and loaned us a jeep. Everywhere we went our guides were the first off the bus to begin handing out Bibles; Russian passengers on the ship at times helped, as well as the police in the cities we visited. Some of the tour ladies started a Bible class for Russian children on the ship, and then the children would work to help get the Bibles ready for dissemination at the next town. At times some of the Bible lessons to the children would take an unexpected turn in translating into Russian. For example, the children would ask their parents: "Where will you go after you go to the morgue?"

The largest city we entered was Gorky, with a population of one and a half million. It was here that we experienced our only problem. The crowds simply got too large, almost rioted, and tied up traffic. The city marshal was unhappy with us, charging that we had turned his city upside-down. Dr. Lindsted calmed his anger by giving him a Bible, which he was pleased to get. When he suggested we give the Bibles to local representatives to distribute, the people, all with one voice, shouted "Nyet!" The people knew that if the Bibles were given to local representatives, they would never get them. However, lines were established for Bible distribution so order could be restored.

At Gorky we understood there were two

churches, a Russian Orthodox church and a Protestant church. The priest at the Russian Orthodox church wanted us to come to his church and hold a service, probably hoping that we would leave him some Bibles, but we did not have the time. Nuns at a local monastery had heard we were coming and cooked dinner for us, but we did not have time to accept their hospitality.

Where Do the Bibles Go?

The only real opposition we encountered was from our own countrymen. The passenger list on our ship included thirty-eight from our tour, approximately twenty other Americans from Ohio, and we would estimate one hundred vacationing Russians. We understood that the Bibles in the passageways were a problem, and that our taking the theater for devotions and meetings might hinder other activities. But the Russians were delighted with us; however, the Americans who were not part of our group were sullen and hostile. They attempted to get the captain to stop our mission activities, and at Gorky they even tried to charter a flight back to Moscow to get away from their embarrassing, Bible-thumping fellow Americans. But we prayed that even they would be convicted by their conscience and the witness concerning Jesus the Christ that they heard.

Rural Russian church

Where Are the Churches in Russia?

In Moscow and along the route we traveled in Russia, we saw hundreds, if not thousands, of beautiful church buildings. Most of these pre-1918 Russian Orthodox churches have been restored, but they are totally empty except for icons, a few hanging bells, and ornaments. The vast majority of Russians relate to these church buildings only as museums of a past socio-religious state order that has passed with time. Today, there is a burning, unquenchable spiritual thirst in Russia, but not on a church basis.

Granted, there are a few churches open in Moscow, including the Baptist Church, but in a city of almost ten million, these are mostly symbolic rather than functional. Evangelical churches in Leningrad do offer hope for the future, but even here, Sergei Nikolov, director of the Baptist churches of northwest Russia, needs funds to establish seminaries and Bible schools to train pastors, evangelists, and church workers.

The Grand Experiment

Communism as exercised in Russia since 1918 began with Karl Heinrich Marx, born in 1818 to Jewish but Christian parents. Karl Marx attended law school at Bonn University. He was baptized in the Orthodox Church and became a faithful attending member. His first literary effort was titled "The Union of the Faithful with Christ." However, young Marx became disillusioned with the church and involved himself with social revolutionaries in an attempt to overthrow the German government. The revolution failed and Karl Marx fled to England where he and a close friend, Friedrich Engels, composed the *Communist Manifesto.*

Having become a total apostate, Marx wrote a pseudo-religious essay entitled *Oulanem,* which in German is an anagram of "Emmanuel." Emmanuel means "God with us"; *oulanem* means, "us without God." In this essay, Marx wrote that he had a new sword given to him by the "prince of darkness" and he would bring civilization to ruin, fling his glove in the face of God, and stride through earth a creator.

Russia is an example of seventy years of "us without God." Communism has robbed the people of Russia, leaving them destitute materially and spiritually. Russia is indeed in ruin, but where is the creator Karl Marx promised? Karl Marx is dead, but God is still alive. Only the statues of Lenin remain in evidence, and according to the June 30, 1991, edition of *Moscow News,* the people are trying to remove them, thus putting to rest all the gods of communism. We heard the phrase, "Death to the Grand Experiment," over and over from Russians we spoke with. They speak of another revolution, but hope change to a new political and economic system can be accomplished without it.

To pronounce the death of communism, however, is premature. According to an article on page two of the June 28, 1991, edition of *European News* (which I picked up at the Helsinki airport), Vladimir Krychov, KGB chairman, is attracting new attention and adherents by claiming CIA agents in Russia are masterminding the movement toward democracy and free enterprise. In an interview carried in the June 28, 1991, edition of *Moscow News*, Eduard Shevardnadze is quoted as saying of the hardline communist bureaucracy that they "plan to make war again . . . to shed blood. . . . These are terrible people . . . who don't wish to understand the terrible consequences." The military is still in command of weapons capable of destroying the world.

The communist bureaucracy still controls communications, transportation, and to a large degree, production. It takes two days to get a telephone call out of Russia, and two hours just to buy a postage stamp. It is in the bureaucracy's interest to see the current freedom movement in Russia fail.

Another Field, Another Harvest

When Jesus was preaching in Israel and the multitudes were interested in the Gospel of the Kingdom, He remarked that the "harvest truly is plenteous, but the laborers are few" (Matt. 9:37). That harvest was lost, Israel was not saved. After World War II, General Douglas MacArthur declared the harvest of souls in Japan was ready to be reaped, but the churches did not respond to the call. Since 1945, tens of millions of Japanese have died and gone to hell.

In 1985, after my second visit to China, I wrote a *Gospel Truth* article on the field in China that was ready for harvest. In 1987 when I returned, the harvest was already wasting in the field. When the harvest of wheat in Oklahoma is ready, it must be gathered quickly. The harvest of souls in Russia is ready to be garnered—now!

Christians in America worry about which of a dozen Bible translations is the best, when in Russia there are no Bibles. We worry about long sermons, air conditioning, or music programs, when in Russia there are neither churches or sermons. We read the words of Jesus, "Go, ye, into all the world and preach the gospel," but what is our world? Our church pew? Our living room?

The Future?

That Russia is the nation of Gog is clearly documented in the *Columbia Encyclopedia* and other books and publications. We read that before Russia comes down against Israel, that God will first turn them back. It could be that Russia is now in this "turning back period," because the Gospel has been withheld for seventy years, and God has never brought judgment without first giving the unsaved an opportunity to repent and come to the knowledge of the truth (2 Pet. 3:9–10).

Without doubt, Russia is at the crossroads today, wanting to turn back from anti-God communism, but strong internal forces are urging the people to remain firm in the promises of a socialistic paradise on earth. Ezekiel 38:4 states that "I will turn thee back, and put hooks into thy jaws, and I will bring thee forth." In spite of wanting to turn back, God will turn Russia around again to come down against Israel with a great army. We have always expressed our view that this will be the first war of the Tribulation immediately after the Antichrist signs a peace agreement with Israel. If our understanding is correct, then Christians should redouble efforts to take God's Word to Russia while there is yet time.

Next Year in Moscow?

As far as I know, none of our tour members received a hostile or unkind remark from any Russian. We did not think of them as enemies or communists. Most appeared to be kindly folks, glad to see Americans, and above all, looking for a light to escape the darkness. When the people received New Testaments or Bibles, they would usually sit down on the curb or stand against buildings and immediately begin reading. If we attempted to guide them to salvation scriptures, they would hold their Bibles tightly, afraid we were going to take them away. The tour itself was highly emotional, with members often returning to the ship with tears in their eyes. Seasoned missionaries and pastors who accompanied us said they had never seen or experienced anything like it.

Should God keep the door open and provide the way, we hope to get back to Russia again next year, charter the entire ship, and take many more Bibles and educational materials. If Christianity is to make a comeback in Russia, evangelical and fundamental churches must be established. Each and every member of our tour said they wanted to return. This year we sowed some seeds; let us now pray for a harvest.

Kremlin, Red Square

I participated in five mission tours to Russia, and all were on the same order, but with some variations. A 1992 Russian tour organized by Dr. Lindsted was the largest. An entire ship was chartered and there were 319 members. I had been so busy in other phases of the ministry that although I had helped finance and organize this tour to Russia, I was too tired to go. However, Dr. Lindsted encouraged me to go and bring Kim, which I did.

From a mission standpoint, the tour was a great success. The tour was well organized, and the ship departed out of the regular Volga waterway into lakes that were inside the Arctic Circle. Bibles were distributed in villages and on islands that probably had not been visited before. On this tour, over three million Scriptures were distributed one-on-one to the Russian people. I brought the early morning devotions and Scripture lessons for the day, and Kim was the most avid Bible distributor and witness on the tour. At times we would literally have to drag her back on the ship. She always wanted to give out that last Bible. With Kim with me I was not bothered by a snoring roommate, so I was able to get some rest. As I remember, it was on this tour that I brought a message to an audience of Russians in a theatre at Yuroslav. At the conclusion of the service a Russian soldier who had fought in Afghanistan came forward seeking forgiveness from God for the people he had killed in that country.

On the 1992 Russian mission, I made two valuable new friends, Kenneth Hill and Robin Horner from the Tri-City area in Tennessee. Robin is a tremendous mission worker and Kenneth is the general manager of a Christian radio station. Kenneth later became vice-president of Southwest Radio Church. In Bible distribution, the tour group was divided into eight sections. Each section was in a separate location because the crowds were so large that until it had been diverted to eight locations, we would have all been overrun and possibly injured in a stampede.

It was evident that the economy in Russia was not getting better, but was going from bad to worse. While there were attempts in some areas to go to a free market, the entire country was being strangled and taken over by the Russian Mafia. While the Communist Party had been outlawed, the leadership remained in the Duma under a different name. The communes were not broken up into private properties. The commune workers had simply gone into their houses and planted gardens in the backyard. As a whole, the land was idle from Moscow to St. Petersburg. What I had predicted was coming to pass.

Along the Volga River there were thousands of cranes puncturing the skylines without moving. I thought about writing a book and calling it *The Land of the Silent Cranes*. While there were certain attempts from neo-evangelical churches and organizations in the United States to bring revival to Russia, these efforts were more of a scatter-gun method that produced no real and lasting results. In the meantime, thousands of missionaries from cults like the Jehovah's Witnesses and the Mormons were crawling over the land like ants. While I was thankful for what we all did on the 1992 mission tour, I returned home with serious reservations and forebodings about evangelical missions and the future of Russia as a whole. Millions of Russians were receiving Bibles, but for too many this was simply a matter of wanting to read something that had been forbidden to them for seventy years, and without a local church where they could attend and grow in the faith of Jesus Christ much of the mission effort was wasted. But as Jesus said, some believed and were saved, for which we thank God.

I believe it was on this tour that Kim and I had a stopover in Helsinki for three days because of airplane scheduling. Helsinki is a beautiful, enchanting city. The tall pine trees seem to reach to the sky, and there was a nice park and lake near the hotel. One of the surprises about Helsinki was that a plant we call poke-salad in Oklahoma grew everywhere. It is a delicious green vegetable if prepared correctly, but I believe the Finns considered it nothing more than a nuisance weed. Another surprise was that the Finns were not very sociable people. In walking through the park, they would look straight ahead or at the ground and pass without speaking. So I would get in their way and force them to look at me, then I would say something like—"Have a nice day, God loves you." Startled, they would murmur something and then pass on by.

At the time of the year we were there, there was only two hours of darkness, so one night we walked to the middle of Helsinki at midnight and stopped at a McDonalds. The fare was the same, but it was four times as high as in the States. I do not know how the company maintains such strict control over franchises all over the world, but I have eaten at McDonalds from Moscow, to Jerusalem, to Beijing, to Bangkok, and Big Macs are all the same. While the food at McDonalds is plain and simple, and high in cholesterol, I have never gotten sick from eating at one of their restaurants. After we had returned to the hotel, Kim asked me a Bible question. My Bible was in my suitcase at the airport, so I opened the drawer of the lamp stand near the bed. Inside, of course, was a Gideon Bible in English. I have been a member of the Gideons for years and thank God for their continuing service for the Lord. Since Russia opened to the Gospel, the Gideons have been sending four hundred thousand Scriptures into the country each month; although with new restrictions, this may have diminished or ceased.

My last trip to Russia was in 1993. This was one of those years when I was running around the world and writing several books. Pastor Mark Hitchcock was president of the board of trustees at that time; Don Glover was acting CEO; and David Ingraham was in charge of programming. I really felt I had no calling from the Lord to go on another mission to Russia, but Dr. Lindsted was busy in other parts of his ministry and thought that I should go. Don Glover and his wife Jane led part of the tour group from Kennedy Airport. Kim and I joined the others leaving from Chicago. My group went by Aeroflot, the Russian airline that was increasingly gaining a poor safety record. The plane we took was an older Russian model with four engines in the tail. Gale Baxter, who was once more taking care of scheduling and logistics, had forwarded suitcases full of tracts and booklets in the Russian language for each member of my group to take on. Some of these cases weighed almost one hundred pounds and I protested because the Moscow airport is a nightmare, and some of the tour members going with me were elderly and could not be responsible for carrying these heavy cases through a crowded, congested immigration checkpoint. However, Mr. Baxter assured me that I had nothing to worry about, that he would personally be waiting at the baggage carousel with porters to take care of the luggage.

Our flight to Moscow was much better than I had anticipated. We made one stop at Shannon, Ireland, for refueling. We arrived at Moscow airport in the middle of the afternoon, the hottest part of the day. It was horribly congested, and I finally got our group through immigration and baggage check, but no Mr. Baxter. There was no way the elderly members of the tour under my responsibility could carry the heavy suitcases with tracts and Scriptures. I had all I could handle just to get them through customs and to the exit, but there were the other suitcases with the printed materials going around and around the carousel.

Some of the people on tour began to cry, wail,

and point to the suitcases, moaning that we couldn't leave them in the airport. I pointed to some of the young bucks on the tour and instructed them that if they wanted the suitcases, then go back in and retrieve them. They protested that this was not their job, and in any event they had already exited customs and could not get back into the area. I was angry, frustrated, and exhausted. I yelled at them to get out of my way, and probably added a few more phrases that would be better left out of print. I grabbed a manifest and worked my way through the crowd to the entrance. I was stopped by a guard, but I pointed to the paper and yelled something in pig-Latin. To my surprise, the guard let me through. I grabbed a four-wheel dolly and began to throw one-hundred pound suitcases on it until it was full to the top. Then I exited and pushed my way through the throng until I again reached the outside exit where the group was waiting.

I was able to obtain a bus to take us to the ship, but there was a protest again that this was a Mafia vehicle and we should not take it. I remarked that I did not care if the Devil was driving the bus, I was going to the ship and all who wanted to go with me should board. When we arrived at the ship there was Mr. Baxter sitting at the bow under an umbrella, sipping on what I trust was a glass of tea. From this point, this particular tour went downhill.

I had assumed that Don Glover and Mr. Baxter were in charge of scheduling and logistics. However, there was no coordination or leadership. We were supposed to have an additional sixty thousand Bibles to distribute, but they never showed up. When Mr. Baxter was asked about where they were, he said: "I don't know where they are, but God knows." I am sure that God knows where every snowflake is in a blizzard, but that does not help a person freezing to death very much.

Many of the problems that plagued this last tour I made to Russia could not be helped. Conditions had continued to deteriorate in Russia, and the Mafia was becoming more involved in the black market. We had contracted for so many buses at each port, but often only one or two would show up, and then would not move unless we paid additional monies. Half of the passengers on the ship we were on were Mormons, and the person who was in charge of ship-to-shore logistics was a Mormon, so the Mormons got first choice on the buses, and we usually ended up having to carry Bibles and tracts on our backs, or in whatever means of transportation we could find.

Don and Jane were sleeping in until mid-morning, and then after lunch might run out on the dock, pass out a few Bibles to Russians, and then run back in and say, "Boy, this is really where it is at." Whatever they meant, I never found out. About halfway through the tour some of the men from Tennessee with whom I had gone on tour before came to me and wanted to know who was really in charge of this tour. I had assumed that Don Glover and Gale Baxter were in charge. So we got them together and demanded to know who was in charge. They both looked at me and said, "Noah Hutchings is in charge of this tour." To say that I was flabbergasted would be an understatement. I think the tour had gone so sour that no one wanted to admit responsibility. At least we did get some order within the tour, and we did the best we could in a bad situation.

After breakfast on the last day of this, my last mission to Russia, it was raining heavily. Ten buses drove up to the ship. At least we finally had all the buses we had contracted for in the arrangements. The ones going back to the States had to get on three buses, the Mormons had to get on three buses, and those staying in St. Petersburg had to get on the remaining four buses. Nowhere was Baxter or Glover to help direct traffic in the rain to see the right ones got on the right buses. Everyone was simply running out in the rain as fast as they could and they just picked a bus. I had to personally get out in the downpour, kick everyone off the buses, and then one-by-one fill the buses with those going to the proper places. After I had finished, soaking wet, I went back into the ship to get Kim when I heard Mr. Baxter on his cellular phone calling someone, I think possibly Dr. Lindsted, and reporting that "*we*" had gotten everyone on the right bus. He will never know how close he came to remaining in Russia permanently.

Nevertheless, I thank God for the opportunity

for this one last chance to somehow reach those who may not have otherwise been reached with the Gospel. Today, Christian mission tours to Russia like we conducted are difficult if not impossible. The Russian Orthodox church has once again assumed ecclesiastical authority. However, God is not willing that any should perish, but that all come to repentance and be saved. The Gospel window in Russia was opened for approximately five years, and we pray the seed we planted will continue to bear fruit.

Faraway Places
with Strange Sounding Names

In this chapter I hope to mention a few of the many places that I have been privileged to see and visit which will be of as much interest to the reader as they were to me.

Singapore

Singapore is a small island at the southern tip of the Malaysian peninsula, approximately fifteen miles long and five miles wide. The city of Singapore covers most of the island. Due to being an English colony before World War II, there is a strong Christian population among its three and a half million people. The racial composition is about eighty-five percent Chinese and the balance is divided among Indians, English, and other Asian races.

The Japanese easily conquered Singapore in World War II because the guns defending the city were pointing seaward, and the Japanese army came from the north down the peninsula. In visiting Singapore the tourist is awed by its beauty and clean-ness. The flowers, shrubs, trees, and grass all appear manicured. The streets are as clean as a dinner plate, and every building is freshly painted. Chewing gum is even against the law, and any found in luggage at customs will be confiscated. There is no jay-walking because a heavy fine can be charged, and one ounce of drugs can get the possessor the death penalty. By law everyone must have a job; by law everyone must own a house or a condominium. From the workers' wages is withheld twenty-five percent, with the employer contributing another ten percent as a pension fund. Fifty-five is the legal age of retirement, and the retiree is then given his investment proceeds, which should sustain him for life if he chooses to retire. There is also zero immigration because no foreigner, even a king or billionaire, can become a citizen. I remember attending a church one evening in Singapore and a member in her advanced years recognized my voice from hearing a ministry program on shortwave.

Thailand

Thailand is a country of mystical enchantment—a land of elephants, snakes, and Buddhist temples. One-third of Bangkok is temples. The gold-leaf plating on the temples is refurbished every fifty years. Christian evangelism in Thailand is very difficult, because Buddhism is the state religion, and if one is a good Thai, he or she is also a good Buddhist. Buddhism in Thailand is mixed with animism and pure demonism. Each Thai residence has a spirit house in front, and each morning a new offering of fruit, flowers, or dessert is placed in the spirit house so that the spirits will give the residents a good day.

There are temple dancers who put on shows for tourists, but these are not the real thing. I usually scout around until I find a temple where a Buddhist presentation is being performed. The dancers take the part of different demons: snake demons, monkey demons, elephant demons, etc. The movement of the dancers' bodies from the head, to the hands, to the legs and feet, is something to behold—absolutely fascinating. A girl with a soprano voice sings to the accompaniment of a stringed instrument. As the dance proceeds the dancers take on the personality of the demons, and the voice of the singer may change from a high soprano to a low guttural growl, and while still keeping in tune, the voice seems to descend into her stomach. In these presentations in Buddhist temples in Thailand is the only place I have witnessed real demon possession.

There is also an unusual tradition in Thailand. Out of the thousands of elephants born there, an occasional albino appears. This young white elephant must be presented to the king. The king calls a national holiday and presents the baby elephant to his biggest enemy or most hated relative. Why?

Because the elephant is to be worshipped, and the new owner must build it a temple. Because this is a Buddhist holy elephant, it cannot be worked. Elephants are expensive to feed and they live a very long time. So, who wants a white elephant? This is where the reference to a white elephant gift originated.

Prostitution in Bangkok is perhaps more flagrant than any other place in the world, with the possible exception of Cuba. I usually have tried to get a five-star hotel on the outskirts of Bangkok for the tour group, but on one tour we were sidetracked into a French hotel downtown. I warned the tour members several times what to expect, and I asked our guide to repeat the warning. The prostitutes in the hotels are very young and pretty. Fathers sell their young daughters into prostitution. In going to the bathroom, there were pictures of the young girls available in our hotel with their room numbers and telephone numbers.

After freshening up and changing clothes after the long plane ride, I went down to the lobby for dinner. There in the middle of the lobby was Mrs. Trayser from Columbus, Ohio, throwing what is commonly referred to as a lily-livered fit. Seeing me, she charged, waving her arms with sounds coming from her mouth that I had heard somewhere before, but had escaped my memory. Finally, as she got within a foot of my face, the sounds became words: "Why would you dare bring us to this Sodom and

Gomorrah?" she shouted. I calmly inquired as to the nature of her problem, and she responded: "My husband and I thought we would walk around the block, but before we got across the street he was propositioned four times, and with me holding on to his arm!" What could I say? I did mumble, "Mrs. Trayser, this is a way of life here, and I doubt if they will change just because a lady from Columbus, Ohio, came to town for the weekend."

South Korea

While traveling in the Far East, I have visited South Korea several times, and many of my books have been published in the Korean language. At times I received the royalty due me, and at others times I didn't. In a foreign country there is usually nothing the author can do if the publisher is dishonest.

I had promised one publisher, who was also the pastor of a large church in Seoul, that I would come to his church for a series of prophetic sermons. It was on Labor Day in 1992 that I took off for Seoul in a Northwest Airlines 747 from Seattle. Taxiing down the runway for takeoff, one of the engines blew, but the pilot stopped the plane in time and we returned to the terminal. Being Labor Day, there was no room at the hotels, so we sat up in the terminal all night, and the engine was not replaced until the next afternoon.

Finally I arrived in Seoul a day late, and the pastor and associate pastor were waiting for me at the airport. I was half dead and looking forward to hitting the hay as soon as I could get to the hotel. But the pastor said, "Thank God, you have arrived just in time to get a bath, change clothes, and get to the church for the afternoon service." I almost sobbed, "How long do you want me to speak." Korean churches have long services, and he replied, "Four hours." I choked and asked, "What about the evening service?" He repeated, "Four hours." After a week, my mouth was still moving, but no words would come out. I was glad that Kim was not with me on this particular mission because I could not have done any shopping with her or anything else, but to just plop down on the sofa and go to sleep.

Seoul is an unusual city in that it was completely rebuilt after the Korean War. There are cross streets, but the main traffic artery is an eight-lane loop. In 1955 this loop was sufficient, but as the population of Seoul grew from three million to thirteen million, the loop actually became a traffic hazard. It took two hours to get from my hotel on the loop to downtown. At two a.m. there is still not more than two inches between cars on all eight lanes, in a complete circle around Seoul.

Approximately forty percent of the population of South Korea belongs to one of the many churches. At the turn of the century, Presbyterians established schools, hospitals, and churches in Korea for a solid Christian foundation. While the Japanese did attempt to destroy Christian missions and churches in World War II, there was a revival after the Korean War in the fifties. The largest churches in the world are reported to be in Seoul, where it is claimed that five thousand have been baptized on one Sunday. I interviewed the pastor of that church in 1982 while visiting Seoul. The church has two main attractions for Koreans:

1. It has a Pentecostal-charismatic connection, which Koreans more easily identify with their Buddhist background.
2. It is on the edge of the largest apartment and condominium complex in the world. The church sends one couple into a high-rise apartment. This couple give parties and share their faith with other occupants, and then bring as many as will come to their church. This is called cell evangelism, and it works, at least in Seoul.

China
On my 1992 mission to South Korea, it was during one of those times when I had attempted to turn Southwest Radio Church over to someone else. I was doing what I really wanted to do, and what I felt the Lord wanted me to do at that stage in my life. I had been to Russia, the Middle East, on a series of meetings in

the United States, and I departed from Seoul to meet up with a tour group in Tokyo that I was to lead to China.

My first visit to China was in 1982, just after the bloody era of the Cultural Revolution had subsided. This was the period soon after the death of Mao and the trial of the Gang of Four. For those interested in a more detailed history of China, including what happened during the years 1949 to 1980, I suggest the book *Forewarnings* published by Harvest House and copyrighted 1998. I have a chapter in the book entitled "The Chinese Tycoon."

Of all the Asian countries and peoples I have visited, because of its history, art, and culture, China is my favorite. The Christian mission effort in China began in the early eighteenth century on the coattails of Western imperialism. As ocean traffic increased, many commercial voyages were made to bring tea, spices, jade, jewels, and silk from China to demanding markets in Europe and the United States. As is still the case today, there was a serious balance of payments problem because orientals, and especially Chinese, neither needed nor wanted Western products. However, Spain discovered there was something that could be sold to the Chinese—and that was opium. Other Western maritime nations followed Spain's example, including the United States. When the rulers of China could not get Western countries to halt the drug traffic, ships were raided, barrels of opium were thrown overboard, and Westerners were held as hostages. England, France, and the United States sent armies to China, burned the Summer Palace, and rescued their citizens. Out of this war, England got a hundred-year lease on Hong Kong, and other nations, mainly the three great powers, got concessions in Shanghai and other areas. In spite of being tainted with Western imperialism, mission efforts did bear fruit and churches were established.

When Mao Tse-tung installed a communist governmental system in 1949, he saw no need for the Church. However, a delegation of Chinese pastors agreed to place the churches under governmental authority. This was called the Three-Self Church Alliance. Even so, thousands and perhaps millions of Christians were killed and many churches closed.

Mao envisioned world conquest and ordered the Chinese women to have children. They did not need much encouragement, as Chinese families have always been large. In 1965 Mao discovered that he had half a billion kids to feed, house, and educate; his economic policies were failing, and he decided to resign. Party leaders convinced Mao that he had not failed; it was the capitalists, counterrevolutionaries, and religionists still in China that were causing the problems. For the next decade chaos and carnage reigned. The Red Guard, young armed hoodlums, pillaged the country killing millions and closing churches and schools. I have not talked with anyone in China who did not have a relative killed in the so-called Cultural Revolution.

In 1982 China was in a pitiful condition. A commune worker made fifteen dollars a month, but from this was taken money for utilities, food, and rent. No one ever got out of debt to the company store. No person could leave the commune to visit a relative without a pass. All the people—men, women, and children—wore drab Mao denims. There were no cars, no markets, and no freedoms. However, the first reversals of communist policies appeared in the churches. A limited number of Three-Self churches were allowed to reopen. I attended services in Christian Mens Church in Beijing and the Mo'en Church in Shanghai. Although in the Mo'en Church windows were still out and damage to the church had not been repaired, four services were held that Sunday just to accommodate the crowds.

However, when communists are left in power, atheistic control will gradually return when their purpose has been served. This happened in Russia, in China, and now probably in Cuba. Although communism in Russia has been outlawed, communists rule in the Duma under a different name.

In 1982 there were practically no hotels in China that met minimal Western standards; the food was absolutely horrible; and the people were afraid to talk with us. But we did find a number of brave souls who would receive the few Bibles and tracts we were able to take in our suitcases. Also in 1982, there was a departure occurring in traditional communist economic policies. Farmers could sell vegetables that were grown in ditches, or a few places that were not a part of the communal farm. The new political leader, Deng Xia-peng, was developing what he called Chinese socialism, which was nothing more than state capitalism, or perhaps economic fascism.

I returned to China in 1985. The change was dramatic. The children were wearing the brightest col-

ors possible. Most on the streets, in markets, or in churches, were quite friendly and talkative.

McDonalds in China

Chinese newspapers were openly advocating capitalism and free markets; and with some assurance of stability, world finance operators and institutions were building hotels, restaurants, and even factories—taking advantage of the cheap labor. However, the Chinese Civil Air Service was still flying old Russian planes, and one miraculously managed to stay in the air long enough to get my tour group to Chungking, not far from Tibet on the Yangtze River. This was the city where the U.S. Air Force volunteers flew P-36s to fight the Japanese. The old air strip was still visible the last time I was in Chungking.

At Chungking we took a river ship and headed north and east down the swift Yangtze, a muddy, raging river, the third largest in the world. The Yangtze River ships carry about two hundred passengers, and the scenery is beyond description. One of the first stops was Fung Du, where thousands met the ship and grabbed Bibles and tracts as long as they lasted. By 1985 there were actually few re-straints against witnessing

Hutchings and guides at Guilin. Leonard is on the right.

or Scripture distribution. The churches were open, and while there were government agents monitoring every service, most pastors seemed to have considerable freedom. There was some growing uneasiness, because church members had to sign their names to receive a Bible.

In the back country in places like Fung Du, we felt at complete liberty to witness and distribute Christian literature. At Fung Du there is also a Buddhist shrine on top of a high, cone-shaped mountain. This shrine is a Buddhist interpretation of hell, and it is called Eighteen Gates and 999 Steps to Hell. And, there may be a half-mile between each gate. Only thirteen of my tour members made it to the top. I held services on the ship every day and some among the passengers came to saving faith in Jesus Christ. I remember one Chinese girl named Rose who was marvelously saved.

At a town below Fung Du the ship docked for a day and we took river skiffs up the Doning River and had lunch in a mountain village. On one trip up the Doning I saw two boys fishing, and they had what I thought was a fifty-pound catfish tied out in our skiff guide to stop at the bank. I could not believe what I saw. It was a fifty-pound salamander, and some of the salamanders in the Yangtze and its tributaries go as high as one hundred pounds. While they are considered a delicacy in China, I had just as soon pass. If a three-ounce salamander in the United States can be a one hundred-pound salamander in China, then we should not wonder that lizards may have at one time been dinosaurs. While the Yangtze was dammed above Wuhan in 1960, another dam is being built further up the river. Much of this incomparable scenery will now be under water.

In 1985 we got off the ship at Wuhan for a couple of days, and I was privileged to visit Wuhan University and speak to the foreign language classes. The president of the university and I got along very well, and I even spoke to a government and politics class on why communists do not believe in God. Below is a copy of a letter I received from a lovely female student at Wuhan University after my return:

Mr. Noah:

I suppose you have been at home for a long time after your marvellous journey. Do you remember last time when we had a very nice talk? At first I was really a little afraid to talk to you because my English wasn't good enough to speak to an American. But gradually, I began to free myself from nervousness. Why? Because of you! It was you who made me happy and free. We talked about journey, sports, politics, and religion. Almost on every topics, you made a speech. I was surprised that you knew such a lot of things to everything, especially to China and her people. What pleased me is that you took no prejudice in your talk. You said that China had changed a great deal and China has a little capitalized factor in her reform. I had to admit, that's true. Perhaps most of our people haven't reached the level which socialism needs.

The Bible tells its disciples to love everyone, which leads you to be kind to everyone. I was very glad. I have the same opinion with you. So I'd like to make friends with you and your family.

Now, let me talk something about myself.

We began our summer vacation 5 July. The weather in Wuhan was very hot in summer. I don't know what is the weather in Oklahoma City like. Within my geography knowledge, I assume in Oklahoma it must be quite cool. Every day I stay at home to read books and listen to music, watch TV. On the national newsstands, I prefer watching American news to watching others. From TV I know that Mr. Reagan had lived in the Army hospital and received a little operation. According to the reports, Reagan had got a cancer. Fortunately he recovered in no time.

Chinese president Li Xian Nian and his First Lady went to America to have a visit. They received a warm welcome by American people and government. Li Xian Nian is the peaceful and friendly emissary. I hope that his successful visit will advance the friendship and cooperation between China and America.

I have read several articles about America. I studied the Political Parties in the United States. I see how do the two major parties—Democratic party and Republican party come from. And I also read the article written by Dr. Melvin Howards dealing with the American adolescent. They are active in the society and they play an important part in American society. So do we. Nevertheless, in spite of the difference of political systems, we have the same task that is to make our life better and to support the world peace.

What's your opinion?

American people and Chinese people want to know more about each other, just as what Reagan said in China. Let me copy down Mr. Reagan's address in Fordham University: "History is a river that makes us as it will. But we have the power to navigate, to choose direction, and make our passage together. The wind is up, the current is swift, opportunity for a long journey and fruitful journey awaits us. We have made our choice. Our new journey will continue. And may it always continue in peace and friendship."

Mr. Noah, I am a student in modern China. Almost every young persons in our country ad-mire modern America. So do I. I want to go abroad to America to study or to work. If I am lucky to have a chance to America, I will be very glad. Perhaps at that time I could go to your house and visit your family.

I wish that one day you can come to China again. Then you would be surprised to find China a very different country from its past.

I wish someday we shall meet again in either Wuhan or Oklahoma.

Hope you happy all the time and long live.

Sincerely,

Louise, Liao Thai Ying

Note: Last time you asked me what I need. Within your ability, you'd better send me one Jackson Michael's record tape and some pictures about your family.

Here I send some addresses of my home. When you write back to me, please put one piece of them on the envelope.

This letter typified the general attitude of Chinese university students in 1985, but when I returned in 1987 there had been a complete turnaround in the relationship between students and government on academic freedom. But in 1985 we were also allowed to visit intermediate schools and kindergartens. The teachers were quick to have the girls in lower grades perform for us and push the boys into the background to offset reports that because of the one-child-per-family law, girls were being killed or aborted in order for the couple to have another child that might be a boy. However, this is a terrible reality in China. Except in rare cases of racial minorities, or farmers and ranchers in remote areas where more than one child is a necessity, the law strictly forbids more than one child per family. If a couple has more than one child, then there are severe penalties which may include loss of jobs, loss of housing, reduction in pay, etc. Then, there may also be mandatory sterilization so that the couple will not have a third child. This dates back to the accelerated population growth that resulted from Mao Tse-tung's earlier policies. Because of this one-child policy, most hospitals now have units like in the United States that will reveal the sex of the unborn child, and abortions may be made in the second trimester of pregnancy. When I was in Shanghai in 1992 I picked up an edition of *China News* and read where eight percent of child-bearing women in China have annual abortions. Of course, the same women do not have yearly abortions, but the percentage stands. This means that there are thirty-two million abortions every year in China. Our local guide at Xion on our 1996 tour related that he and his wife decided to finally have their one allotted child, but an examination revealed that it was to be a girl. However, he said that he and his wife had decided to have the girl. As a result, relatives every night came by to mourn for him as his name will never be passed on through a son. It is extremely important in China for a man to have a son, and this is one reason why girls are either aborted or killed at birth.

After we had gotten to the Wuhan airport on the 1995 tour, we were told that a Japanese tour would get preference, and the Japanese luggage would be taken, but ours would have to come later. We knew that if we left our luggage behind we would never see it again. The plane left without us. At midnight an airport attendant arrived and informed us that another plane was ready. This was a small airport and there were no lights. While we could not see the airplane, we could tell it was a fairly large twin-motor prop. Upon climbing aboard, I looked out the window and the man taking care of the baggage crawled up into the cockpit, which was not altogether assuring. At that time, so many Chinese planes were crashing that they did not even bother to remove them from the runways. After the pilot finally got the poor thing off the ground and up into the air, we could tell that one engine was sputtering. Sitting across the aisle from me were two Germans who were evidently in China on business. I asked the one nearest me if this were not an old World War II Russian cargo plane. He responded, "Not only that, but it is one we shot down over Leningrad!" By God's mercy and a strong tail wind we did make it to Shanghai by sunrise.

In 1987 I led a third mission effort to China. We

had contracted for Scriptures and teaching materials in Chinese to be picked up in San Francisco, packed in suitcase–appearing boxes so that each tour member could include one along with one suitcase at baggage check-in. But when we got to our San Francisco check-in, all the Scriptures and literature were delivered to the airport in regular packing boxes.

On previous tours we had scheduled arriving on the last flight before midnight to avoid a close baggage inspection, so I thought perhaps we might just get by customs anyway. However, when we arrived in Hong Kong I was advised that our national guide was bringing us in at Guilin, not far from Canton; therefore, we would land two hours earlier than anticipated.

We landed at Guilin at nine p.m., and our guides were there to meet us. The baggage handlers had put all the boxes containing Bibles and other material on a large dolly, and I had just about got through customs when a loud-talking female with a red star on her hat demanded to know what was in those boxes. I doubted that she would believe Chinese fortune cookies, so I opened one of the boxes. This disturbed bureaucrat began yelling in an unknown language, at least unknown to me. I was informed in English that I had broken a law of the People's Republic of China, for which there could be serious consequences. I asked to see a copy of the law, and a copy of China's immigration and customs laws was

presented to me, with the one I had broken under-
scored. I carefully read the article that pertained to
me which said in essence that no literature of any
kind constituting political or any other harmful propaganda would be allowed into China. I argued that
Christian Bibles were not harmful propaganda, but
would actually help the Chinese people to become
better citizens. The customs people didn't buy my
opinion, and I was placed under temporary arrest.

Our national guide appeared on the scene, a
lovely young lady whom I later learned was the secretary of the China Travel Agency. Her father was a
member of the Communist Party and governor of
the province where Guilin was located. There was
some discussion, and then our guide, Chiang, advised me that the boxes of literature would be confiscated, and I would be asked to sign a legal document admitting my crime against the state. If I did
this, I would be allowed to join my tour group. If
not, I would be taken to detention to await deporta-
tion. I looked out the window where my tour group
was standing in the rain outside the bus. They were
not even allowed to get out of the rain until my immediate future was decided. I wondered what would
happen to them if I were taken to prison, so I signed
the blasted document. We had not eaten, and the
delay caused us to miss the dinner that had been
prepared for us at the hotel where we were to stay.
Our national guide and our local guide, a delightful
young lady, took us to a place where there was a

kitchen and prepared Chinese noodles with a curry flavor. I was in no mood to eat anything, especially curry noodles, as I had gotten sick on curry in China on my first tour and couldn't stand even the smell of this bottomless-pit concoction. So I made up some excuse to keep from casting aspersions on their culinary skills.

The next morning I was really down. Sitting on a bench with my head in my hands I must have presented a forlorn picture, and Chiang came up to me, put her hands on my shoulders, and apologized for the loss of our materials which had included several thousand copies of my salvation booklets entitled *Happiness*. Romans 8:28 never failed me before, so I again claimed this promise, got up out of my misery, and joined the tour group on the bus.

As we got on the bus I asked Chiang why, as secretary of the National Tourist Agency, she was guiding our tour group. She replied that there were so many young people in China converting to Christianity she wanted to know what this religion was all about.

As we started our first day of touring in the Guilin area, as usual, I led in prayer, read a scripture, and presented a devotional. The driver wanted me to read also from Mao's *Little Red Book*, but when I declined he remarked that Mao was greater than Jesus. I replied that Mao did indeed rule a country of over one billion people, but Jesus said that His Kingdom was not of this world; and, Mao had been given credit for killing over sixty million people, but Jesus never killed anyone, and in fact, Jesus came to give life, not take it. Therefore, I told him, if we wanted to consider greatness in the eyes of men on this basis then he would be correct. The driver never bothered me again.

One of the first stops we made was a beautiful park next to a clear, placid lake. The only Bibles and tracts we had left were in our suitcases. There was a man sitting on a bench, throwing pebbles in the water, watching his two daughters play (which in itself is unusual, a family having two daughters). The same Mrs. Trayser I referred to earlier said to me that she only had two Bibles in Chinese, and she felt that the Lord was leading her to give that man on the bench one of them. I watched as she got off the bus and gave him the Bible. He spoke some English and thanked her kindly, and then grabbed her and began to jump and shout. I thought he was going to throw her in the lake and rushed to help. After quieting the man down and getting him to release a rather frightened Mrs. Trayser, I found out his name was Phillip and that he was a Christian. He said that he had been praying for a Bible for over ten years, and today this strange woman gets off a bus and gives him the Word of God. He considered it a great miracle. Our national guide took all of this in with considerable interest.

Our local guide at Guilin was not a Christian, but her fiance was. I had lunch with him and found him to be a fine young man with aspirations of becoming a pastor, but he confided to me that this was very difficult in China. That afternoon we passed out some of the tracts we had hidden in our baggage in a large park in town. A student came up and questioned me about what I was doing, and asked for one of the tracts. After he was convinced I was who I said I was, he asked if I would like to attend a church service that night. He said that he could not come to my hotel, but if I would meet him back in the park he would guide me. After dark I slipped out and went back to the park, which was about one-half mile from the hotel, and there he and another student were waiting. He went down side streets and through dark alleys for another mile and finally came to a two-story house. We went up the stairs and joined a small underground church service already in progress. The leader of the church group was a professor at Guilin University. I kept in contact with him until after the Tiananmen Square affair.

The next day our tour group took the customary fifty-mile river barge journey on the Li River. This incomparable scenic wonderland is beyond imagination to anyone who has never experienced it. The following day we departed for Beijing in one of the few small jet airliners available in the China national air service at that time. While in Beijing we visited the usual sites, including the Great Wall and the Ming Tombs in Inner Mongolia. I had given our national guide a copy of my tract entitled *Happiness* and the only Bible in Chinese that we had left. Chiang asked me if I thought our God really answered our prayers. I replied that if we did not think so, we would not waste our time in prayer. She looked at me and said, "This is the rainy season in China, but I notice every morning when you pray and ask your God to give your group a good day, it stops raining. It is raining on every tour group in China but this one."

Our local guide in Beijing that year was a woman about thirty years old named Ping. Ping had been caught in the Cultural Revolution and shipped to the border of Outer Mongolia in the midst of winter. She and others were given some lumber and told to build their own houses and start their own farm. She said most of those with her either died from the cold or starved to death, but that she survived out of pure desperation and will power. However, Chiang told me not to trust Ping too far because she was a member of the Communist Party.

After our tour of the Beijing area was completed, we were bused to the airport to catch a plane for Chungking. After an hour Chiang came to me and reported that our plane was down and needed a part, and she did not know if or when we would get to Chungking. I had to get our group to Chungking because there was no place else to go. I asked her to call the government and see if we could charter an airplane. She returned and informed me that it was possible, but the cost would be nineteen thousand dollars. I told her that I just happened not to have nineteen thousand dollars on me. She responded with what was obvious to her, "Why don't you ask your God to fix the plane?"

Should I accept the challenge or not? Would I lose face with this young Chinese girl who was already obviously under conviction?

I called our tour group together, and right there in the middle of a busy airport in a communist country we held a prayer meeting. Not more than five minutes after we had ended the prayer meeting, I saw Chiang trying to get to us through the crowd, jumping up and down, waving her arms. She shouted, "The plane is fixed, and it will be here in one hour." We arrived in Chungking before the ship sailed, and Chiang, secretary of the China Travel Agency and daughter of the communist governor of one of the provinces of China, received Jesus Christ as her Lord and Savior.

As was customary, the last night on the ship there was a farewell dinner. A lovely Christian girl who had taken the name Josephine was the hostess on the ship, and a young Chinese man who was also a Christian, and also named Phillip, was in charge of logistics and activities. The captain of the ship was an old warrior who had been personally decorated by Mao. Josephine and Phillip came up with the idea that at the end of the party, I was to present the captain with a Bible in English and a Bible in Chinese. Also, there was always dancing at a Chinese party, and I was to begin the party by dancing with

Josephine and end the party by dancing with Chiang. I had not danced but two or three times since I became a Christian. I had forgotten even which hand was to hold Josephine's hand, and which hand was to be put on her waist. After I got that straightened out, lucky for me the first dance was a waltz, and after stepping on her toes a time or two, everything went pretty well, and we got a big hand when we finished.

As the dinner party progressed, the Chinese on board, and especially the ship's officers, began toasting each other with what I assumed was hard liquor. Josephine and Phillip brought me the Bibles to present to the captain, but I voiced extreme objections because he was drunker than a skunk. But they literally lifted me out of my chair and pushed me to where two officers were holding him up. I made my little speech; it was interpreted; and I hurriedly pushed the Bibles toward the captain. He mumbled something back in Chinese, and Phillip, interpreting, said that he did not care much for religion, but he would place the Bibles in the ship's library. The floor was cleared, and I ended the party by dancing with Chiang to the same waltz that was played at the beginning.

The next year, in leading a tour to the Middle East, I shared my experiences on the China tour the year before. Our Israeli guide was a Jewess named Audrey who had immigrated from Vancouver, Canada. Audrey was a good guide, but she was rather loud and aggressive. When I had finished, Audrey snorted, "Well, if you have such a direct pipeline to God, why don't you get Him to give us some cooler weather." The date was in late September and cooler weather was late in arriving. The temperature was still hovering near one hundred degrees Fahrenheit. I tried not to respond in kind, and replied that we would certainly pray for the Lord to grant us better weather, or give us the grace to bear up under what we had. She almost angrily retorted, "Prove to me that you Christians are closer to God than we Jews. I don't want cooler weather next week, next month, or next year. I want cooler weather today."

I replied, "Well, how about high noon." Half kidding, I added, "If we get cooler weather in the middle of the day, will you let me baptize you in the Jordan this afternoon?" She returned, "Bring me the cooler weather and we'll see."

It was at that time eleven a.m., and at exactly twelve noon while we were going through the Jesus Boat Museum (this boat had been discovered in 1986), the wind shifted sharply to the north and the temperatures dropped twenty degrees. I looked at my watch to be sure of the time, held it up to Audrey, and asked if she had a change of clothes for the baptism. She snipped, "Well, you read the weather report this morning. It means nothing." Audrey's reaction reminded me of Paul's words in Acts 28:27–28:

For the heart of this people is waxed gross, and their ears are dull of hearing, and their eyes have they closed; lest they should see with their eyes, and hear with their ears, and understand with their heart, and should be converted, and I should heal them. Be it known therefore unto you, that the salvation of God is sent unto the Gentiles, and that they will hear it.

There are readers who might question some of the accounts I am relating, but there are thousands across the country who have gone on tours with me, and many of them will be reading this book. I would not dare write anything that would be false and untrue.

I continued to hear from Chiang until Tiananmen Square. In subsequent tours I tried to locate her, but to no avail. In China, people just disappear without any record. The Tiananmen Square affair was not just in Beijing; it was all over the country. In 1985 students were hopeful they would be given academic freedom to choose their own future. In 1987, because of rising conflict between student aspirations and the government's iron rules, tensions were rising. This is why we were not permitted to visit schools in 1987.

The news media covered only the Tiananmen Square revolution, but the entire Chinese army was mobilized, and divisions were sent into larger cities like Nanjing, Xion, Chungking, Shanghai, Guilin, and others. Parents were warned that their children would be killed and they would be sent to prison or labor camps. Many student leaders and professors were put in prison, and in 1992 I was told many of them had not been released. School officials and even local mayors were hung in main city squares, even though they were not involved. The Tiananmen Square massacre was indeed a horrible thing, almost three thousand students machine-gunned and their bodies thrown on trucks and picked up by helicopters to be hurriedly mass buried so there would be no news coverage or subsequent protests.

When I returned to China in 1992 I found that one of the aftereffects of the student revolution in 1989 was that the United States had lost face, and the Chinese young people had a stoic posture. We had preached to them liberty, but the liberty we had was not for them. My 1992 tour was mainly a fact-finding venture, but we still took Bibles and salvation tracts with us, and we did distribute them without much opposition. The underground church had gone further underground, and the leaders were not trusting anyone, even us. However, I was still able to visit some of the pastors in the Three-Self churches. Huge hotels had been built in major Chinese cities by major hotel chains like Hilton, Sheraton, etc. But in 1992 in the aftermath of the Tiananmen Square massacre, they were only about thirty percent occupied.

In 1996 I again joined with my good friend Dr. Robert Lindsted for another tour to China. Dr.

Lindsted had hopes of distributing thousands of Bibles and tons of witnessing and teaching materials to the house churches and the underground church. I cautioned Dr. Lindsted that China was not Russia, but he said that he had already made plans to ship them into the country through commercial avenues. I agreed to participate on the basis that this could be done. So, the funds were raised and plans proceeded. I continued to have reservations because the Communist Central Committee had on January 14, 1996, criminalized all Christian activities in China not associated with the Three-Self Church.

About a month before we were to leave for China, Dr. Lindsted called me and reported there had been a hitch in our plans. Things had tightened up, and the men in China who had been instrumental in receiving and distributing materials sent in with commercial shipments had been arrested, so this avenue was closed.

We had already received funds for the Bibles and other materials. Eighteen members going with me had already paid for their tour expenses and most of the funds had already been forwarded for plane fares and logistics. We had already gone beyond the point of no return. Some at the office suggested I plead old age and urgent business responsibilities as an excuse to pull out. But I just could not do this. While I certainly was not fearless or perfect, there are some things that men who are men can't do, and there are things that men who are men must do. I assured our office staff that the battle was the Lord's, and if this mission effort was according to His will, we would return safely.

The logistics for the taking of what materials we could into China was left in the hands of Dr. Lindsted and his tour assistant, Mr. Baxter. As we had done before on foreign missions, each tour member was to take one suitcase, and later I found these huge suitcases weighed approximately one hundred pounds—some less, some more. I was to lead my group through Beijing, and the group led by Dr. Lindsted was to go through Shanghai. We landed at Beijing at half past ten in the evening, just as we had planned. Even so, I thought there was no way, except by God's power and might, that we were going to get all this material through customs. I was expecting to be arrested at passport check and customs inspection. I, outwardly confident, led my group up to immigration check, trying not to show my forebodings.

I presented the group visa with passports. The immigration officer informed me there was a problem. There was no exit visa with the entrance visa. I was told we could not enter China. Why had Mr. Baxter not included an exit visa for the group? Was it on purpose? Why had I not been told? I later assumed that it was because after we left China we were to go back through at Hong Kong to take more Bibles in the back door at Gangzhou. If this was the case, the plan did not work, and I was left hanging out on a limb with an intolerable situation. What was I going to do with eighteen people hung up at customs with no place to go?

I collected our local guide, named Jack, and our national guide, Leonard (not their Chinese names), and we began negotiating, calling government immigration officials, and praying. After a couple of hours it was agreed that another exit visa would be granted, on the basis that I pay for another exit visa. By this time it was after one a.m., everyone was gone from the airport except for two or three. We were waved right on through without a customs inspection. Although not including an exit visa was a serious mistake, had we had one we might have all been arrested and the materials confiscated. Mission impossible began to be mission possible, with all the glory going to God.

At the hotel I did not allow any of the suitcases with Bibles in my room, because if there was trouble mine would be the first room to be checked. The next morning our schedule called for a tour of Beijing, including Tiananmen Square and the Forbidden City. The square in the heart of Beijing is approximately one-quarter mile wide and one-half mile long, adjacent to the headquarters of the Communist Party and the Forbidden City. In the middle of the square is the mausoleum of Mao Tse-tung where his body lies in a vacuum glass coffin, looking like a painted penguin. While the lines of people to see Mao's body is shorter today, thousands still go by every day. Everyone first goes through a metal detector before being allowed to enter, because if someone should break the casket Mao would go up in a puff of dust. I remember on our tour our guide was a young man named Lee, and as we got to Mao's casket I asked rather loudly, "Lee did you bring the hammer." I thought Lee would pass out.

As the tour group was browsing through the square, I went off by myself. I just had to talk with the people to find out present attitudes toward the government, to us as Christians, and to the United States. I had previously been warned that I would be watched, but I was no novice, and I thought I would be very careful. I would cut through the crowd, look around as I went, and then select a young couple with their one child to approach. As usual, the Chinese couples were friendly, warm, and happy to talk with me, and overjoyed that I wanted to take a picture of their offspring, usually a boy. As I left I shook their hands and slipped them a thumb-nail tract with a brief message from one of the gospels. I only gave two of the little tracts out on the square. When we got to the Forbidden City I sent Kim into one of the buildings to pass out tracts, and she came back empty, reporting that everyone was glad to get them and she had no trouble. I again gave two couples in the Forbidden City one of the little tracts. As we were about to leave this site, our guide Leonard came to me and said that I had been observed giving out literature in both sites, and I would be arrested at the gate, which I was. Another one of our tour members was also observed giving out several tracts, and she was arrested with me.

We were taken to a police station just off the square and booked. I knew what to expect. I emptied my pockets and someone was sent to check my hotel room. We were interrogated and the Chinese police are very good at that sort of thing. They wanted to know where I got the tracts,

Me standing in front of Chinese police station where I was taken for questioning.

where they were received in China, whom I had contacted, who I knew in China, etc. One just has to be very careful not to contradict oneself. After filing charges on two sides of a legal-sized sheet, we could sign the document or be sent to jail. Of course we signed it because the only thing we really confessed to was witnessing for the Lord. We were allowed to return to our tour group, and that was that. However, someone in our group advised the group in Shanghai that I had been arrested. I assumed that group was to try to contact the underground church in Shanghai, and then take the rest of the materials they had by train to Nanjing and Xion. They panicked and hid all of their materials in the duct work in the hotel; as far as I know, it is still there. It may have been just as well, as surveillance was exceedingly tight in all major cities in 1996.

In Beijing our problem was still unresolved. We were not able to contact the underground church. I told Dr. Lindsted that I knew the pastor of Christian Men's Church, and I would contact him, and perhaps he would at least put me in contact with a house church. When I called the church, a government agent answered the telephone and told me in no uncertain terms that I could not talk to anyone at the church without a government permit. This had changed since the last time I was there. A couple of the brethren went with me in a taxi to the church, and we encountered the same roadblock. So, what to do? We could not leave the Bibles at the hotel because they would be checked to us, and we could not take them with us on a Chinese airplane because baggage was limited to forty pounds. The materials had become a millstone around our necks, and we were to leave for Nanjing the first thing the next morning. At midnight one of the tour members, Mrs. Ford from Washington, D.C., called my room and reported that someone in broken English kept calling her room wanting to know if we had anything for them. We knew immediately who it was, and we smuggled all the suitcases with Bibles out to the front while the guards were occupied. The underground church people went rumbling off in a broken-down van singing "Hallelujah." The battle was indeed the Lord's.

At Nanjing I did some research on the Japanese massacre in that city which occurred in 1937. Tens of thousands, and possibly hundreds of thousands, of men, women, and children were hunted down and shot in cold blood. Japanese soldiers who killed the most were given prizes. But what I really wanted to see in Nanjing was the great seminary I kept hearing about. I had never been to Nanjing before on any previous tour. The seminary was a disgrace. There were only about one hundred students. No teacher or administrator could talk with us. The library had only about two hundred books. Our student guide was terrified to even answer questions, and finally on the outside he confided that they had to wear two faces. If they said anything the government would not like, or even visit a house church, they would be sent to prison. So much for the freedom of religion in China about which the Billy Graham organization broadcasts to the world.

We continued on the tour to Xion and Guilin. Our local guide in Guilin was a delightful young man who offered to rent me a house on the Li River for only fifty dollars a month. If possible, I would like to do just that for one summer, but with my record it may not be possible.

Our young guide Leonard was a member of the Communist Party, but I have never met a communist in China who would not jump at the chance to come to the United States. He was only twenty-five and quite smitten with a girl that was in Dr.

Lindsted's group. Leonard attended every devotion and group fellowship that we had, and even went out of his way to see that everything needed connected with these activities was furnished. He also invited others. He also asked me if it were possible for anyone in the United States to buy a Bible. I assured him that this was so, and that when we left him at Gangzhou I would give my Bible to him, which I did.

Because of my heavy schedule I was unable to go back to China in 1997, but Bob Glaze from the ministry went in my place. Twenty-five thousand of my salvation tracts entitled *Happiness* were taken into southern China for distribution to house churches and underground churches, and since 1997 many additional copies have been printed and found their way into the hands of unsaved Chinese men, women, and children to witness of Jesus Christ in my absence.

There are many other countries that the Lord has in His will and purpose allowed me to visit and uphold His Word. In 1996 I was in Honduras to preach to churches and establish headquarters for Profecías Bíblicas in Central America. In March 1998 I was on a humanitarian mission in Cuba and witnessed the economic, social, and spiritual poverty in that country after forty years of communism.

However, it is not possible to recount all the places and events in my travels to far away places with strange sounding names, and I pray that those who have been saved by the gospel that we shared will be our crown of rejoicing, as the apostle Paul prayed, at the glorious Second Coming of our Lord and Savior Jesus Christ.

Life's Little Surprises

One of the more popular series presented over Southwest Radio Church (and made the entrance into the eighties easier for the ministry) was a two-week segment of programming I did with Constance Cumbey. In 1977 I included in a book I wrote, *Satan's Kingdom and the Second Coming,* a section about a rising new religious cult in Washington and Oregon called the New Age movement. This cultic, esoteric religion was traced to one Foster Bailey in 1917 and his two wives, Mary Bailey and Alice Bailey. In 1978 this collective hodgepodge of supernatural ideas burst out of the closet and began to be accepted by the yuppie generation.

The New Age was identified as the Age of Aquarius, and it encompassed everything from reincarnation to holistic health. The central emphasis was on the Eastern religions of Buddhism and Hinduism with a Western flavor. Businesses, clubs, government agencies—both state and federal—large corporations, and even liberal churches, embraced New Age teachings because they was thought to release the mind from rigid concepts of the past. It was the "now" religion, the religion of the future that man would finally become his own god. One day in full-page notices in newspapers around the world, even in *Reader's Digest*, appeared the startling news that the New Age Christ, Maitreya, had arrived.

Constance Cumbey, a lawyer in Chicago, compiled all her research into a book titled *Hidden Dangers of the Rainbow*, the rainbow being an emblem of the New Age movement. I did a two-week series with Constance on this subject. We mailed out thousands of copies of the series on cassette tape, plus thirty-five thousand copies of the book. This series was not only beneficial as far as the dissemination of this information was concerned, it was also beneficial in increasing the outreach of Southwest Radio Church. And, of course, the series catapulted Constance into prominence as an authority on the subject, and demands for her as a conference speaker snowballed.

Later, Southwest Radio Church scheduled Constance as a speaker in a Southwest Radio Church meeting in Independence Hall in Washington, D.C. Constance called me and wanted to know if she could bring her son as she had been out on the road a great deal and had not been with him as much as she should. Of course, we said it was all right and that we would take care of his airline fare and accommodations. The meeting at Independence Hall had been scheduled in conjunction with the National Religious Broadcasters convention.

Once a Christian decides, or is led, on an attack or exposé ministry, they have to be very careful to stay within well defined biblical guidelines. Constance became so involved in investigative appraisals of the New Age movement and its adherents, that many began to accuse her of thinking everyone else in the world besides she was a New Ager. It was reported by some attending the NRB convention where Pat Robertson spoke that Constance passed out a leaflet, "Eighteen Reasons Why Pat Robertson Is the Antichrist." Whether this was the reason or not, or if Constance simply got tired and did not have time outside her practice to continue her own particular ministry, she faded from the conservative speaking circuit. However, Constance Cumbey is a very brilliant person. In 1996 I did a few programs with her on the European Union which were well received.

In the expanding years of the ministry in the early eighties, the news that made the headlines was:

1980

January 3: Laetrile Tests Authorized by the
National Cancer Institute

January 29: Jimmy Durante Dies

April 28: Attempt to Rescue U.S. Iran Hostages a
Disaster

April 29: Alfred Hitchcock Dies

May 19: Mt. St. Helen's Explodes

July 23: Peter Sellers Dies

July 27: Deposed Shah of Iran Dies
September 13: Iran and Iraq War
November 4: Reagan Wins
December 8: John Lennon Killed

1981

January 28: Mao's Widow Gets Death Sentence
January 31: Iran Hostages Released
February 2: Converted Jew Lustiger Made
   Archbishop of Paris
March 30: Reagan Wounded in Assassination
   Attempt
May 13: Pope Wounded in Assassination Attempt
June 24: Israeli Planes Destroy Iraqi Atomic
   Reactor
July 7: First Woman on Supreme Court
July 29: Prince Charles and Lady Diana Marry
October 6: Anwar el-Sadat Assassinated
October 16: Moshe Dayan Dies

1982

March 5: John Belushi Dies from Overdose
March 16: Claus von Bulow Found Guilty of
   Killing Wife
April 30: Argentina Invades Falkland Islands
June 20: Israel Invades Lebanon
August 12: Henry Fonda Dies
September 10: Princess Grace Dies in Car Wreck

1983

January 26: Bear Bryant Dies

March 8: Reagan Says Soviet Union "Evil Empire"

June 24: Sally Ride First U.S. Female in Space

June 27: New Death Plague AIDS Identified

September 15: Russians Down Flight 007, 269 Die

October 14: National Council of Churches Denies
   God Is a "He"

October 18: Famine Threatens 22 African Nations

October 25: Terrorists Kill 216 Marines in Beirut
   Barracks

In 1982 I received a call from my sister, Geneva, that Mother was in the hospital with serious complications from pneumonia. The doctors had indicated that her lungs were no longer functioning and that she could not live without a respirator. I picked up my younger brother, Harold, and at the hospital in Paris, Texas, it  *Mother, a few years before her death.* was the consensus of the family that the respirator should be turned off, as mother was too old to even contemplate a lung transplant. First, I went into the ICR unit. Mother was breathing with the help of the respirator. It appeared she was unconscious, but I took her hand and told her to squeeze if she could hear me. In response she firmly gripped my hand.

Then, I asked her to squeeze again if she wanted the respirator to be turned off. Her hand squeezed mine. I had prayer with her, told her goodbye, and that I looked forward to seeing her and Dad again in Heaven. In four hours Mother was dead and then buried beside the grave of my father at Mt. Olivet Cemetery in Hugo. Mother was a good mother. She did the best for us kids she could with what she had.

In 1984 there arose a serious matter at the ministry. As radio coverage to new stations expanded even more, which was accompanied by a drop in the mail, the debt problem became a factor. Also, the delay in paying the stations due to having to send funds by check to the agency in California, and then have the agency send checks to the station, often required an extra month. As more and more radio stations were added to corporations presenting Christian programs for profit, owners and operators put more pressure on program producers. In order to reduce payment time by a month and at the same time assume more control over reducing the outstanding radio bill, I exercised my authority as secretary and treasurer. Radio stations were paid directly by check from our office, and I began to drop stations that were not sustaining. The debt had increased to over one million dollars, and in six months I was able to reduce it by half. Even though I would send the agent the commission on every station paid, he was not happy. The agency had lost control and clout in dealing with stations.

Evidently the agent began to play economic politics with David and two other trustees without my knowledge. One day David dropped into my office and gave me a direct order as president of Southwest Radio Church to once again begin sending all monies for stations directly to the agency. I responded that while I respected David's authority as president, I could not comply because this order would not be in the best interest of the ministry, and I exercised my rights under the bylaws to call for a trustees' meeting. At the meeting I presented complete accounting records to show how I had reduced expenses, reduced payoff time by more than a month, and without decreasing income. Imagine my amazement and disbelief when three of the trustees voted against me. Only Lucille Andrews of Olney, Texas, stood with me. I had no alternative but to resign as secretary and treasurer. But in six months the financial status had reversed back to what it was. Mrs. Andrews filed a report to the entire board, and this began a process that eventually led to David's resignation in 1988.

My connection with Southwest Radio Church after the trustees' meeting in 1984 continued in the areas of writing, programming, and leading missionary tours. At the time I bowled as a member of two leagues, and while bowling one evening on my team's competition I ate a piece of pizza. After I returned to my apartment, I had heartburn and an upset stomach. I thought it was the pizza. The next morning I went to work, but the burning and gas got no better. That night my pains were severe, and I assumed that I had developed an ulcer. I called my daughter Cheryl, and she insisted that I see her doctor, so I made an urgent appointment for eleven a.m. By the time for the appointment came, I felt so much better I almost cancelled it. The doctor I met with was in a clinic adjacent to the Baptist Hospital in Oklahoma City. He gave me some medicine to quiet my stomach and the pain that was remaining disappeared, but he said at my age he should check my enzymes. I came back at two p.m. to get the results, and I was told that I had suffered a heart attack and should immediately check into the hospital. An attendant rolled me over to Baptist Hospital in a wheelchair, and I was checked in and was put on oxygen. While the pain was gone, when I tried to get out of bed the next morning to go to the bathroom it was extremely difficult to walk even those few feet. There was no doubt then that I had experienced a moderate heart attack.

After a five-day stay in the hospital I stayed with my daughter Cheryl for two weeks until I was able to take care of myself and resume physical exercise. After the two-week convalescence period I returned to work at Southwest Radio Church and gradually regained my strength.

At the annual board meeting in 1986 there was considerable unrest among the members about my position with the ministry, and the debt which had again become quite large. While David was retained as president, Ben McCammon was elected as chairman of the board of trustees, and a new office was created for me, CEO, which meant I could run the ministry with the board's approval. The ministry's contract with the agency in California was abolished, and over the next two years the financial status improved and most of the displeasure by board members over the conduct of affairs disappeared. My three daughters were happily married, and I had adjusted to living by myself in an apartment.

In the spring of 1988 I noticed that I could not maintain a satisfactory level of physical exercise in jogging, bowling, or playing golf, without pains in my chest. I checked with my cardiologist, and after a stress test he advised that if I was to continue my present activities and quality of life I would need a heart bypass. While such operations in 1988 had attained a ninety percent success rate, there was still a chance I might not make it. Cathy was to give birth to my first grandchild in July, so I waited until after Kelly was born to schedule the operation for July 15.

I checked into Baptist Hospital at one p.m. on July 14. There were preliminary tests and instructions. The head surgeon, who was assisted by the best team available in Oklahoma, came by at two p.m. My son-in-law Chris was with me, and so we asked Dr. Hawley about checking out to play golf that afternoon, as the Hefner golf course was just across the street. He responded, "Such a thing is utterly out of the question, but do have a nice game." I checked back in at six p.m. and Dr. Hawley came back to see me at eight p.m. In the course of his final appraisal of my condition before surgery, he mentioned the number of pints of blood that would be needed. No one had said anything to me about blood before and in 1988 adequate safeguards against AIDS-contaminated blood had not been established. I protested and said that if that were the case, then put off the operation until I could give enough of my own blood to save for the operation. Dr. Hawley asked if I were nervous, afraid, or would need anything to put me to sleep for the night. I remarked that I was in excellent spirits, I was not afraid, because I knew where I was going in the event I never woke up from the operation. He replied that if I didn't need to take anything and got a good night's sleep, that maybe we wouldn't need any blood. Dr. Hawley said that he would get me out in a hurry.

I went to sleep immediately after Dr. Hawley left the room and was awakened at half past five the next morning to be bathed and shaved. I was due to be put under at seven a.m., but after getting to the outside entrance room, the attendant informed me that Dr. Hawley had an emergency and the operation would be delayed. The time was almost a quarter to nine when I was finally put to sleep.

Although the heart bypass procedure has changed somewhat since 1988, then it was to open the chest and completely stop the heart while a blood pump took over. Arteries taken out of the legs re-placed the clogged arteries. After this was done, an electric charge was made to the heart which the phy-sician hoped would start it beating again, and then the heart pump was turned off. A respirator was used during the procedure and continued after the pa-tient was revived as long as deemed necessary.

At 11:20 a.m. I woke up in the recovery room. There was no respirator. I was breathing normally, and I asked the nurse when the operation would begin. She replied that it was over. I was kept in the recovery room another hour to make sure my blood pressure and my breathing had stabilized, and then I was put in a room for two days in the ICU ward. Dr. Hawley did have the best bypass team in Okla-homa, but no one has ever understood how a qua-druple bypass was performed and the patient was wide-awake and off the respirator in two and one-half hours. I checked the hospital statement to see if I had been charged for blood, but there was no such item listed. I was released on the eighth day to go to my daughter Cheryl's home. Cheryl lived near Bap-tist Hospital.

What the results of the operation would be was the question. Would I be able to resume my work at the ministry? Or being sixty-five years of age, I could draw Social Security and, with a little added income from royalties, I could live quite comfortably. I could play golf, go fishing, write books, and live the re-maining years of my life out quite peaceably and comfortably. I thought to myself, why not? I have paid my dues!

Little did I realize that, for better or worse, my life would take a dramatic turn within the next two weeks.

After transferring from the hospital on August 23 to my daughter's home, I was to remain fairly immobile for six weeks, meaning no heavy work to negate the possibility of something breaking or coming loose. Carol was in Minneapolis working at *USA Today*, and Cathy was at home in Choctaw, Oklahoma, with a new baby. Cheryl had her work to take care of, and I was interfering with her schedule, plus she was running back and forth to see that I had everything I needed. She was insistent that I lie in bed most of the day and she would not even let me make more than one or two telephone calls. On the third day I determined that all this was for the birds. My car was parked in the driveway, so I found my keys and returned to my apartment.

That evening I was besieged with calls from all three daughters demanding that unless I returned to Cheryl's home so that she could take care of me all kinds of nasty things would happen, from being bitten by bedbugs to expiring in my sleep. I had intended never to remarry, but that night I reconsidered, thinking that it might be the best thing to do. I had been involved in humanitarian mission work in saving Cambodian refugees who had escaped from the Killing Fields era. One of the immigrants that I had become somewhat more than just a friend to was Kim Ky. Kim Ky had lost her mother and father, and also seven brothers and sisters during the Khmer Rouge genocide period against her own people. Kim had received the gospel, was born again by faith in Jesus Christ, and had a tremendous testimony. That night I called Kim and asked if she would like to get married. While it must have been a tremendous shock to her, she agreed, and we set the wedding date for November 5. That I was twenty years Kim's senior was something we would have to deal with later. My daughters were happy to hear the news.

The annual prophecy conference was held the last week of July, and the annual board meeting was held on the last day of the conference. I had not really been kept up with the progress of the conference; however, I did show up on Saturday morning for the board meeting. As I remember, David was not at the meeting, and Ben McCammon, who was president of the board of trustees, was in charge, assisted by Lucille Andrews, who was secretary of the board. I sensed that there was something wrong, and Ben advised me that he and another board member had met with David over a problem that had occurred during the conference.

At the conclusion of the board meeting, Ben announced a special meeting of the board of trustees for Sunday afternoon and asked if I felt like being present. Later that afternoon Ben advised me of the nature of the problem, and said that he and the other trustees had drawn up resignation papers for David to sign. The bylaws of the organization stipulate that a board member or an officer can be requested to resign voluntarily. If the member chooses not to resign voluntarily, then the matter can be brought before the board of trustees, or the entire board, for a hearing.

Ben McCammon had been quarterback of the Oklahoma A&M football team in the late thirties and early forties. He was a no-nonsense, black-or-white type individual. He was seriously involved in the Gideons and the Christian Businessmen's Organization. Ben had a reputation of being a stalwart Christian leader, and at six foot, five inches, he made an imposing figure. On one occasion my brother Harold and I were on a fishing trip at Eufaula Lake, approximately one hundred and fifty miles east of Oklahoma City. We stopped at one of the bait houses in one of the lesser frequented parts of the lake. As our bait was being readied, we stopped by the counter for a Coke. A man sitting at the counter who had obviously had six or seven too many beers, slapped me on the back and shouted, "Friend, do you know Ben McCammon?" Surprised, I replied that by chance I did know Ben McCammon. This drunk went on until our bait had been put into our bucket about what a tremendous Christian gentleman Ben was. It must have been one chance in millions that I would run into a drunk on a lake far from home who would suddenly begin extolling the virtues of one Ben McCammon, but this was the kind of man Ben was. Thousands of people in Oklahoma knew Ben as one of the finest Christian gentlemen in the state.

On August 1, 1988, I showed up at the Southwest Radio Church offices. The board of trustees was called to order in an official meeting. Five minutes later David joined the meeting. Ben read to David and the board a resignation statement, and to my surprise David signed it and left without comment.

Shootout at the OKC Corral

On October 26, 1881, a famous shootout occurred at Tombstone, Arizona. The marshal of Tombstone was Virgil Earp. Marshal Earp was assisted by his two brothers, Wyatt, who was acting marshal, and Morgan, who was a special policeman. Marshal Earp also deputized their good friend, John H. "Doc" Holliday, a Georgia dentist who had turned gambler and gunfighter because he had contracted tuberculosis and did not have long to live.

Marshal Earp had dedicated himself as a lawman to make Tombstone a safe place for decent citizens to live. The bad hombres were just as dedicated to keep Tombstone a safe place for outlaws. The tough guys were Tom and Frank McLaury, and Ike and Billy Clanton, cattle rustlers and robbers. The Earps had posted notice that no guns would be allowed in Tombstone. The McLaurys and the Clantons came into town wearing their guns, and let it be known that they were making their stand just west of C. S. Fly's Boarding House and Photo Studio in a vacant lot near the intersection of Third Street and Fremont Street behind the OK Corral.

The Earps and Doc Holliday marched side by side up Fremont Street intent upon arresting the outlaws, but when Frank McLaury and Bill Clanton drew their guns, the lawmen drew theirs and the fight was on. When the smoke cleared, Tom and Frank McLaury were dead, and so was Billy Clanton. Ike Clanton ran away. Virgil and Morgan were wounded, but lived. Doc Holliday suffered a bruise, and Wyatt was not even scratched. Doc Holliday died in 1886 of tuberculosis, but Wyatt lived to be eighty and died in 1929. After the gun battle, the Earps and Holliday were arrested by Sheriff Behan and tried for murder, possibly because Behan thought the Earps were taking over his territory, or perhaps Behan was a friend of the outlaws. In any event, at the trial all four of the accused were found innocent.

There have probably been a thousand shootouts between lawmen and outlaws in the United States as dramatic as the "Shootout at the OK Corral," but this one stands out as an example of courage, duty, and human interest. Murder and shootouts not only occur in the area of civil government, they also occur in the spiritual realm of the Church. We read in 1 John 3:15, "Whosoever hateth his brother is a murderer. . . ." After being in the ministry for forty-seven years, I am convinced that Christians can be more cruel, vengeful, hateful, and untruthful, than the unsaved. Yet they manifest these acts while fooling themselves that they are doing God's will.

Going all the way back to the early Church we

find Peter and Paul yelling in each other's faces at Antioch. We discover Paul being accused of blasphemy by members of the Jewish church and having to go up to Jerusalem to defend himself. In Paul's letter to the church at Galatia we see within the context backbiting, character assassination, and blasphemy. On one mission trip we see Mark deserting his fellow missionaries because he was homesick. In another epistle we discover Paul trying to referee between the feuding divisions within the church at Corinth, and when the apostle returns to Jerusalem, James tells him that he has forsaken the law of Moses and must commit blasphemy by making a sacrifice for his sins in the Temple. When Paul was sent to a Roman prison, almost all forsook him, and he referred to the "false brethren" who had departed from the faith. Finally as he awaited his execution, Paul mentioned that all the churches and Christians of Asia had turned against him, and this would include the seven churches of Revelation. I have witnessed Christians who were friends and fellow laborers for God in the church one week turn against one another the next week, angrily charging one another with every sin mentioned in the Bible, as well as some that are not mentioned. In the last two Southern Baptist churches I have belonged to, there have occurred bitter fights that would never occur in secular organizations. I have never personally gotten involved in interchurch politics. If I cannot agree with the pastor or be satisfied spiritually with the membership, I will leave and find another church. I am sure that most pastors who have been in the ministry for ten years or more have experienced their own OK Corrals. Of course, in divisions that cause split-offs, the losers will go off and establish their own church, and then work harder to build it up. God will often use church controversies to expand the gospel witness and save souls.

In 1988 I had nothing at all to do with David's problem and controversy with the trustees. Any negotiations with David or anything I did, which was very little, was at the instructions of the president of the board of trustees, or by majority vote of the trustees. I have not been with one Christian organization for forty-seven years by disobeying the legal ordinances of the board as stipulated in the bylaws. Even though I was, for the most part, a bystander trying to recover from serious heart surgery, I was drawn into a vicious conflict for the control of the ministry.

A week had passed since David had resigned to the board of trustees. During this week I had to think about the October mailing and publications that were involved, as well as programming, three meetings in other states featuring David which had been set for the middle of August, and David had a tour to England, Jordan, and Israel scheduled for the last week of August. I had asked the trustees about approaching David about fulfilling the meeting engagements and leading the tour, but they refused to allow it. I called Texe Marrs, who had been a guest on the program several times, and he agreed to take the meetings. David was the principal speaker on the program and the only Webber left to identify historically with the organization. Now he was gone. What was I going to do in bringing about a transition without losing the supporting constituency? I had been a regular on the program, but I had a voice like a Boggy Bottom hog caller. How could I find a suitable host for the program?

But my problems had only begun, because on Sunday, August 8, Ben McCammon called me at my apartment to tell me that David had joined with two trustees and a former business associate in making serious charges against me, and they intended to take over the ministry. I was still having angina chest pains, and in fact, I had to continue using nitroglycerin patches for two years after my operation. I suggested to Ben that we must meet with them and let them have the ministry, because I was sick and I was tired and I really wanted to retire. However, Ben yelled at me over the telephone that I was their leader and I could not just lay down and quit. The other parties were probably thinking that I would resign, or the stress would throw me into another heart attack. However, many have misjudged me. Although I am outwardly humble and the opposite of aggressive, I can be as hard as nails when backed up against a wall. So for Ben's sake, and I hoped for God's sake, I would make a fight of it.

If those who were interested in restoring David

to Southwest Radio Church had simply contacted me first, I probably would have resigned voluntarily rather than risk a confrontation that could have ended my life. But now my honor and credibility were being challenged. It was high noon and time to put up or shut up. The participants were:

David Webber: David evidently had contacted several friends who had been involved with the ministry to help him regain control, even though he had resigned voluntarily.

Participant "A": I understood this gentleman orchestrated the effort and stood to gain thousand dollars a month if David regained control.

Participant "B": According to Mr. "B"s own words, he promised David he would do everything possible to get his ministry back. Others told me later that even if I were removed, David would not again be the host of the program.

Particpant "C": Mr. "C" was a generous giver to extra-church organizations, as long as he could evidently have a voice in the operation and outreach of these organizations.

The first attack came in the form of postcards and letters mailed to board members accusing me of all sorts of incompetency and related sins. At first I answered these charges and accusations, but they were spaced two to three days apart, and before the board members could receive my defense, a new barrage was already in the mail. It was obvious that these attacks were so spaced that I could never answer them. First there were cards, then letters, then telegrams, then special delivery letters, and then Air Express letters, Federal Express packaged letters, etc. Each new set of accusations was mailed in a more desperate manner to impress the board members that something had to be done, and quick.

I had to admit these people were real professionals. They really knew what they were doing and I complimented them on their research and methods. Next, they sent letters to members of the staff indicating that they were going to take over the ministry and any employee who remained faithful to me would be fired. I began to wonder how these people knew every move I made, every contract I signed, and almost word for word, everything I said. I soon discovered that the person in charge of the secretarial pool was copying papers and sending notes on my daily activities to one of the leaders of the opposition. Of course, we dismissed this person immediately.

Next, the tone of the accusations against me became more frantic and demands were made for an immediate and special meeting of the board. I could not allow this to happen, because I was extremely busy with writing, programming, and trying to keep the ministry going while raising three hundred thousand dollars a month to meet the bills. They sent out letters requesting proxies so a majority of votes could be gotten to force the meeting. So, I had to call and convince enough board members to stay put until pressing business was taken care of, including a tour which David had set up that would cost the ministry two hundred thousand dollars if it were not completed. Ben McCammon and Texe Marrs took care of the meetings, and I left to lead a three-week tour. This was an extremely dangerous and difficult time for me to be away from the ministry. It was also hard on me physically, as scarcely a month previously I had undergone the heart bypass.

When I checked the tour members in at Kennedy Airport to board the British Airlines 747, there were two missing. Either two had not shown up, or they did not check in with me. As we left the plane at Heathrow Airport in London, there was a rather hefty woman in her forties hanging on the arm of an older woman in her late seventies or early eighties, while the older woman was bouncing along in a horizontal position on a horizontal escalator. Evidently she had fallen down, and the younger woman was yelling and screaming at her, "Get up! Get up! Old woman, I knew I should have left you home!" I thought, what a vulgar and gross person. I felt sorry for the older woman and helped her get to her feet. After we went through immigration check, you may have guessed, these were the two lost tour members.

After I got the tour members checked into the hotel, I had to catch a cab to go back to the airport to pick up a second group from the West Coast who came over the North Pole. No one on the tour would go for me, and by the time I got into my own room I must have been half dead. The next day was Sunday and our bus took us to St. Paul's Cathedral for morning service. About halfway through the service I saw the old woman get up and go back to the rear. I assumed she was going to the bathroom. But after the service we could not find her. We looked and searched through the cathedral and within a half-mile around it on all sides. We called the police and they looked and searched, checked hospitals and stations in the event she had been picked up. I was extremely worried, but by three o'clock we gave up and went back to the hotel. There in the lobby of the hotel was the old woman. During the church service she had dirtied her panties and was afraid to tell her mean daughter. This dear soul had walked five miles through London to the hotel, all by herself.

In talking with the mother, I found out that it was her lifelong dream to go to Israel and walk where Jesus had walked, else I would have sent them both back home. But the daughter gave me one trouble after another. In Amman she cursed me out for not having the tour group stand still and bow their heads while a Moslem prayer call was in progress. I finally had to demand that she shut up and not say anything on the bus or at meals. Her husband, an attorney, would call me at one a.m. each night for the rest of the tour demanding that I apologize to his wife, or he would sue me. I never apologized and he never sued me. This was one tour I was glad to see come to an end, but when I returned to the office the same problems confronted me. In leaving the tour group I had asked them to pray for me and the ministry, because I did not know if I could continue at Southwest Radio Church much longer.

The second day after I returned Mr. "C" called me, pretending that he was behind me and said that regardless how things looked, everything would turn out all right. He wanted something, and that something was for me to have Edgar Whisenant on the program to offer his book *Eighty-Eight Reasons Why Jesus Christ Will Return in 1988*. It seems that Mr. "C" had helped finance the publishing of a million copies of the book. I would have liked to have incurred favor with Mr. "C," but not at the expense of blasphemy. Three times that week Mr. "C" called me back and asked me to air Whisenant, and three times I refused. The last time he called was to inquire about the condition of the finances, and to encourage me to quickly get up the *1989 Prophecy Calendar*, as the *Prophecy Calendar* had become our most popular item. Mr. "C" then went on to say that he was behind me and that he would see that everything came out okay. But as the Hertz commercial goes, this was not "exactly" so. I was told, although I cannot document it, that some received "contributions" from fifteen thousand dollars to seventy-five thousand dollars a person to participate.

Next, former employees were contacted. Some had left of their own accord and others had been dismissed because of incompetence or because they could not do the job for which they were hired. Some had been fired by John Stowe. These past employees were given the opportunity to have their day in the sun. They were invited to attend a meeting of past employees and record on tape (which was to be sent to the board members) their reasons why Noah Hutchings was the worst individual who had ever walked the face of the earth. For ten hours a dozen or more former employees stood up at this meeting and recorded on tape their gripes, dislikes, and contempt for one Noah Hutchings. Some light was shed as to one of the reasons why these people were on a shark feeding frenzy to eat me up. The announcement was made: "We're going over to the board meeting at Southwest Radio Church and throw Noah Hutchings out, and when we do, I am going to give every one of you a good job."

When I returned from the tour I personally set the date for the board meeting so I could control the conditions under which it would be formatted. But the tapes made at the "Noah Hutchings Roast" were sent by Federal Express to every single board member. I had no intention of listening to all this garbage. I knew who I was and what I was. But when I was contacting the members about the forthcoming general meeting, Mrs. Greathouse advised me strongly to listen to the tapes. I cannot refer to all the sessions on the tapes, but below are just a few examples:

Mrs. "D": Mrs. "D," her husband, father, and mother, and attended my classes in Sunday school and training union in church for at least ten years. Never had I had a cross word with her or any member of her family. She had worked at Southwest Radio Church for several months, but when summer came she wanted to take a four-month leave to stay with her children while school was out, and then come back in the fall. We could not do this because then half the staff would have wanted to arrange their working days, weeks, or months also. However, Mrs. "D" left seemingly understanding why we could not comply with her wishes. Before I went on tour the month previously I went to have my glasses changed where Mrs. "D" then worked, and she was so happy to see me that she hugged my neck and thanked me for all the years I had ministered at her church and told me what my ministry had meant to her and her family. But here, one month later, she attends the bashing session and testifies against me.

Mr. "E": Mr. "E" had worked for Southwest Radio Church for about a year in 1986–1987. He was hired to help constituents with wills and trusts. As far as I know, he never helped anyone with a will or a trust, and we finally transferred him to help in the Spanish ministry, Profecías Bíblicas. In

December of 1987 David terminated Mr. "E." In the spring of 1988 I received a call from a national fast-food franchise company asking for a resume on Mr. "E." I knew this fellow had some problems, but I thought that his talents and personality would permit him to be a good sandwich maker or fry cook. The company was wanting someone to also manage this fast-food unit, which was probably no more than fifteen feet by thirty feet. Seven times the company contacted me by telephone or by mail. Had it not been for me, this person would not have gotten the job. Now here he was on tape telling the board members how I cruelly fired him at Christmas time, and what a terrible business person I was. Mr. "C" chimed in to also add his two cents worth about how I had fired this top-notch proven business genius. In the first place, I did not fire him—David fired him—and the rest was nothing but baloney and garbage.

Mrs. "F": A letter from Mrs. "F" was sent with the tapes. In the letter she referred to something my daughter Carol had said about my being a mean old father and a reprobate, or something to that effect. It was rather a terrible, stinging accusation against me as a father and a person. When I showed the letter to my girls they were all horrified and Carol was exceedingly angry. All three girls wrote Mrs. "F" about their own appraisal of me as a father and demanded to know why she had lied. I had worked with Mrs. "F" and her husband for ten years; we had been the best of friends in the ministry, so why? Mrs. "F" was the only person who responded to apologize. She wrote me back that the reason she did it was because she had been told I had stolen the ministry from David and this would help him get it back.

As I have noted before, the opponents were extremely efficient and compelling. The *coup d'etat* was the accusation that three young teenage girls who cleaned my apartment and did my laundry once a week were also there for other purposes. This accusation came from a person involved in church youth work. This charge was a bad one. I could not imagine anyone doing such a thing, especially me. If I could not disprove this one, I was through. I did indeed pay these girls ten dollars apiece to take care of my apartment, which involved only a couple of hours a week. The family was in need and even this small amount doubtless helped. However, the family had moved and no one knew where they had gone. I had to locate them. Finally, after questioning friends and associates, they were found in the Boston area. Dortha and her husband took a plane to Boston, and the girls were interviewed on video tape. All three girls and their mother denied that I had ever been anything to them except as a kindly grandfather. At the conclusion one said, "If these people are Christians, why are they telling these lies?" I still keep up with the girls. Two are married and have children, and they would still come to Oklahoma City and testify under oath in a court of law.

On November 5, ten days before the set board meeting, Kim and I were married in Northwest Baptist Church in Oklahoma City. We went on a brief honeymoon. I was determined not to allow people or circumstances to control my life. All during this extreme trial I never felt under stress, I was never distracted from what God set before me, I continued confident that all things do work together for good, to those who love God and the called according to His purpose.

We read that Noah before the flood was perfect in his generation. But even Noah had his own problems. Neither was this Noah perfect in his generation. We are all humans; we all have faults; and we all have sinned and come short of the glory of God. But God is sovereign and He is our judge, and I knew my own heart and my own will to do His will even in trials and tribulations. I can in all good conscience affirm that my own needs and wants have been subservient to the ministry which the Lord has tendered to my care.

On November 15 the big day came. Karen Howick, the attorney for the ministry, was present. My own personal attorney was Pat Castleberry. Both did a stellar job. The opponents had their own attorney. Mr. "C" had previously called about getting a couple of Pinkerton agents to be present in the event they were needed. We assured him that we had already made provision for the police to be present.

Fifteen board members out of the twenty-five remaining showed up. Ten had resigned on the grounds that they did not know enough about the actual facts and their continued presence on the board would only confuse the proxy ratio. The minutes of the last meeting were read. I was to chair the first half of the meeting. It is easy to accuse and get false witnesses, but proving what is accused is another matter. I had done my homework. A TV was set up with the video tapes on top. For two hours the meeting progressed with a couple of test votes taken on relatively minor issues. The meeting was not going well for the other side. Finally, someone asked for a recess. I asked why. The reply: "To go to the bathroom." I asked for how long. He replied, "Fifteen minutes." I called a ten-minute recess. I went downstairs for a Coke and to confer with my attorney. In ten minutes I went back into the room, but everyone had gone except us and the board members. David, Mr. A, B, and C, and their company had packed up their briefcases, gone out into the parking lot, and were leaving in their limousines. After spending all that money and time, they all simply left. It did not make sense to me, but it must have to the Lord.

The shootout at the OKC Corral was over!

The next Monday Rev. J. R. Church, of Prophecy in the News, came by the office and asked, "What are you going to do next?" I replied that the first thing

I had to do was talk with David and see if I could get him restored to Southwest Radio Church. Pastor Church was shocked.

Jesus said that we were to love those who persecute us. Hatred of one's brother in Christ makes one a murderer, and that works both ways. Hatred, envy, and jealousy will kill the spirit, destroy a testimony, and make a Christian unfruitful, miserable, and dejected. I do not hate those who had a part in this episode. This trial made me a better Christian, and I am sure it did them, so God gets all the glory, regardless.

On Tuesday I called and made an appointment with Jerry Crabb, a ministry attorney and friend of long standing. Jerry called David and we met in Mr. Crabb's office the next day. David appeared sullen, angry, and defensive. I finally got through to him that the best I could do was to get the board to reinstate him on a probationary basis. Even so, it was very difficult, as the board was not as forgiving as I. However, after much prayer, pleading, and promises, David was reinstated on a trial basis until the next annual board meeting.

Some readers may conclude that in this chapter I have been too defensive, gone into too much detail, or perhaps complained too much. I want to set the record straight as to just why and how I became the ministry's leader. I still receive telephone calls about this matter from constituents who have supported the ministry over these many years. They have a right to know. At every meeting I am asked the same questions. What sixty-five–year–old in his right mind, who had just undergone a heart bypass and several heart attacks, would want to assume such a tremendous burden and responsibility?

Also, few, if any, have ever been told that immediately after the board meeting in November that I pressured the board to bring David back into the ministry. I have no animosity toward anyone involved in the November 1988 affair. I have always wished them well and prayed for them. And to be considered after 1988 incident is the number of books I have written, the number of missions I have been involved in, and the number of times I have tried to turn this ministry over to others. Surely, this is evidence that the Lord's will was done. After all, He is the final Authority.

It is evident that this was a pivotal time in my life, and had I not dealt with it in this book, I would not have been honest with myself or the readers.

Many personalities involved in the 1988 shootout at the OKC corral were not mentioned, and many incidents connected with this episode have been passed over. Dwelling too long on the mundane and the profane does no honor to God or the testimony of this ministry, which has now endured over sixty-five years. And after all, as I noted in the foreword, who wants to dwell too long in the swamps with the alligators, snakes, and creeping things?

It Ain't Over Till It's Over

After David was reinstated, his participation in the program and contacting the constituency continued, but on a reduced basis. There was the possibility that full reinstatement could occur at the next board meeting. News of David's collaboration with John Barela on special meetings representing Southwest Radio Church, however, infuriated some of the trustees. I cautioned David about this matter, but it continued. When the next board meeting was scheduled for July of 1989, I advised David of the date. He informed me that he and John Barela had a meeting in Albuquerque, so he would not be present. I advised him that it was absolutely necessary for him to be at the board meeting, but he insisted that he would not be able to come. When the meeting was convened, a motion was made to withdraw all fellowship from David. Minutes of the meeting will note the vote was fourteen to one for permanent separation of David from Southwest Radio Church. The one vote for David was cast by me. So no one took the ministry from David, he gave it up by default. It has been charged that the board members were my picked friends, but David had recommended all the board members for approval. I had not picked even one.

After the July board meeting I contacted Dr. Robert Lindsted about becoming host of the Southwest Radio Church program, but he had too many irons in the fire already. Next, I approached Rev. J. R. Church about merging Prophecy in the News with Southwest Radio Church. The board was interested, but one was a TV ministry and the other a radio ministry, and there was a large difference in salaries, so the board declined.

Next I called Texe Marrs and asked him if he knew anyone who might make an acceptable host and leader of the ministry, and Texe indicated that he would be interested. I set up a meeting between the trustees and Texe at Embassy Suites on South Meridian in December 1989. After the interview exchange, an agreement was reached and duly recorded that Texe would work with me in programming and administration for the first six months of 1990. After the six-month trial period, if Texe was satisfied and the trustees were satisfied, Texe and Wanda would move to Oklahoma City and assume responsibility for the ministry. A salary arrangement was also worked out.

For the first six months of 1990 Texe and I did work together, with Texe being mainly responsible for programming. Texe and I worked together without tensions or problems. In the latter part of May the time was rapidly approaching for Texe to make a decision. He came into my office and informed me that he and Wanda had built a new house in Austin, or were building a new house, and their business was in Austin, so they had decided not to move. He continued that inasmuch as my health had improved and there was no one more capable of running Southwest Radio Church, that I should again take over full responsibility for both management and programming. I reported this to the trustees and began planning future programming. However, the next day I received a communication in writing that Texe had changed his mind and would continue to produce programming for the ministry in Austin. I called Ben McCammon to check with him, and Ben stated emphatically that this arrangement would not be in agreement with the contract, and to tell Texe thanks, but no thanks. Subsequently, I wrote Texe a very nice letter thanking him for his generous offer, but that the trustees agreed that according to the contract his services should end on June 30. I went on to compliment Texe and Wanda on their ministry and services to Southwest Radio Church, and also included a warm invitation to again be on the broadcast as a guest at any time. I also invited him and Wanda to go on a tour with me to the Middle East in the fall.

In the past six months there had not been a cross word between Texe and me, yet in one day, according to a response from Texe, I became an enemy. Texe had set up a two-week series of one-night meetings throughout the Midwest. He was to have been the principal speaker at these meetings. Advertising announcements, programs, and schedules had already gone out. When I asked Texe if he intended to honor his commitments and take care of the meetings, I got a not-on-your-life response.

David Ingraham, myself, and Johnny Ray Watson, took off in a van with a trailer to keep the meetings. Texe had not been knowledgeable regarding suitable sites for ministry meetings, so the selection of some of the cities was very ill-advised. We probably did not average over one hundred people per meeting. Our low mark was Louisville. We were on an FM station forty miles north of Louisville, but evidently no one in Louisville listened to it. About four o'clock in the afternoon we pulled up to the address where the meeting was to be held. We went inside and looked at the auditorium. Plush red cushioned seats started at the back and seemed to run forever toward a stage that was barely visible. I remarked that even three hundred attendees would rattle around like a dozen peas in a large bowl.

At seven p.m. we had set up for the meeting and were waiting for the crowd to rush in. No one showed up, not a single soul. Finally, ten minutes later, three old timers on Social Security came hobbling in, and five minutes later in came a widow with four children ranging from two years to eight years. We did the best we could to put on the program promised, but even David Ingraham did not have the nerve to take up an offering. And not only that, but the widow and her four children were hungry so we had to take them to a restaurant and feed them.

The next morning I sent the entire crew (which included David Ingraham and two members of the staff) home. Only Johnny Ray and I stayed behind to take care of the final meeting in Nashville, and as fate would have it, this was the largest meeting of all.

Bott Broadcasting was one of the primary carriers of the ministry in the seventies and eighties, but in 1991 Dick Bott, Jr., and I got into a squabble over the cancellation of our program over KCCV in Kansas City. Senior did not like some of my comments, which he interpreted to be my casting aspersions upon Junior, so he sued me for libel. Southwest Radio Church in turned sued Bott Broadcasting for several million dollars on RICO charges. Texe Marrs wanted to get his two cents in, so he was included in our suit against Bott. Dick Bott, Sr., requested a Christian conciliation meeting, which was held just before Christmas of 1991. Like most meetings, it was neither Christian nor conciliatory, and ended with the participants being even further apart than when it started. Finally, in the following February, just before were were getting ready to go into district court at Denver, both sides agreed to a settlement and all legal action and proceedings were cancelled. Because I did not want to go to court in Denver, we also dropped the suit against Texe. Texe called me and was greatly appreciative, and said that he was going to pray for me every day of his life. The trouble with this is that I do not know how he is praying for me. But since that time there have been no problems between us, except he recently made a crack about one of my books in his newsletter, which is okay because more readers will probably go out and buy the book.

I think the majority of radio station owners and operators respect me and the ministry because I keep my word. Two of the best friends and Christian gentlemen I have known in Gospel communications have been Robert Ball of Salem Broadcasting, and Don Crawford, Jr., of Crawford Broadcasting. Salem and Crawford are two of the largest, if not the largest, corporations in the nation presenting Christian programming.

In the spring the ministry was in fairly good condition financially, and with Rev. David Ingraham at the ministry, I turned it over to Ben McCammon and Dortha. I left for tours, missions, and meetings. Ben was indeed a good man, but leading a ministry like Southwest Radio Church was beyond his talents and experience. When I returned in the fall, the finances had gone from bad to impossible. We owed on taxes withheld from employees wages to both state and federal, plus interest and penalties, which amounted to almost one hundred thousand dollars. Because I had not been at the ministry, Mrs. Harvey led a tour to the Middle East and the books had not been kept current. I had to get hold of the finances immediately, and the only way I knew how to keep up with the bank accounts was to have the bookkeeper call each morning and get the balances. About the third day I asked Teresa to call the bank. We had five accounts, and she returned with the information that by strange coincidence, all our account balances were zero. This was no coincidence to me. I knew the Internal Revenue Service had bled every bank account of every cent, and we had thirty-eight thousand dollars worth of checks outstanding. I called Mrs. Andrews, one of the trustees, and asked her to rush me twenty-five thousand dollars as soon as possible to salt the bank accounts until I could get more funds. I hurriedly wrote five thousand letters to our most generous supporters, and I personally signed every one.

By the end of January 1992 the finances were again in pretty good shape. This time I turned the ministry over to a gentleman who had experience in Bible publishing and distribution, Don Glover. David Ingraham was to pretty much take care of the program. However, I continued to be on the program from time to time, as well as occasionally write the monthly letter. Mark Hitchcock, pastor of a fundamental church in Edmond, Oklahoma, was elected president by the board. I moved my office about one mile north on Classen. Besides missions to China, Korea, Russia, and the Middle East, I wrote three books that year: *Why So Many Churches?*, *Rapture and*

Resurrection, and *The Revived Roman Empire.*

From the time I left, the ministry again started to go downhill. The management was given every chance to get things together. Finally in September 1993, Pastor Hitchcock called me and said the ministry would have to be closed unless I returned. There was much wailing and gnashing of teeth, but with determination and an iron fist I just had to get things back together. I told Teresa and Nena, the bookkeepers who were in charge of the vendor accounts and the radio station accounts, to direct every credit investigation call to me personally. It was extreme mental torture to have to talk with creditors who needed their money and had not been paid in over a year. The first month I probably took over two hundred calls from disturbed or angry creditors. Half of the supporting constituency had been lost, and at least half of the radio coverage had been lost. The old building we were in needed repairs badly.

I asked God if He had one more miracle. If so, then give me the strength and wisdom to be able to move the office to a better location, get the debt paid, and restore the ministry's radio coverage.

By the first of the year credit calls began to subside, and we began looking for a better office location. Mrs. Betty McCammon, Ben's wife, had served on the board of Southwest Radio Church with her husband. Betty informed me in January that Ben just seemed not to be able to get over a severe case of flu, and he was losing weight rapidly. Kim and I visited Betty and Ben, and while Ben had lost considerable weight, he still seemed fairly active. In February Betty called and informed me that Ben was in St. Anthony Hospital, just three blocks north of the office. I do not know what was really wrong with Ben, whether it was his lungs, heart, or cancer, but when I saw him in the hospital he was almost skin and bones. Betty said no one could get him to eat anything.

I knew Ben liked McDonalds sausage biscuits and hash browns. For two weeks on the way to work each morning I would pick up two McDonalds sausage biscuits and two hash browns. I would sit by Ben's bed and pull out a contract form I had written, showing that when I took a bite, Ben McCammon by contract and covenant was to take a bite. Although it took thirty minutes, I could get Ben to eat both the biscuit and the hash brown. After two weeks Betty called me one afternoon and said that I need not stop at McDonalds the next morning because Ben had gone to be with the Lord. I gave part of the memorial service, and I endeavored to present Ben as he was and his love for the gospel. Everyone said it was the best memorial tribute they had ever heard. I wish I had written it down.

Funerals are not necessarily a sad occasion. I remember a Christian friend whose name was Mary Green. Mary was a member of the Roman Catholic Church, and because of her family she would not leave it. One day Mary told me she had cancer of the lungs, and in about one year Mary died. Under her pillow was a note that she wanted me to bring the memorial at her funeral. Although I did not know what to expect, or even if I would be allowed in, I showed up at the church. The priest was sprinkling water around with one hand and had a pot of smoke in the other. I showed him a copy of the note. He shrugged his shoulders and gave me a paper, and pointed to where I should read and where he would read. I responded: "I knew Mary. I know she was saved and is now with the Lord. I know what I am to say. If I have to read from that paper, I will leave." The priest again shrugged his shoulders and pointed to the podium. As I should, I not only paid tribute to Mary and her faith, but also gave the gospel. There was a large audience, and every eye looked directly at me. Not a head moved. Mary's son later came by the office to thank me for such a wonderful memorial service and gave me a check for two hundred dollars.

In 1994 I reached one of the goals I set when I returned to the ministry in 1993, and that was to move the office to a better facility and location. The old building we were in was only a few blocks from the Alfred P. Murrah Federal Building and was later damaged in the April 19, 1995, explosion. In 1997 the debts were eliminated, and in 1998 the effort to restore coverage of the program from coast to coast was accomplished.

As far as my own personal affairs are concerned, I draw approximately twelve hundred dollars a month from Social Security. I have paid my own money into this system since 1935, so I feel that I am entitled to get as much of my money out of the system as I can before it goes bankrupt. Also, I get some monies from royalties, plus a very small remuneration from Southwest Radio Church.

Although the life status of my three daughters, Carol, Cheryl, and Cathy, is not perfect, I am sure it is bearable. When Kim and I married in 1988 there were serious reservations because she had five children. Most of the children in the years of the Killing Fields in Cambodia died of disease or starvation. There was not enough food to keep both children and parents alive. Rations consisted of one cup of rice per day per family. Kim kept her children alive by feeding them first before she would eat. It doubtless seems extremely unwise to most for a man of sixty-five years to take on a new adopted family of six. As it has turned out, Pola married a fine young Cambodian in Washington, D.C., and they are well on their way to becoming millionaires. Poline graduated from Oklahoma State University with a degree in business administration and accounting. She married a caucasian and now has two children. Sothea, the oldest boy, graduated from Oklahoma State University with honors. And although losing eighty percent of his eyesight in Cambodia because of illness, he has spent two years in the Peace Corps in Jamaica, and is now teaching school. Sothy lacked one semester getting his degree in automotive engineering at Oklahoma State before deciding he wanted to do something else and started working toward a degree in hospital technical services. During his first week in his required internship, he decided that he did not want to work where people were sick and dying. At the writing of this chapter he is back at Oklahoma State completing his last semester in automotive engineering. Phaly, the youngest, is rapidly hurrying toward her degree in nursing.

While all the kids speak English fluently, at home they mainly communicate in Cambodian. People ask me if it does not disturb me for them to speak Cambodian in my presence. My response is that I do not mind at all, because I don't have to listen. Actually, raising a second family of Cambodian refugees has kept me working and mentally alert. God knew what I needed at the time, and again after all, all things do work for good to those who love God and the called according to His purpose. Most men, when they retire at sixty-five, sit around bored to death, trying to think of something to do that will keep them from going crazy, and end up in the grave before they are seventy. At seventy-five I am still working at least ten to twelve hours a day, running all over the world, writing books, and producing a daily thirty-minute Christian program. At least for the present all the parts are still working, and I am looking forward to living until the Rapture (translation) of the Church.

To quote a famous American, Yogi Berra, "It ain't over till it's over."

Foreclosure

Longfellow wrote, "Life is real, life is earnest, and the grave is not its goal." In this book I have attempted to reflect the image of my life, experiences, and circumstances. One of the primary objectives I purposed to attempt was not to bore the reader, whether he or she be Jew or Gentile, Christian, agnostic, infidel, or heathen.

As indicated in the foreword, I really do not know if I have written anything herein of great importance. If so, then it would have been the importance of doing the best you can, with the talents God has given you, in the time He has given you to do it, then going home and going to sleep. Also, that all things in the lives of Christians work together (inclusive) for good, to those who love God, to those who are the called according to His purpose. God is sovereign, and absolute faith in this truth is paramount. Faith dictated the words of the three Hebrews in the fiery furnace, and Job in the midst of extreme tribulations, that although God even fails to deliver us or even slays us, yet we must trust Him.

The definition of "foreclosure" as given in the dictionary is, "An act or instance of foreclosing; specif.: a legal proceeding that bars or extinguishes a mortgager's right of redeeming a mortgaged estate." Death can exercise a foreclosure on my body at any time. In fact, death kills more people than anything else I know of. But only God can foreclose on my soul and spirit; or have the legal power and authority to redeem my body at the resurrection (Ephesians 1:12–14).

As far as this book is concerned, as the author I have been trying to foreclose on this rambling effort since I wrote the foreword. With these last few sentences, I think I shall finally realize some success. As I look forward to beyond seventy-five, I hope I will be able to visit a few more countries, write a few more books, catch a few more fish, hit a few more golf balls, enjoy a few more meals of Kim's excellent cuisine, win a few more souls to Jesus Christ, and escape a few cases of litigation by people I may have offended in this book.

If I should die before the Lord comes, then perhaps there shall be a few dollars left of my worldly possessions after funeral expenses to inscribe in twelve point type on my tombstone:

He did the best he could,
  With the talents God gave him,
In the time he had to do it,
  Then:
He fell asleep and went home.

May God bless each and every one of you, and keep looking up, for God is still on the throne, and prayer changes things!

Acknowledgements

We would like to think all those who helped in the publication of this book by lending their financial support:

Jean Abrahamsen	Marcia Berger
Leo Affi	Mr. and Mrs. Edwin R. Bergman
Mr. and Mrs. Leonard Alford	G. Berka
Diane Allen	Mrs. T. F. Blaauboer
Mary L. Allen	Charles Black
Henry Francelia Alonzo	Lucy Blanch
Rod Anderson	William Boess
Steve Andrewson	Wayne J. Bokum
Charlie and Mary Angal	Jill Bolakas
Marie F. Armstrong	Ruth Bolin
Bradley Arndt	Margaret Borneval
Rudolf and Inga Arnold	Ronald Boryla
Evelyn Aurnhammer	Dorothy Bowden
Tony and Joanne Avans	Andrea Bozeman
Bill Barnes	Frances Bozarth
Mr. and Mrs. James Bator	Mr. and Mrs. Paul Bracewell
Rev. Edmund Bauer	Shirley Brad
Mrs. Jean M. Bell	Mildred Brand
Ada Bentley	Richard M. Briles

Arthur and Alicia Brown

James P. Brownlow

Mr. and Mrs. G. F. Bryan

Mrs. E. Bunniss

Wilmer and Lois Burns

Helen E. Burnson

Dorsey and Phyllis Buttram

James A. Byrd

Mrs. Joe M. Cable

Roger and Rose Marie Cadena

Jesse Cantu

C. A. Carlson

David Carnahan

Albert and Louise Castaneda

Leta Cate

Salvacion Celestial-Brown

Mrs. Earl Champion

H. G. and Zelma Chrisman

John Clapp

Lucille Clark

Mary Clark

Elizabeth Coakley

Frank and Bertha Cobb

Clifford H. Cochran

Donald J. Cogley

Kinnard T. Cole

Mrs. Rise Cooper

Mrs. Harold Coover

Mr. and Mrs. Dino Costanzo

Louise Craddock

Dorothy M. Crary

Mr. and Mrs. Ron Crosby

Daniel M. Crutchfield

Thomas D. Cusack

Joe Daluz

Melba Jean Day

Jack and Debbie Deetjen

Patrick Deleon

Elyse B. Delucie

S. P. Demoss

William Dettling

Mr. and Mrs. Robert D. Dick

Rutherford Diehl

George A. Dippner

Bernice Divornicki

Thomas and Dianna G. Dixon

Judy Doerr

Jimmy Dossey

Ilona Dragert

Mrs. Eugene Drainer

Don Duff

Phyllis Dvorak

J. William and Betty Elliott, Sr.

Lillie Elliott

Mr. and Mrs. Verne Ellis

Rocky E. Ellison

Mrs. Cecil W. Ely

Darold Eslinger

George Esquivel

Annie Jo Evans

Gary Eyler

Bernice H. Fahlberg

W. C. Farber Sunshine Bible Shop

Richard Ferris

Charlotte Fertich

Beatrice Findlay

First Baptist Church, Maywood, CA

Rhonda Fischer

James S. Floyd

Robert G. Floyd

Michael Flynt

J. H. Forwood

David and Betty Fowler

Willard O. Galery

Clara Gerig

Helen M. Gibson

Dr. and Mrs. Marc D. Gilbert

J. Ruel and Marian Glover

Joseph Godwin

Craig Goodenow

Kenneth Grave

Mary Green

James and Judy Grissom

Freda L. Grist

Henry and Helen Gross

Don Guidry

Vela Gwin

Wilbur Haeseker

Gloria Hall

E. L. and Betty Hamilton, Jr.

Carl and Lucille Hanks

Mrs. Alvin Hansen

Mr. and Mrs. Gerald W. Hardy

George Harms

William Harriman III

Richard and Teresa Harrington

Mr. and Mrs. M. F. Hartley

Neal Hartman

Mr. and Mrs. John Harvey

Mrs. Troy Hataway

K. Hawk

Fred Healea

Gerrit Heeg

M. Louise Henderson

Glenn Herbst

Howard Herm

Grace Ann Hines

Keith Hinson

John T. Howell

Lawrence B. Howie

Melvin Howland

Mrs. Harold R. Hudson

Alice A. Hughart

Kathleen Hurley

Elliot Ingram

Mr. and Mrs. Weldon Ivey

Thomas and Doris Jackson

Charles J. Janda

Mr. and Mrs. Wayne C. Jenkins

Mrs. Duane Johnson

Dr. Pauline B. Johnson

Ronald and Susie Johnson

Eliza Jones

John Jorgenson

Pauline Kauffman

Donald and Dale Kehoe

Jeff and Tracy Keiser

Michael Kerkhoff

Douglas Kern

Mrs. Ken Kiester

Gary and Carine Kinsel

Mrs. John H. Klein

Gail Knutson

Bob Konkel

Rose Montagna Kovaks

Mr. and Mrs. Frank M. Kozlik

Josephine Kremer

Mary Kujawa

Conni Kuykendall

Grant and Carol Lamb

James and Roma Lang

Steve Larmer

Mrs. and Mrs. Larry Larson

Barry D. and Joanie B. Leichty

Jean Leichty

Gary R. Letsinger

John Levesque

Mr. and Mrs. Robert Lind

Buzz Lindstrom

Phyllis J. Loehden

Mr. and Mrs. Sidney C. Lord, Jr.

Stephanie Lorenzen

Alfred Lowe

Gary and Sandra de Luna

Carole A. Lunders

Terri Maas

Edward and Beth Mack

M. Maddox

Hank Mahley

Mrs. Raymond A. Malone

Barbara Manaka

Jake T. Manchesian

Linda Marten

Dorothy Mastin

Mrs. Hodie Maxwell

Jerome McCabe

Barrett McDonald

Robert B. McFatridge

T. H. McGraw

Mrs. Mel McIntire

Mr. and Mrs. D. L. McKay

Elia V. Medrano

Adeline Metz

Carol J. Middleton

David E. Miller

Rose Mitchell

Frances Mitten

Patricia Mobberly

Jane Q. Mole

Stanley Monteith

Eduardo Monzon

C. E. Morris

Mr. and Mrs. L. Gary Morrison

Mrs. Homer Moseley

Raymond L. and Gene C. Moses

David R. Moss

Marilyn Moyer

Kirk Mueller

Lorn Mullenix

William E. Munther

Lt. Col. Valeska Musselman

Mrs. Ruth Myer

Gerald Nave

Irene R. Neff

Alice Wells Nelson

Paul and Pamela Nelson

Gertin and Donna Ness

Marlana Nevitt

Michael Nix

Robert and Kathryn O'Brien

Regina Osborne

Mary Paisley

Michael Palmer

Richard E. Parish

Thelma Parker

Anita Parks

Laverne Partin

Robert O. Paske

Evelyn Susan Patterson

Lorraine Peck

Louis E. Pedulla, Jr.

Mary L. Peterson

Una T. Petry

Linda Plett

John Polansky, Jr.

David J. and Gail Ponesse

Ray and Joie Poulsen

Travis Proctor

Dr. and Mrs. Robert L. Ramus

Bradley Rash

Mr. and Mrs. Floyd P. Ray

Jeff Reagan

Mrs. Jay B. Reid

Wilmer J. Rentsch

Greg Rhine

Paul E. Rhodes

Esther May Richardson

Paul Rinear

Kelly Rinehart

John G. Roberts

Margaret Roberts

Harve and Barb Robinson

Michael Sankowski

Roger Saunders

Jack and Jean Scheehle

Iva Schildroth

Robert E. Schmierer

Charles and Gloria Schnell

Harol R. Schrag

Lowell and Betty Schroeder

Mrs. J. Schroeter

M. J. Schroeter

Laes Schuler

Eugene and Beverly Schulte

J. Doris Scofield

Irene Scott

Sheila Selby

Willie and Eva Self

Mrs. A. R. Seltenreich

Charles T. and Geneva Servais

Alton and Billy Shumate

Irma M. Siemens

Mr. and Mrs. Eugene Silvus

Mr. and Mrs. N. O. Simonsen

Paul B. Skinner

Mr. and Mrs. Robert Skold

Gene Smith, M.D.

J. Allen H. Smith, Jr.

Ruth E. Smith

William J. Smith, Jr.

Julia Snyder

Eugene and Cindy Sole

Shirley Somers

Brian Souders

Elizabeth Stauffer

J. T. and Vivian Stenner

Jim Stevenson

Marion E. Stief

Kyle Stoltzfus

Wanda Stuart

Gary L. Suchy

Gary Sudela

Wesley and Kimberly Supak

Jane Tallant

Eddie Teague

Karen Tellor

Joan Terwilliger

Mr. C. Thurlow

Louise Thut

Jim Tillery

Eposi Tittfon

Craig Tittsworth

Kathryn M. Toncy

Mark Trombly

Wanwan Tzeng

Mr. and Mrs. Donald Underwood

Mr. and Mrs. Jules L. Ursin III

Barbara Vandegrift

Elizabeth Vanderhoof

Mr. and Mrs. Lowell Vanskike

Mildred A. Vaughn

George Verciuc

Steve and Sandy Vetter

Cecilia A. Vickery

E. Voelker

Larry Voss

Mr. and Mrs. Lloyd A. Wagner

Wade and Barbara Wamsley

Mrs. L. S. Wanslow

Richard and Maxine Warner

Tom Wasson

Mrs. Bennett B. Watson

Harold and Helen Weaver

Stephanie Weaver

Volker and Iris Weise

Marcella Weisgerber

Nell Westbrook

Mr. and Mrs. Joseph L. Wieser

Don and Cheryl Williams

Donald G. Williams

Esther Williams

W. L. Witschey

Mrs. Roland Wolseley

Lee Woodward

Anne Wright

Kenneth Yoder

Iona J. Young

Helance Youngbauer

Phillip and Donna Yowell

William Zlobik

Cut-out silhouette of Rev. Hutchings done by a Chinese student in Xion, China, while the bus Rev. Hutchings was riding in was stopped at a traffic light.